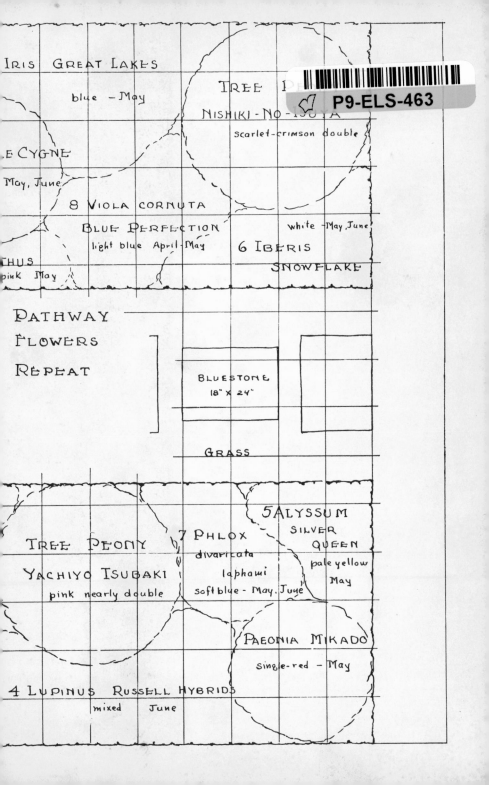

IRIS GREAT LAKES

blue – May

TREE P[E...]
NISHIKI-NO-[...]A
scarlet-crimson double

E CYGNE

May, June

8 VIOLA CORNUTA
BLUE PERFECTION
light blue April-May

6 IBERIS
white – May, June
SNOWFLAKE

THUS
pink May

PATHWAY
FLOWERS
REPEAT

BLUESTONE
18" X 24"

GRASS

5 ALYSSUM
SILVER QUEEN
pale yellow May

TREE PEONY
YACHIYO TSUBAKI
pink nearly double

7 PHLOX
divaricata
laphami
soft blue – May. June

PAEONIA MIKADO
single-red – May

4 LUPINUS RUSSELL HYBRIDS
mixed June

PEONIES, OUTDOORS AND IN

Peonies, Outdoors and In

by
ARNO & IRENE NEHRLING

drawings by
Charlotte E. Bowden

HEARTHSIDE PRESS, INC.
PUBLISHERS • NEW YORK

Dedicated to Amy Irene

Contents

BLACK AND WHITE PHOTOGRAPH PORTFOLIO
Between pages 144 and 145

COLOR PLATES
Courtesy Horticulture Magazine

On the cover—Japanese tree peony Tama-fuyo (Jeweled Lotus), in the garden of Mr. and Mrs. Ellery Sedgwick. *Emily Henry Bush photo*

Between pages 96 and 97:

I. Tree peony Virginia Irving Pierce, in the garden of Mrs. Irving C. Wright, Chestnut Hill, Mass. *Paul Genereux photo*

II. Brilliant peonies and snow-in-summer dramatize a wall in the garden of Mrs. Edwin S. Webster, Chestnut Hill, Mass. *Paul Genereux photo*

III. Tree peony Hinode-no-seki with 39 blooms. Garden of Mr. and Mrs. Ellery Sedgwick, Beverly, Mass. *Emily Henry Bush photo*

IV. Peonies and bearded iris in the garden of Mr. and Mrs. Stedman Buttrick, Concord, Mass. *Paul Genereux photo*

Between pages 192 and 193:

V. Nine hardy singles and Japanese varieties from Gilbert H. Wild and Son, Sarcoxi, Mo. Reading across from top row: Tamate Boku, Krinkled White, Neon, Aztec, Sword Dance, Mrs. Wilder Bancroft, Golden Arrow, Sunup, Battle Flag. *Courtesy A. B. Morse Co., St. Joseph, Mich.*

VI. Fifteen doubles in pinks and reds from Gilbert H. Wild and Son, Sarcoxi, Mo. Varieties included are Mrs. Harry F. Little, May Morn, Blanche King, Sarah Bernhardt, Mons. Jules Elie, Lady Kate, Felix Crousse, The Mighty Mo, Prairie King, Queen of Hamburg, Ozark Beauty, Karl Rosenfield, Andy, Dixie, Pierre Dessert. *Courtesy A. B. Morse Co., St. Joseph, Mich.*

VII. Japanese and double peonies from Cherry Hill Nurseries, West Newbury, Mass. Top: Frances Willard (double). Second row: Two blooms of Matilda Lewis (double). Third row, center, Hari-ai-nin (Japanese), left and right, Hakodate (Japanese). Bottom: Jeannot (double). *Ralph Sanborn photo*

VIII. A fine semi-double, Phyllis Kelway, grown at Cherry Hill Nurseries, West Newbury, Mass. *Paul Genereux photo*

IX. Double old-fashioned Paeonia officinalis is still a garden favorite. In the garden of Mrs. Irving Fraim, Waltham, Mass. *Paul Genereux photo*

X. Ten varieties for the home garden. Back row: Festiva Maxima, Currant Red, Annisquam, King of England. Center row: Therese, Le Jour, Thomas C. Thurlow. Bottom row: Amberglow, Hari-ai-nin, Walter Faxon. *Paul Genereux photo*

12

FOREWORD

During the past quarter century miracles in plant breeding have brought to the modern garden plants of hitherto undreamed utility and beauty. Many of these plants have been praised in books and plant catalogs. For instance, scarcely a year goes by without one or more excellent books on roses. One great nursery advertises it has to grow nine million Rose plants a year, so great is the demand from amateur gardeners.

The production of new types, new forms, and new colors of Peonies has been no less spectacular than that of the Rose, Daffodil, Iris, Chrysanthemum and other flowers so widely seen in our gardens. Curiously enough no Peony book designed for the home gardener has been written for 25 years, and it, as well as the larger one 42 years old, is out of print.

The splendid publications of the American Peony Society have been of untold value to a comparatively small group of Peony specialists. These publications, however, are not often seen by the hundreds of thousands or possibly millions of those persons who now comprise our gardening public, and who should be growing and enjoying at least a few of the newer Peonies.

It is, therefore, very gratifying to all who love gardens that Arno and Irene Nehrling have prepared this present book. Mr. Nehrling has unusual qualifications for presenting practical advice for the amateur. He is, and long has been, secretary of the Massachusetts Horticultural Society, the largest and most active horticultural society in the country. In that position he is in daily contact with amateur gardeners and their problems. He is responsible for the magazine "Horticulture," the official organ of the society, which has a nationwide distribution. Year after year he has staged the Boston Peony Shows, as well as similar shows of Daffodils, Tulips, Dahlias and Chrysanthe-

mums, and the much larger spring show which has consistently
been one of the greatest shows of the country.

Mrs. Nehrling, in addition to being a good gardener, has been
particularly interested in arrangement of flowers for the home,
and has written much on this subject in the past.

From beginning to end the book abounds in plain, practical
advice that the home gardener needs in order to take advantage
of the great development of Peonies during this past quarter
century. While much of the information is aimed at beginners,
the advanced gardener and even the Peony specialist have not
been neglected.

The authors, in addition, have done a great service to the
American Peony Society and its many experts by assembling
and publishing, for the first time, a complete list of varieties
registered by that society during the more than half century
of its existence.

I hope the present book will have a wide distribution. I am
sure that it will greatly increase the number of gardeners
growing Peonies.

John C. Wister

Swarthmore College
Swarthmore, Pennsylvania
September 1, 1959

IN APPRECIATION

First of all we want to thank George W. Peyton, secretary of the American Peony Society, for his splendid cooperation and assistance, certainly far beyond the call of duty. His wonderful spirit and genuine interest were an inspiration. He writes a fine letter, too, and we'll miss them, now the book is completed.

Our sincere thanks to Miss Silvia Saunders of Clinton, New York, for reading the material on herbaceous hybrids and tree peonies, and for her good advice and suggestions.

We are grateful to four landscape friends: John Brimer, Suffern, New York; Allen C. Haskell, New Bedford; Ruth D. Leiby, Weston and Harold D. Stevenson of Marshfield, the latter three from Massachusetts, who took time out from their busy spring schedules to draw garden plans featuring peonies.

Our thanks to Myron D. Bigger of Topeka, Kansas, President of the American Peony Society, for his comments on herbaceous hybrids; to Miss Dorothy Manks and her fine staff at the Massachusetts Horticultural Library for research and for the compilation of a list of all peonies registered with the American Peony Society as published in its bulletins through 1958; to John C. Wister and Miss Gertrude Smith for lending us the "Scott Foundation" tree peony pictures and answering many questions; to Winthrop Thurlow for his cooperation and assistance; and to the accomplished arrangers who supplied us with excellent photographs of their fine work.

We are particularly appreciative of all those who answered our questionnaire; they are listed in the supplement. We thank those who added extra interesting information about their peonies or personal good wishes and wonder if writers in other fields receive the same generous, enthusiastic response!

We are grateful to Horticulture and Paul Genereux for the use

15

of photographs; to Mrs. Charlotte Bowden for her lovely sketches and to Miss Ann White who was helpful in so many ways.

Finally our deep appreciation to Nedda Anders of Hearthside Press for her encouragement and assistance in helping us plan, organize and edit the book.

Arno and Irene Nehrling

Needham Heights
Massachusetts
July, 1959

WHY GROW THEM?

The modern peony now surpasses all other garden flowers for sheer majesty and splendor. Its natural beauty has been enhanced by peony experts and hybridizers who for a century or more have worked devotedly in developing and improving this favorite perennial. Their efforts have produced improved types of exquisite distinction and magnificence. Here are eight reasons why peonies are called the "Queen of Flowers":

1. Superior blooms of breathtaking loveliness are available in a wide variety of forms and colors. Starting with the lovely singles, some like huge, beautiful anemones, and the semi-doubles resembling water lilies, to the gorgeous double forms, there is great variety. The glossy, satiny petals come in hundreds of shades, tints and combinations of white, pink, red and yellow. Some of the flowers, which are outstandingly beautiful, also have a delightful fragrance.

2. Its wide diversity of foliage and habit of growth. The leaves of some are much divided and fern-like while others are strong and broad, usually lustrous and frequently with leather-like qualities in a range of greens, often tinged with copper or red. Some sorts are dwarf and bushy, some medium in height and spreading, yet others tall and bold in silhouette.

3. Excellent for use in the landscape, it is the glory of the spring and early summer garden. For the home grounds its substantial size and beauty make it valuable. Magnificent in mass, yet its individual size and perfection of detail make it an

excellent specimen or accent plant as well. And after the blooming season it still has landscape value since the shining foliage
remains attractive throughout the growing season and takes
on interesting coloring in the autumn.

4. The peony provides excellent cut flowers. The exquisite
beauty and infinite variety in both flower and foliage, plus lasting qualities, make it an ideal cut flower.

5. It is extremely hardy and dependable, thriving in severe
climates, enduring temperatures fatal to many other perennials.
All have a sturdy quality and self-reliance.

6. Of easy culture, once planted it requires a minimum of
care and expense.

7. The peony is practically free of disease and pests if a few
simple rules are observed.

8. It is a permanent investment and will bloom for years
if it is not disturbed.

PART I — THE QUEEN OF FLOWERS

1

A Fascinating History

Copy of woodcut in herbal published
by Peter Schoeffer at Maing in 1485

The peony, according to legend and Greek mythology, was named for Paeon, a physician of antiquity. Zeus and Leto were the parents of Apollo, god of healing and the father of Aesculapius, god of medicine. Paeon was his pupil and the physician who attended the Greek gods. Paeon was first given the potent peony by Leto on Mount Olympus. With it he is said to have cured Pluto of a wound inflicted by Hercules during the Trojan war, the first to have used the peony as a medicine. He is also credited with healing Mars of a wound with this powerful herb. These successes so aroused the jealousy and envy of his teacher, Aesculapius, that he secretly plotted Paeon's death. Pluto, grateful to Paeon for saving his life, when he heard of the plot, saved the physician from the fate of mortals by changing him into the plant that had been used in the cure, and the plant has ever since borne Paeon's name.

In prehistoric Greece many magical attributes, myths and legends centered around the peony. A familiar flower that glowed in the dark when the moon was full surely must possess great and supernatural powers. Thought to drive away devils and evil spirits where it was growing in the ground, a piece of the plant worn on one's person might be equally potent as a protection, not only against evil spirits but as a magic for healing. Its medical history is by far the most interesting of any flower and the most consistent in ancient folk medicine based on magic.

Pliny in his Natural History (about 77 A.D.) gives the first detailed description of a peony plant and seeds. He sets out twenty ills which it will cure. Another early herbal, the work of the Greek author and medical man, Dioscorides, was written in the first century, A.D. and includes about five hundred medicinal plants. This treatise was accepted as an almost infallible authority throughout the entire Middle Ages. In it Dioscorides describes as the medical peony what is apparently P. officinalis and growing wild in Europe. These writings take the peony back to a folk medicine of undeterminable antiquity.

According to Banckes' Herbal, the peony is "good for women for diverse sickness. Peony seed when it is black, it maketh deliverance ... of the child in her womb, and at every time when she shall use to drink it, she must drink fifteen seeds at one time. ... Also, for a man or woman that has the falling evil (epilepsy), eat it and drink it with wine, also hang the root about his neck and it will save him without doubt within fifteen days." As

late as the nineteenth century, faith in the value of the peony
for epilepsy still hung on here and there, its magic power still
potent in the minds of simple people.

The peony also served a career in the kitchen; P. edulis, a deep
crimson peony, was so named because its roots were eaten in
soups in Siberia.

In China in 536 A.D. the peony was fairly well distributed
over the country and used for both medicinal and kitchen purposes, as was the custom with herbs in early days. (The scholar
Alcuin is said to have inquired of his pupil, Charlemagne,
"What is an herb?" "The friend of physicians and the praise of
cooks" was his reply.)

The peony seeds were used as a seasoning in food and drinks.
Along with pepper, salt, garlic and other spices, they added
flavor to soups.

The rich in England during the medieval fourteenth and fif-
teenth centuries used its roots (P. officinalis) as a fine accom-
paniment with roast pork. The poor could only afford it as a
seasoning. Much was written about herbs for the medieval house-
hold, for cooking, healing virtues and divers uses. The Alewife
in Piers Plowman (1362) says "I have pepper and peony seed
and a pound of garlic and a farthingsworth of fennel seed for
fasting days."

Practically the national flower of China, the peony figures
often in its poetry, linking it by legend, history and romance to
the golden age of Chinese poetry and to the most famous of
Chinese love stories. In China its name "Sho Yo" means most
beautiful and it is considered the aristocrat of all the flowers.

P. lactiflora, which was a pure white, has been in cultivation
since time immemorial and the tree peony (P. suffruticosa), a
native of China, has been domesticated since the seventh century, during the Tang dynasty (619-906 A.D.), when it appeared
first in the imperial garden. The gardeners of those days, realiz-
ing the ornamental possibilities of the peony, "with the use of
strong fertilizers and great diligence in cultivation", began to
produce flowers of larger size.

The fields where the peony was grown were consecrated by inscriptions of a religious enthusiasm. Its culture was the favorite amusement of the nobility, the literary and the rich. Some varieties were held in such high esteem, far above the ordinary rates of barter, they were exchanged for gold. Some were considered heirlooms and willed to descendants. Frequently a prize plant was offered as a portion of the marriage dowry.

The tree peony of ancient lineage has been known as the "King of Flowers" since time immemorial in its native China, and as a symbol of royalty, wealth and rank, and one of the main motifs in their art. The herbaceous peony "Prime Minister Of All Flowers" is second in grandeur only to the tree peony. The lofty position of the peacock among birds is just like that of the peony among flowers. Both are a symbol of splendor. Peacocks and peonies are frequently associated in pictorial and decorative arts and found together in paintings on silk, screens, woodblock prints, porcelains and tapestries of the past, from the twelfth century down to the eighteenth.

Introduced into Japan by Buddhist monks, the peony is one of its most highly prized flowering plants and held in high esteem by the flower-loving Japanese. It is known in Japan as the flower of prosperity, an age-old association and symbolism, which came about because the difficulties encountered in its early cultivation caused it to be confined to the gardens of the wealthy.

The history of the peony in England is largely the story of its cultivation in gardens from early times. In 1157 an English writer gives a description of what a noble garden should contain and includes the peony, perhaps P. officinalis. From early poems it would appear that by 1375 the use of peonies in the hardy border had begun. The first printed picture, in England, a woodcut, appeared in 1484. In Tudor times the peony is described as "coming into fashion, widely grown and regarded with affection." Shakespeare, in "The Taming of The Shrew" (1603) refers to the peony in his line "Thy banks with peonied and lilied brims."

During the nineteenth century French hybridizers became very

1

much interested in the peony and their efforts produced many fine new varieties. An early and still well beloved variety is the large double white with crimson flecked center, Festiva Maxima, originated by Miellez of France in 1851. Beginning around 1898 Victor Lemoine of Nancy, France. became recognized as one of the world's greatest peony hybridizers; his introductions were notable for their distinction of form and coloring in addition to their rare beauty. He produced some very fine varieties crossing P. lactiflora with P. wittmanniana. A very remarkable race of hybrids was produced by crossing the tree peony, P. suffruticosa with the yellow P. lutea. Breeders also crossed an improved type of the Chinese lactiflora with the European officinalis to obtain new varieties.

In America, as in France, peony experts, collectors and commercial growers became interested in producing new improved plants, not quite like any others yet on the market. Although there have been many discards, many wonderful and unique varieties of startling beauty have been produced.

From Thomas Jefferson's Garden Book, we know peonies were grown in Virginia as early as 1771. This knowledge gives those in authority in Virginia at Mount Vernon and eighteenth century Williamsburg the privilege to grow peonies in their restored present day gardens.

The introduction of a number of varieties of the species of P. lactiflora from China around 1850 caused an increase in the popularity of the peony. The fragrance, hardiness and erect habit of growth, variability as to color and form of flowers combined to create a demand for this new Chinese peony. The tree peony also arrived in America at about this same time.

OLD-FASHIONED PEONY RECIPES

Liber Cure Cocorum

Liber Cure Cocorum, a copy of the Sloane manuscript by Richard Morris, published by Asher and Co., Berlin, 1862 has a recipe for "Peions istued" (stewed peonies) that goes as follows:

"Take peions and hew him in morselle smalle,

Put hom (them) in a erpyn (earthen) pot, pou (thou) shalle;

Take pilled garlek and herbys anon,

Hack (cut) hom smalle er pou more don (when this is done)

Put hom in po pot, and per (then) to take

Gode (good) brothe with wyte (white) greece, pou nost forsake; (do not forget)

Do (to) powder them to and gode verius (to powder them very well)

Coloure hit with saffron and salt inow (enough);

Pou (then) put in pote pese pyngs alle, (all these things)

And stue py peions pus pou schalle.

(And stew thy peonies thus you shall)

The Complete Confectioner

The Complete Confectioner, by Hannah Glasse, published by J. Cooke, 1782, has the following recipe.

COMPOUND PIONY WATER: Take eighteen *piony roots* fresh gathered, six ounces of bitter almonds, the leaves of rosemary, rue, wild thyme, and flowers of lavender dried, of each three ounces; of cinnamon, cubebs, seeds of angelica, coriander seed, carraway and anniseeds, each half an ounce, one gallon of rectified spirits of wine, with five gallons of soft water, and draw of three gallons by distillation. This is good in all nervous disorders.

THE USE OF THIS WATER: It is strong and powerful that it cannot be taken without the assistance of some other thing; but when dropt on crumbs of bread and sugar, you must take it the first thing in the morning, at four in the afternoon, and the last thing at night; you must not eat for an hour either before or after you take it; it is exceeding efficacious in all swoonings, weakness of heart, decayed spirits, palsies, appoplexies, and both to help and prevent a fit, it will also destroy all heaviness and coldness in the liver, restores lost appetite, and fortifies and surprisingly strengthens the stomach.

2

Peonies Classified

BOTANICAL CLASSIFICATION

Family — Ranunculaceae

A plant family is made up of a group of related plants (genera, plural for genus) sufficiently alike in general characteristics to show relationship and to justify being classed together into a family group. This relationship is based on similarities in structure in relation to their evolution or descent from common ancestors. The grouping of plants into families is essential for purposes of systematic classification.

The peony is a member of the Ranunculaceae, also called the buttercup or crowfoot family. This hardy group is mainly herbaceous but it also includes some shrubby and woody climbing plants. The family is widely distributed over the Temperate and Arctic regions.

Genus — Paeonia

A genus is a subdivision of a plant family, designed to simplify identification of plants and indicate relationship. It includes a group of species more or less closely related, having certain obviously structural characteristics in common. Members of a genus resemble each other more than they do members of other genera. The first part of a plant's Latin or botanical name is that of the genus to which it belongs. The Latin or botanical name is universal and precise and means the same thing to botanists in all countries, while common names are frequently

27

colloquialisms and a single plant may have a dozen different names in different parts of the country.

Paeonia is by far the most important garden genus of the Ranunculaceae family although the delphinium, anemone, aquilegia (columbine), clematis, pulsatilla and aconitum (monkshood) are also extremely popular garden plants in this same family.

Species

A number of species, there may be many or few, make up a genus. This group of plants is so nearly alike in their more stable characteristics they differ no more than offsprings from the same parent and represent a collection of closely related subjects. The plants may differ among themselves within a species to some degree by minor and less stable variations. The second part of a plant's botanical name is that of the species to which it belongs. To illustrate: Paeonia lactiflora is the Latin or botanical name of the common Chinese peony. Paeonia is the genus, lactiflora the species. If a third word is added, as P. lactiflora var. festiva, it refers to the variety, a variation derived from P. lactiflora.

The species of the genus Paeonia are composed of both woody and herbaceous perennial plants, an interesting, attractive and valuable garden genus.

Three Groups Under Paeonia

Paeon, suffruticosa and onaepia are the three divisions that make up the genus, Paeonia, which supplies the spring and early summer garden with beautiful, showy flowers in a wide assortment of color and form. At the height of its blooming season one is held spellbound in admiration.

1. *Paeon* includes all the herbaceous species native to Europe, Asia and Africa. This hardy group of perennials forms bushy plants 2' to 4½' high that die down to the ground in the autumn and now includes hundreds of named varieties. In a large measure this group is indebted to P. lactiflora (native of Siberia, Manchuria, Mongolia, China and Tibet) as the progeny of the modern herbaceous peony, familiar and popular with garden enthusiasts today. While this parentage is responsible for the

larger group, P. officinalis from southern Europe has also contributed its share to the present day race. Since its flowers usually begin to bloom about ten days before the "Chinese" or P. lactiflora peony descendants, they make a welcome extension to the blooming season.

The botanical names lactiflora or albiflora denote and refer to the same species and are synonyms. It has been found recently that lactiflora is probably the more correct name for the species. Botanists have adopted this term so we too are using lactiflora to denote that species in this book, but albiflora, through usage, will long remain in the trade and in common usage.

2. Moutan, suffruticosa, arborea, or the tree peony, native of China and Tibet, is a much branched shrubby or woody type plant (a shrub, not a tree) which grows from 3 to 6 feet in height. Its woody stems do not die down to the ground in the fall but it does lose its leaves. Truly the aristocrat of the flower kingdom, prized for its bushy habit and wide range of jewel-like flowers, it is a beautiful sight to behold when in flower.

3. *Onaepia* is composed of two low, fleshy species native to California and Washington, the only peony species found on this continent. This group has no importance in commerce.

FLOWER PARTS

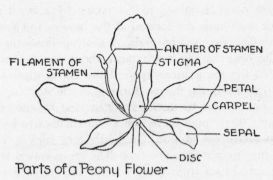

Parts of a Peony Flower

1. SEPALS—which make up the calyx, the outer green covering of the bud.

2. PETALS—which make up the corolla. There are five or more depending upon the flower type.

3. STAMENS—the male, pollen bearing organs composed of the:
   Anther—which develops and contains the pollen, usually yellow.
   Filament—a thread-like stalk which supports the anther, may be yellow or some other color, as pink or crimson.

4. CARPELS—the female organs, which when impregnated form the seed pods, usually some shade of green; may turn to other colors with age.
   Stigma—the sticky tip or end of the carpel which receives the pollen, of many different colors varying with each variety.

5. DISC—the base to which petals, etc. are attached on which often appear around the base of the carpels seed-like bodies of many colors. In some hybrids and tree peonies, it takes the form of a sheath surrounding the carpels.

PLANT PARTS

The peony plant consists of a crown underground from which all growth originates. The roots grow downward and outward. In some species they taper to a point while in others they grow like sweet potatoes joined to the crown by a small stem. The "eyes" or stem-buds are formed at the base of the stems shortly after the flowering season ends. A sharp-pointed sheath covering splits open as the stems push above the ground in early spring. As the stems grow upward the leaves gradually unfold from a tight head, the flowers forming at the stem tops.

Each variety has its distinctive stem and foliage color. Some are green, others pink or red or a combination of both as they push up above the ground. Gradually they turn green, though the red may persist for some time. The green leaves are of many shades and shapes from the grass-like foliage of the tenuifolia to the broad leaves of the wittmanniana macrophylla group.

The plants vary in height from low or dwarf forms 6″ to 2½′

to medium heights of 2½′ to 3½′. Five feet is considered tall but sometimes the tree peony grows taller.

The size of the bloom will vary from 2″ to 12″ and all colors except a true blue are included. The flowers begin to bloom in early spring with the first tulips and by careful selection of varieties peony flowers may be enjoyed over a blooming period of eight weeks. Occasionally the tree peony, lutea, will have a few flowers in the fall but there are no fall blooming varieties.

FIVE FLOWER TYPES

Peonies are classified according to the varying forms the flower parts take and there are five distinct types. For varieties see pages 73-77.

Blooming times will vary a great deal according to the season and many other conditions but to generalize we may say for regular herbaceous peonies the early doubles come into bloom in the North around Decoration Day, May 30th. Mid-season is approximately from June 10 to 20 and the late varieties bloom the last 10 days or 2 weeks in June. If you disbud, the blooming season will be shortened to about three weeks. If the side buds are left on, the blooming season should extend over a four week period.

Singles are early except for one or two and usually come five or six days ahead of the early doubles. If not disbudded they last almost through the entire blooming season. The Japanese are usually early mid-season and mid-season but a few may be late mid-season, Semi-doubles are usually mid-season though some bloom at all times.

1. SINGLE—This type has five or more petals around a center or cluster of pollen bearing stamens and carpels. The single-flowered types are of exquisite form and grace having the same purity of form that makes a water lily so exciting, some look like over-size buttercups or huge anemones. They usually have one or two rows of petals accentuated by conspicuous centers thick

Peony Types

Single

Semi-double

Japanese

Double

Anemone

with yellow stamens and open three to five days earlier than double varieties. The flowers hold up well on stiffly erect stems. While they do not last as long as the doubles they are more adaptable to wind and bad weather and are particularly useful and effective for indoor decoration as well as in the garden, where some of the doubles may be too heavy.

Favorite whites include Krinkled White, Pico, Le Jour and Exquisite. Seashell heads the list of pinks which also includes such favorites as Helen, Mischief and L'Etincelante. Arcturus is a favorite red as are President Lincoln, Imperial Red and Kickapoo.

2. JAPANESE—This type has five or more petals and a center of stamens bearing abortive anthers, nearly or completely void of pollen, commonly called *staminodes*. The staminodes appear in many different forms and surround the carpels and disc. Akin to the singles, the Japanese types form an unusual and lovely group. Similar in form, although usually larger than the singles, they are distinguished by their modified stamens which look like clusters of thinly shredded petals. These charming blossoms never become pollen spotted. Completely or nearly void of pollen, it may sometimes be found by splitting the edges of the staminodes.

Frequently the open flowers have fluffy centers different in color from the outside collar of petals, providing vivid color contrasts and giving the flower a richness of form and color, providing an outstanding feature in the spring garden. The flowers hold up their heads in wind and rain better than most doubles, do not get waterlogged and their strong stems do not need supports. Like the singles the plants are graceful in appearance and make very satisfactory garden plants, lending themselves particularly well to Japanese type flower arrangements. Many of the varieties have picturesque Japanese names, subtle colors and a striking overall effect.

Favorite whites include Isani Gidui, incomparably lovely in white and gold and resembling a large white poppy, Lotus

Queen, Moon of Nippon and Plainsman. Among the pinks Westerner, Tamate Boku, Ama-no-sode with rose pink petals surrounding a yellow center and Largo are especially popular.
Nippon Brilliant, Nippon Beauty, Hari-ai-nin and Mrs. Wilder
Bancroft are outstanding reds. Dignity is a giant dark but brilliant red. Mikado has crimson petals with red and yellow centers.

3. ANEMONE—Few catalogs list the anemone type as such, clas-
sifying them either as Japanese or doubles, for the garden trade.
This type is made up of five or more petals; usually it has several
rows of outer petals. The stamens in the center are fully transformed into small narrow petals called petalodes, usually yellow
or the same color as the outer petals which are white or light
pink. In novelty varieties the center may be of other colors, often
quite different in color from the guard petals. The so-called
yellow or near yellow lactiflora herbaceous peonies belong to
this group but with age the yellow color always fades to white.
The carpels are usually normal.

For Show purposes in entering specimen classes it is important
to enter "anemones" in their correct type class. Listed in catalogs
under doubles you will find such popular anemone type peonies
as Primevere, Laura Dessert and J. C. Legg, all whites with
lovely yellow centers. Nippon Gold, a dark pink with purest
golden-yellow staminodes, is tops in popularity in the anemone
group listed in catalogs as Japanese. Other favorites in this
same group are Gay Paree, a pink with white center, and
Prairies Afire, a pink with red center. Carolina Moon and Ada
Priscilla are both lovely whites, with yellow centers that fade
to white with age and are listed under doubles. Cathedral, a
lovely pink with yellow center fading to white, Do Tell, an
orchid pink, Leto, white with yellow center, and Mad. Butterfly,
a pink, are popular anemone types listed under the Japanese.

4. SEMI-DOUBLE—This type has five or more outer or guard petals
and a center of broad petals intermixed with many pollen bearing stamens which are sometimes grouped together in the center

or in other varieties, form rings among the petals. They are always a prominent and interesting feature of the flower, which includes some of the most artistic of peony blooms. The carpels may be normal or transformed either in whole or in part. The center may be made up of a greater or lesser number of broad petals.

Although the flowers of some are flamboyant they are never heavy and will not overwhelm a small planting or an indoor arrangement. Excellent for the suburban garden and for cutting they are long lasting and with the doubles are the most widely grown of all the peony varieties.

Dependable semi-double whites include such favorites as Miss America, Minnie Shaylor, Mildred May and Margaret Lough. White Rose is one of the most exquisite of all. In the pink group Lady Alexandra Duff, Silvia Saunders, Phyllis Kelway and Auguste Dessert are popular. Red Goddess, The Mighty Mo, Rosalie and Chippewa are lovely and popular reds.

5. DOUBLE—This type has five or more outer or guard petals with a center of stamens and carpels, more or less fully transformed into petals, which make up the main body of the flower. Often no trace is left of these parts. Sometimes the carpels appear with the stigmas either normal or partially transformed into petalodes or petals. When the outer or guard petals are shorter than the transformed petals the flower takes on a globular shape. When the transformed petals are shorter a so-called bomb shape is formed. Sometimes hidden stamens may appear imbedded in the flower.

The magnificent double kinds with their solid mass of petals, some looking like huge roses, are the most familiar, most grown and most loved of all and include many old favorites. Besides the white and blush kinds, many shades of pink and red are available in early, mid-season and late varieties. Some of the doubles owe their beauty to informality but almost all of the great exhibition varieties are prized for their symmetrically arranged petals. One of the earliest to open is the old favorite

Bomb-shaped double   Globular-shaped double

the lovely white, Festiva Maxima, with flecks of crimson in
the center. In spite of its weak stems requiring support it heads
the list of popular early, double whites along with varieties
like Kelway's Glorious and Le Cygne. Elsa Sass which blooms
late, is a fully double, creamy white, veiled pink, with a true rose
form, nice fragrance and unusually strong stems. Solange, Moonstone, Alice Harding and La Lorraine are good representatives
and favorites in the "blush" colored group.

Therese flowers early, is satiny pink changing to lilac-white in
the center, with heavy foliage and strong stems. Mrs. Franklin
D. Roosevelt also comes early to mid-season with exquisite rose-
shaped, light pink flowers. Reine Hortense, a delicate pink with
occasional crimson flecks has a crisp look, is wonderful for both
cut flowers and garden display and blooms in mid-season.
Hansina Brand's flowers are flesh pink with salmon tints. They
have splendid substance and good stems, are late to flower.
Nick Shaylor and Myrtle Gentry are also dependable in the light
pink group and late season bloomers.

Monsieur Jules Elie blooms early and is a joy to grow with its
huge, fragrant rose-pink flowers. Sarah Bernhardt and Walter
Faxon are two other reliable dark pinks which flower mid-
season to late. Blanche King, immense and fragrant with never
failing blooms of sparkling deep pink, is late to flower. Never
disbud it except for exhibition purposes.

Louis Joliet is an early dark, lustrous, non-fading red. Felix
Crousse and Karl Rosenfield are both fine, mid-season reds;

Felix has weaker stems but is a better cut flower. Philippe Rivoire and Mary Brand are also popular in the dark red group.

HOW THE TREE DIFFERS FROM THE HERBACEOUS PEONY

Although the tree and herbaceous peonies have much in common, they also have distinct differences. The tree peony develops rough-barked, woody stems that do not die down to the ground in the fall, continuing to grow year after year so a bush is formed. Their leaves are dissimilar in outline and the tree peony foliage is usually of a paler shade of green. Its buds are larger and flatter and are raised to a sharp point in the center. Its flowers, like the herbaceous, have both single and double forms; however, they usually attain a larger size, eight to twelve inches

A TREE PEONY
Its woody stems do not die down to the ground in the fall. Leaves are dissimilar in outline and usually of paler shade than herbaceous. Buds are larger, flatter and raised to sharp point in the center

A HERBACEOUS PEONY
Stems die down to the ground in autumn. Both tree and herbaceous peonies have single and double flowers. Tree peony flowers usually attain larger size

across, and flower about two weeks earlier than the common herbaceous peony. In the Orient the tree peony has had a more extended history and wider cultivation than the herbaceous, the reverse being the case in Europe and the United States.

The tree peony's requirements are more exacting than those of the herbaceous type, yet it is not fragile or as difficult to grow as many less rewarding plants that require greater care and attention. Although the original cost for tree peonies may seem high both type peonies are notably long-lived and improve with age, so considered as a longtime investment, peonies are not expensive but a real bargain, giving much in return for the minimum attention they require.

WHERE THEY WILL GROW

Peonies are easy to grow and do well in all sections of the country except Florida, southern California and the deep south where lack of winter cold prevents dormancy. In dry areas like northern Arizona and California plenty of water must be supplied every few days.

The South

As a rule easy opening varieties of loose petalage and the earlier blooming kinds of the single and Japanese types are best for the south or any locality where extreme heat comes quickly. Very late sorts with tight buds and full flowers need cool, somewhat moist weather to make them open best. Two year plants will give better results than smaller ones and the "eyes" in the south should be planted not more than one inch below the surface.

George W. Peyton, secretary of The American Peony Society, writes, "We run into some curious facts. A great many of the full doubles do as well in the South as the others but the extra late ones are almost always so badly damaged by either heat or thrips that they will not open. Yet some almost never fail, like Nick Shaylor, Mattie Lafuze and others. We also find that the kinds that do best in the further north sections like Duluth, Minnesota and the Peace River Country of Canada are exactly the same that do best in the South and the lates fail for one of the same reasons, excessive heat which almost always comes at the end of the peony season. And again we find a rather strange thing that the variety Mrs. A. M. Brand, a late white double, which almost never opens anywhere, is one of the best bloomers in the state of Georgia.

"Better results will be obtained in the South by always spraying the later doubles for thrips as they are primarily responsible for many failures of these to open."

Further south where the winter climate is very mild tree peonies do not flower as well as in the north since they may start into growth during warm January and February spells and then get nipped by later frosts. If they are nipped, protect them from the strong morning sun after the night of the frost so they will thaw gradually. We know of some tree peonies growing satisfactorily as far south as Northern Florida.

To force dormancy in the warmer climates, withhold water from around September 1 until October 15, and cut herbaceous varieties back to the ground.

California

Secretary Peyton writes: "There are successful plantings in California as far south as San Diego in the higher altitudes. South of Sacramento tree peonies seem to do better than the herbaceous at the lower levels, often blooming over a six months period from Christmas until June, though the bloom is sparse except in March and April. This is especially true where there is little frost. The late full doubles should be avoided." If you live in California and want advice on varieties that do best contact some successful, reliable peony grower in the state (see supplement, page 230).

The Far North

Peonies are hardy and do well in Canada where they are at their best in late June and early July. Where winter temperatures range 20° below zero or lower for any length of time, especially if there is little snow covering, winter protection is recommended. In severe climates protect the tree peony if you want to preserve the growth above ground. If not protected and the above ground growth dies, cut it off at ground level like an herbaceous peony. With this treatment it will perhaps not live to as ripe an age, but should do well for several years.

In parts of the north with low temperatures and no or little snow covering, a winter mulch or covering for the herbaceous hybrids and tree peonies is imperative to prevent losses. The lac-tiflora varieties can take such conditions as a general rule, but the hybrids need protection.

MAY STARTS THE PEONY PARADE

Peonies dominate the garden when in bloom and with care in selection of species and varieties it is now possible to have flowers in blossom for at least eight weeks. Plant breeders, with their many new fine hybrids and by their methods of selection, are constantly increasing the flowering season.

Our daughter attended Swarthmore College and we frequently made trips from Boston to Philadelphia during those four years. In comparing vegetation it seemed to us that Boston was always about two weeks later than Philadelphia. Of course, in the very early spring during forsythia time Boston is perhaps a month behind Philadelphia but as the season progresses by about June, Boston catches up to within a couple of weeks of the more southerly city. Mrs. Arthur Hoyt Scott told us she read some-where that the season progresses north 17 miles a day and according to her observations she thought that this was quite true. It is helpful information in approximating blooming dates in other sections of the country by comparison with your own location. Of course, the season and local conditions, whether protected, in the open, etc. must be considered, too.

1. Of the garden peonies *P. tenuifolia* is the earliest to bloom. Peony lovers can extend the season two or three weeks by planting this old time favorite. The little plant grows to only 16″ or 18″ in height, has fragrant, bright blood-red flowers, both single and double, which make up in brightness for their smaller size. Its distinctive, lacy, finely cut, fern-like foliage dies down to the ground a few weeks after blooming, differing in this respect from the other species whose foliage remains lovely and decorative all through the growing season. Their space in the garden may be filled in with annuals. These peonies make fine accents in the rock garden or in city gardens where space is at

a premium. P. tenuifolia latifolia, sometimes sold as P. officinalis tenuifolia, has fine grassy, emerald-green foliage to set off its open blossoms of rosy-red. The variety flore pleno has deep-red double, 3" blossoms.

2. P. WITTMANNIANA and the beautiful wittmanniana hybrids (crossed with lactiflora) closely follow P. tenuifolia, blooming early in May, a month ahead of the Chinese varieties. They are frequently referred to as the May-flowering peonies. The flowers are single with large firm petals, the first yellow peony to be discovered, although not a strong yellow. Its seeds are bright coral red. Crossed with the Chinese varieties valuable early-flowering hybrids have been devoloped. They have large, fragrant, single flowers of great beauty in delicate tints of white, yellow, rose and salmon. Their thick leaves are of vigorous and luxuriant growth. Excellent for cutting.

3. P. OFFICINALIS, in the North, blooms around Decoration Day, near the end of May. It grows to three feet in height, has coarsely cut foliage and wide-open single flowers varying from white to crimson, set off by recurving stigmas forming crimson centers. The double variety rubra plena is the familiar "piney" so common in our grandmothers' gardens, and characterized by its vivid ruby-red blossoms, large size and persistent growth. The variety rosea superba plena is a double variety of almost watermelon pink. The tuberous roots of these species are more delicate than the lactiflora varieties so plant them carefully. Up until about 1850 P. officinalis was the only peony grown to any extent in America. It has become one of the parents of some of the beautiful peonies in today's garden: alba plena has pink buds but the flower is a double white; and rosea plena has full, bright rose double flowers.

4. THE LOVELY TREE PEONIES, Japanese and European, come into bloom in the North around the middle of May. Remarkable for their beauty, the flowers are large, some measuring 8" to 12" across. P. suffruticosa varieties come in a wide range of colors from purest white and pale pink through rose-pinks, vermillion, scarlet, crimson and purple.

5. THE RESULTANT TREE PEONY HYBRIDS from interbreeding P. delavayi and P. lutea with P. suffruticosa, bloom about ten days to two weeks later along with many of the herbaceous hybrids. P. delavayi, the first maroon species discovered, probably enters into the parentage of most of the darker hybrid varieties. P. lutea, a wonderful golden yellow, is the parent of the yellow and orange colored blooms. These excellent strains are responsible for wonderful new colors, shapely and attractive plants with great vigor which transport and handle easily and extend the blooming period by at least two weeks. One may now have tree peonies in bloom over a period of a month. P. lutea will occasionally have a bloom or two in the early autumn, but there are no fall blooming peonies.

6. P. LACTIFLORA, (syns.— albiflora, chinensis, edulis, sinensis) the so-called Chinese peony, flowers in June and is the last to bloom, and one of the finest. One of its most famous varieties, Festiva Maxima, has large, white, double flowers flecked in the center with carmine. There are several thousand named double varieties of lactiflora on the market today. It has been crossed with other species. While originally white, pink or crimson, these crossings have produced a wide range of color and form. The newer introductions include clear tints and intermediate tones of shell pink, bright rose and deep velvety red. Other exciting colors are deep black-reds, brilliant orange-scarlets and pastel salmon. The inter-specific hybrids are well known for their precocity and beauty. These hybrids make possible a sequence of bloom which is remarkable.

3

Calendar of Things To Do

Peonies will do surprisingly well with little attention but special care will bring rewarding results.

January

1. This is the month for armchair reading and browsing. Study the catalogs and look over your peony notes taken the previous year, so you won't make the same mistakes twice. Figure out ways to improve on your previous methods.
2. Look over any new literature on the peony and reread some of the old.
3. This is a good time for garden clubs to sponsor a talk on peonies with colored slides showing gardens, varieties, care, culture, etc.

February

1. In the event of a mild winter make the rounds of the garden, pressing back into place any newly planted roots that may have heaved or been raised due to intermittent frosts.

March and April

1. Remove any mulch or hilled soil from around new plants early to avoid breaking the new young, tender shoots as they come up.
2. Cut out any dead tree peony wood on the older plants, keeping the plant vigorous, neat and trim in appearance.
3. If you want large flowers, thin out the clumps leaving fewer

43

stems, cutting away the weaker shoots soon after they appear above the ground.

4. To prevent botrytis, burn or destroy any material removed, including the mulch, and soon after the young shoots appear spray or dust with bordeaux mixture, fermate or any good modern fungicide at ten day to two week intervals; repeat at least two or three times.

5. As early as the ground can be worked, cultivate but be careful not to cut into the crown or new shoots when hoeing. Go no deeper than 2″ up near the plant, farther from the plant you can cultivate deeper.

6. If the peony has been planted three or four years, a handful of well rotted sheep manure to a plant, worked into the soil, will improve the bloom. Liquid manure may also be used. Some say manure should never be used. It must be well rotted and great care must be taken to keep it from getting over the crowns of the peony plants.

7. Tiny seedlings may come up around established plants. You may want to mark, later transplant, and coddle them to see what results you can get if you have the patience to grow peonies from seed (see page 119). It takes 4 to 10 years.

May and June

1. Continue to keep plants cultivated to cut down the weeds and keep the soil well aerated. Cultivate after each hard rain to prevent soil from hardening on top.

2. If the spring season is very dry, and the plants begin to wilt from lack of moisture, give them a good watering, a thorough soaking, once a week, enough to wet the ground down to the bottom of the roots. Repeat when the soil becomes dry.

3. If you want fewer and larger herbaceous flowers rather than a quantity of smaller ones, pick off the side buds while they are small, leaving only the terminal bud on each stalk.

4. Heavy double flowered peonies or varieties with weak stems should be staked before the plant becomes very large. An inconspicuous support that will encircle the whole plant loosely is best (see sketch, page 112).

5. If ants become annoying treat the soil around the plants with a strong solution of nicotine sulfate or chlordane to get rid of them.

6. Cut flowers and foliage for fresh arrangements and also to dry for dried arrangements for the winter. See page 187 for instructions.

7. Always cut flowers left on the plants as soon as they fade to keep the garden looking tidy and to keep the flowers from forming seed pods, except for the few you want for arrangements or for seeds. *Never* cut herbaceous plants to the ground until they are killed by frost.

8. While enthusiasm is high, at the height of the peony season, visit other peony gardens, see peonies in bloom in nurseries, and make out your peony order for September delivery. See supplement with peony sources, page 229, and variety lists pages 67 and 155.

9. Visit and participate in peony flower shows.

July

1. If you wish to grow peonies from seed, watch the seed pods from late July on. Collect as soon as the seeds can readily be removed from the pods, before they spill out. Only hard seed is good. Soft seed will not germinate.

2. Remove any seed pods you let form on the plants to use in fresh arrangements or later in dried arrangements.

3. Continue to cultivate as long as weeds grow.

August

1. If the summer is very dry, water thoroughly once a week to insure good blooms the following year. If you haven't already done so, order peonies for September planting.

2. Cut some of the lovely autumn peony foliage to dry for winter bouquets and to use fresh with fall flower arrangements.

September and October

1. Plant a peony for posterity. This is the best time to plant new peonies and to divide old clumps that must be divided so they will become established before hard frost, September in the north and October in the south. In sections in the

north where hard frosts come in late September, plant and divide old clumps earlier.

2. When the herbaceous foliage turns brown in the fall, cut stems to the ground. Brush away any partially rotted leaves, weeds, stems, or any material that has collected at the base of the plant and burn or destroy along with the foliage and stems as this material may harbor trouble, especially botrytis fungus for next year.

3. If the peony has been planted for three or four years, use about half a handful of commercial fertilizer like a 20% superphosphate or one handful of bonemeal to a plant, carefully working it into the soil, to build up the plant so it will flower well next season.

November

1. Peonies may be planted or transplanted until the ground freezes.

2. If you haven't already made a dried arrangement using flowers, buds, foliage and seed pods of the peony, now is the time.

3. Herbaceous hybrids and tree peonies in those below zero climates must be protected to prevent severe damage or loss from lack of snow covering.

December

1. Winter protection for herbaceous peonies is only necessary the first winter to help prevent heaving by frost. Mound the soil over the new planting for several inches, or after the ground freezes hard, mulch with evergreen boughs or straw, anything that will not mat down as leaves do. In extremely cold climates, 10°-20° below zero, protection is necessary for hybrids and tree peonies.

2. Why not join the American Peony Society! A membership will entitle you to the quarterly bulletin, which will keep you up to date on latest developments, give you information on peony culture, relate experiences in growing peonies in various sections of the country and give reports on local and national shows. While primarily an organization for amateurs,

all the prominent peony growers belong since the Society is open to both professionals and amateurs. Getting together for fellowship and discussion of mutual problems at the annual meetings and shows of this organization is no small part of its value. The American peony world revolves around this Society.

At present the membership fee for a calendar year (January 1 to January 1 is $5.00, and the secretary's address is: George W. Peyton, Box 1, Rapidan, Virginia. Mr. Peyton is also editor and chairman of the nomenclature committee.

PART II — THE HERBACEOUS PEONY

4

In Garden Design

LANDSCAPE IDEAS

One of the most decorative of all garden flowers, the sturdy, free-blooming peony is the glory of the spring and early summer landscape. It has justly highlighted the May and June gardens over the years. Permanent perennials, by nature they will stay put for years. Some have been known to thrive and bloom in the same spot for more than half a century. Time-tested, they have proven absolutely hardy even in very cold climates and their needs are simple. They grow from 2 to 4½ feet high, producing outstanding masses of brightly colored, exquisitely shaped blooms in a wide range of colors from white through the pinks and various shades of red to darkest purple with some yellows among the newer types. The much divided, attractive foliage is highly decorative from spring until late fall when it turns to lovely gold and bronze. If you want an attractive garden with a minimum of work, the enduring peony is your flower.

What a joy each spring, after the bleak months of winter, to watch the first little coral points or tips break through the ground, a certain sign spring is on its way. The tips grow into sharp red spears, these tender young stems and foliage then turn from shades of red and bronzy green to various shades of green, slowly the leaves unfold and then finally in May and

Peonies In The Landscape

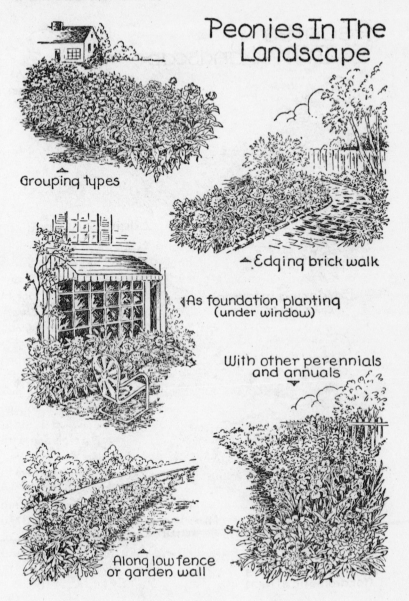

Grouping types

Edging brick walk

As foundation planting
(under window)

With other perennials
and annuals

Along low fence
or garden wall

Peonies
In The Landscape

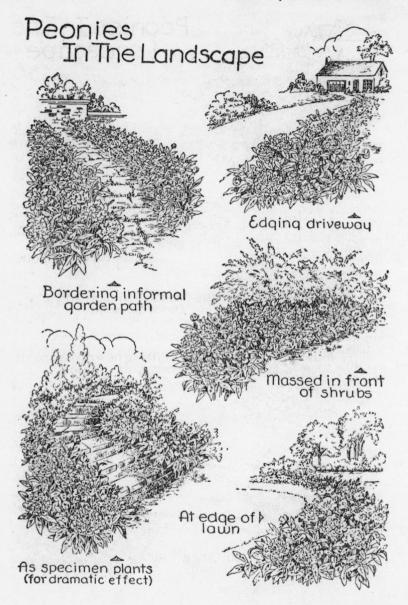

Edging driveway

Bordering informal
garden path

Massed in front
of shrubs

At edge of
lawn

As specimen plants
(for dramatic effect)

June comes the burst of glory of the beautiful flowers. An appealing subject all through the growing season, the gold and bronze autumn foliage is highly decorative. Truly "the old reliable" of the garden, the peony just goes on growing, blooming and surviving winters, year after year. Plant a peony for posterity. Some old clumps may have 50 or more blossoms open at once, a really spectacular sight.

Everybody loves the peony and anybody can grow it. It is fortunate that the peony can be utilized in so many ways in the landscape.

A flower for everyone, it is found growing at the back steps of many farm houses, as well as in the gardens of the most elaborate estates. The peony fits nicely into many situations. Where space is adequate landscape architects like to use it in strategic well placed areas for masses of color. It is also useful for small-scale landscaping. The very smallest garden may have a peony. Used instead of a small shrub one can find many places for it even in a small area.

Peonies may be planted in broad masses at the lawns edge, grouped in front of evergreen, deciduous and flowering shrubs are used as accent plants. Interplanted with other perennials or annuals in the border or grouped in special beds of their own, peonies make an elaborate show when at their peak.

Perhaps the choicest perennial from the standpoint of both flowers and foliage, its nicely cut, dark green leaves remain crisp and attractive all through the growing season. Planted as a hedge along a garden path, driveway, low wall or fence the massed border of peony foliage is as bright with the reds and golds of autumn as the nearby oaks and maples.

An old timer, the peony has long been a dooryard plant in New England and is still enjoyed as a specimen plant near the doorway or some other prominent place where its lovely blossoms may be appreciated to the fullest. As a foundation planting under a picture window, the peony may be enjoyed from both indoors and out providing there is ample root space, good soil, good drainage and sun to make it thrive.

Peonies are at home in the old fashioned garden, informal and unstudied in appearance with an abundance of bloom and color from early spring until late in the season. The newer and better varieties of such old-time favorites as peonies, hollyhocks, roses, phlox and lilies in no way spoil the character of the garden but rather improve the general effect. Used together harmoniously the large masses of plants give a delightful feeling of luxury and opulence. Once established in good fertile soil, these hardy favorites, if given sufficient moisture, do not require coddling.

For an attractive color effect in a long peony border, commence at either end with the whites and paler shades, working gradually from blush through the pinks to the center using a grouping of brilliant and dark reds in the middle. The reds and pinks make wonderful splashes of color.

Many fine color effects are possible or an all white garden is always effective, relaxing and cool looking in the summer. Spring and early summer white blooms may be had from azaleas, rhododendrons, dogwood, daphne, deutzia, kalmia, lilacs, spirea, viburnum, buddleia, climbing roses, peonies, iris and clematis, to mention only a few.

SPACE REQUIRED IN BORDER

In the smaller gardens with limited space which many of us cultivate today, we usually use peonies in combination with other perennials so we are of necessity limited in the number of peonies we can plant. Care must be taken not to overcrowd or dwarf a small suburban planting.

As to the space required for peonies, Secretary Peyton writes, "It will depend a great deal on the situation and the other material used in the border. While peonies vary in height, they rarely increase in number of stems or spread at the base after they put out 20 to 30 stems. They rarely grow over 18 or 20 inches in diameter at the base and 30 to 40 inches at the top or widest part. When almost any peony plant is full grown if the clumps were planted 4 feet apart, they will touch and there is little room for anything else. If grown with other material, however, they will not increase much after 5 or 6 years, especially if somewhat crowded. Tree peonies will expand more, if given a chance, than the herbaceous kinds. Some tree peonies will make a spread of 4 to 5 feet in diameter or even more if kept growing in good conditions".

Mr. Peyton also writes, "The peony rows in my garden are only 30″ apart and the plants not more than 18″ (not ideal), but I took notes for you on two plants planted ten years ago. Mildred May has 15 stems with a spread at the base of 12″ and it is 36″ tall, the widest part measures 30″. It is a good grower and makes a nice garden plant. Lady Aroostock, put out by Cherry Hill Nurseries, has 20 stems and a 14″ spread at the base, measures 40″ at its widest part and is 40″ tall. It makes one of the finest plants I have. Though its bloom is good and of large size it is not one of the top ten in beauty but it surely makes a beautiful garden plant. An old friend, Festiva Maxima, planted in 1907 and still growing vigorously makes blooms often 8″ in diameter. This variety frequently grows 4 feet in height with a spread of 40″, yet with only 10 to 20 stems".

Secretary Peyton advises, "Plant any herbaceous variety you like if height does not matter. Expect a base spread of from 12″ to 18″ as a maximum and a spread at the top of from 30″ to 40″. If height is a factor, choose lower growers".

He further states, "Hybrid herbaceous peonies will vary from small plants 6″ to 10″ in height to some that may reach 5 feet, their ultimate behavior depending largely on the cross and the individual variety".

BORDER IDEAS

Most borders are backed by a fence, garage, wall or a hedge of evergreens or semi-evergreens, interspersed now and then by groups of tall flowering shrubs. The tallest plants are placed at the back in front of the hedge, the other plants arranged to

Peony and Perennial Border
OF SOFT TONES

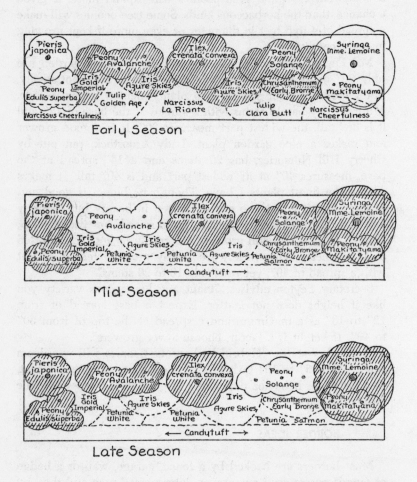

Early Season

Mid-Season

Late Season

Ruth D. Leiby, Designer

Plants Not in Bloom
Scale 1/2" = 1'-0"

Peony Border of Bright Colors
(Using early, mid-season and late peony varieties)

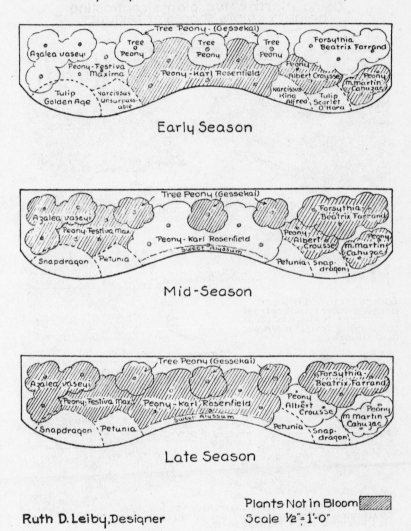

Early Season

Mid-Season

Late Season

Ruth D. Leiby, Designer

Plants Not in Bloom
Scale ½"=1'-0"

Accent Borders or Garden Enclosures
To Create Interest
Using distinctive plants, contrasting heights, colors, shapes or textures

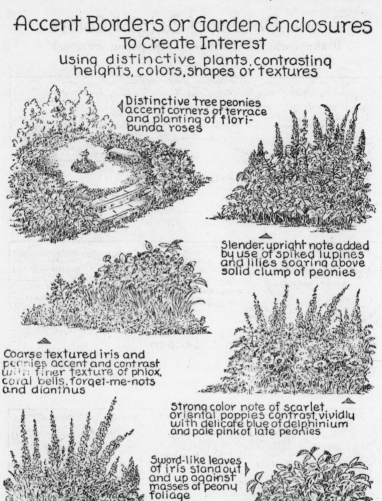

Distinctive tree peonies accent corners of terrace and planting of flori- bunda roses

Slender, upright note added by use of spiked lupines and lilies soaring above solid clump of peonies

Coarse textured iris and peonies accent and contrast with finer texture of phlox, coral bells, forget-me-nots and dianthus

Strong color note of scarlet oriental poppies contrast vividly with delicate blue of delphinium and pale pink of late peonies

Sword-like leaves of iris stand out and up against masses of peony foliage

Spiked flowers of delphinium, lupines, foxglove, columbine and veronica contrast nicely with peony, iris, lily and phlox flower forms

grade down to the lowest ones which are at the front. Occasionally a tall plant like hollyhock, peony, boltonia, lily or Iris kaempferi is brought forward to break the monotony and serve as an accent.

Along the walk or grass use edging plants 6" to 18" tall like dianthus, Iberis sempervirens, Nepeta mussini, Veronica latifolia, viola, sea-pink (Armeria) or white rock-cress (Arabis). Gradually fill in behind with taller plants 1' to 1½' to 2' to 2½' in height, plants tall and sturdy in growth, using color masses which form a continuity and add special interest.

At the back tall, heavy foliage plants fit in well. Use material of special interest as some of the newer and unusual peony varieties that will attract attention. When the garden is new, in the bare spaces between these important plants use filler material or plants which you do not mind sacrificing later as they are crowded out by the growth of more important neighbors. Some good filler plants are the false dragonhead (Physostegia virginiana), globe thistle (Echinops ritro), goatsbeard (Aruncus sylvester), monkshood (Aconitum fisheri) and white snakeroot (Eupatorium rugosum).

Special interest plants should be used for variety and to draw emphasis to the good elements or features of the garden design or to special plant combinations. Accent long borders by using contrasting heights, colors, textures and shapes. Lilies soaring high above a grouping of peonies complement them and will draw attention to the peonies. Bright roses on a climber backing a clump of white peonies add interest and by contrast emphasize the peonies; both show off to better advantage. A strong color note among paler shades can be very effective. The heavier, coarser textured foliage of the peony contrasts interestingly with finely dissected, almost fernlike leaves of the garden heliotrope (Valeriana officinalis). Although the leaf of the iris is also of a heavy texture, its spear-like form contrasts nicely in shape with the large, compound foliage of the peony.

Peonies, iris, chrysanthemums, phlox and a few other hardy

perennials are excellent stand-by plants in the border throughout the season.

GOOD COMPANION PLANTS

(see book endpapers and plans by landscape architects, which appear elsewhere in this chapter)

While peonies are attractive alone, their fine qualities show off to best advantage when judiciously combined with other plant material. Backed by lilacs, deutzia or mockorange flowering at the same time, peonies are in harmony with the old-fashioned character of the plants. The common white flowering lilac (Syringa vulgaris alba) forms a bold, tall growing plant that blooms in May. The Persian lilac grows 5 to 6 feet tall and has fragrant pale lilac flowers on gracefully arching branches in May. There is also a white flowering form. Philadelphus coronarius (sweet mockorange) grows 10 to 12 feet high and produces fragrant white flowers in May and June.

Sir Thomas Lipton is a fine Rosa rugosa hybrid, a semi-double fragrant shrub rose; it has pure white flowers and is one of the earliest to bloom, in late May on through the season. Plants reach a height of 4 to 5 feet. R. rugosa alba and the cherry-red Grootendorst, another rugosa hybrid, are also good shrub roses to plant with peonies. The creamy white flowers of the fragrant viburnum (V. carlesi) are at their best in April and May and it is one of the most fragrant of the deciduous flowering shrubs. It forms a compact plant 5 to 6 feet in height. Often overlooked and delightful backing up peonies is Neilla sinensis closely allied to spirea, a small dense graceful shrub not over 6 feet high with showy dainty pink terminal clusters. There are many, many fine shrubs that bloom with the peony and combine beautifully with it in the landscape. Weigela, white, pink or red, with its foxglove-like flowers blooms in May and June as do some of the interesting honeysuckles. Both make excellent companion plants in the landscape and in arrangements.

In the spring when peonies thrust up their soft red shoots they are especially pretty with the green leaves of white and yellow daffodils. The leaf buds unfold remarkable form and color with red stems and sea-green leaflets varying in hue from one plant to the next. As the peony leaves expand, they in turn hide the drying daffodil foliage. As the new shoots of the peony come up in the spring, before the foliage is fully developed, the extra space may be utilized by some of the other very early spring flowering bulbs; like the crocus, snowdrop, scilla, chionodoxa, and extra early flowering tulips. These blooms may be enjoyed while the peonies are making their new growth. The foliage of most die down naturally and the luxuriant peony foliage as it develops will do them no harm. Hardy lilies do well interplanted with peonies. Summer flowering bulbs such as the ismene (Peruvian daffodil), lycoris (Wonder Lily) and summer hyacinth add color and interest when the peonies are through blooming.

Grouped together in a border, peonies contrast massively with the spiked, more slender vertical flower forms. A fine mixer, many delightful and exciting color combinations are possible when peonies are interplanted with late iris, early phlox and the triumphant poppies or clumps of spire-like lupines in deep pink and rose, spikes of blue delphinium or the tall stately foxglove.

Some of the early flowering hybrid hemerocallis or daylilies make excellent companion plants. The Madonna and regal lilies can be used effectively between peonies. Other tall growing perennials which give picturesque effects are the spikes of yellow thermopsis (T. caroliniana) with pea-like foliage or the wild false indigo (Baptisis australis) with its blue-green foliage. Also the long-spurred columbine, coreopsis or pyrethrum (both single and double), and the early-flowering spireas all make charming peony companions as do feverfew, garden heliotrope and filipendula.

Late peonies are good with plants like gladiolus which, when set out in the spring, flower shortly after the peonies have finished. Since gladiolus corms must be taken up each fall and

Lilacs bloom. Viburnums just beginning and Althaeas in small leaf stage. Tree Peonies in bloom with early and midseason in full to opening stage, midseasonlates and lates in bud. Border plants in bloom. Others in various stages of shoots, small to medium in height, filling in between peonies, small iris in front of tree peonies partly in bloom, many in bud

May: Introducing the Peony Display

Lilacs gone by. Viburnums in full tilt. Althaeas in full leaf. Tree peonies gone by, earlies also. Midseason and lates in full bloom. Delphiniums in just opening to full open stage. Siberian iris in full bloom. Good clump in center. Border plants in bloom. Those gone by now mounds of leaves, others in bloom but tapering off as in case of edging plants

June: "The Queen of Flowers" in all its glory

Only Althaeas now in bloom. Delphiniums in second blooming with verbascums, lilies, Jap. iris, daylilies and other lilies carrying on, chrysanthemums and fall asters making nice mounds but not yet in bloom, while dianthus carries on and chrysanthemum arcticum is now in bloom. All peonies in leafy stage making fine mounds

July: Other flowering plants supply the color

(plan by John Brimer)

Peony Garden
(Plan by John Brimer)

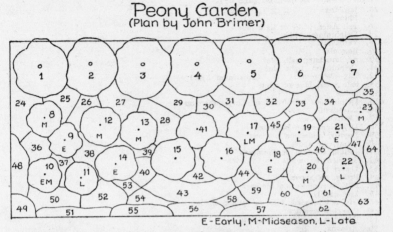

E-Early, M-Midseason, L-Late

The above plan is for an area 12' x 25' which includes the space devoted to the shrubs backing up the peonies and other perennials. The shrubs give some auxiliary bloom with a couple for late summer. The peonies give a range of bloom, form and timing as well as utilizing all colors.

The border is one which might extend across the back yard at the rear of a lawn patch with the shrubbery masking a vegetable garden or maybe up against a garage or other building .or maybe just a property line fence. The herbaceous plants mixed in among the peonies were chosen for size, for blooming time and to give some kind of color all season long with the main emphasis on the peony-time bloom. However all will be good looking most of the season (not ragged or unkempt in appearance) with a minimum of care.

1. Althaea, Snowdrift
2. Viburnum tomentosum
3. Hybrid French Lilac, Firament
4. Hybrid French Lilac, Miss Ellen Willmott
5. Hybrid French Lilac, Ami Schott
6. Viburnum tomentosum plicatum grandiflorum
7. Althaea, rubis or Celestial Blue

PEONIES: E-Early M-Midseason L-Late

8.	Irwin Altman	M. Rd
9.	Pico	E. Single white
10.	Hargrove Hudson	EM Pink
11.	June Brilliant	L. Red
12.	Lottie Dawson Rea	M. Pink
13.	Rashoomon	M. Jap. Red
14.	Festiva Maxima	E. White
15.	*Tree Peony* Reine Elizabeth	Salmon Rose
16.	*Tree Peony* Comtesse de Tudor	Salmon tipped white
17.	Better Times	LM Rose
18.	Mrs. F. D. Roosevelt	E. Pink
19.	Roberta	L. Jap. white
20.	M. Martin Cahuzac	M. Dark red
21.	Kansas	E. Red
22.	Solange	L. Ivory White
23.	Mandaleen	M. Light Pink

40. and 44. Fern leaved single and double peonies.

List continued on page 64

PERENNIALS (see plan on page 63)
24. Jap. Iris
25. Phlox
26. Fall Aster, white or light blue
27. Delphinium, white
28. Verbascum
29. Boltonia
30. Autumn aster, tall, pink
31. Delphinium, light blue
32. Lily—Western . . . Pardalinum hyb.)
33. Fall Aster, blue or white
34. Phlox
35. Delphinium belladonna or Chrysanthemum
36. Late daylily, yellow
37. Chrysanthemum
38. Lily—midseason blooming
39. Daylily, midseason bloomer
40. Peony, see above
41. Lilium auratum or Eremurus
42. Siberian iris, white
43. Dwarf bearded iris
44. Peony, see above
45. Lily, late midseason bloomer
46. Late daylily
47. Iris, tall breaded. Pink or salmon shades
48. Creeping veronica
49. Dianthus deltoides, "Brilliant"
50. Armeria
51. Arabis
52. Iberis
53. Heuchera, red
54. Dianthus heddewigi
55. Aubrietia or Arenaria
56. Cerastium
57. Creeping Veronica
58. Heuchera, pink
59. Dwarf fall aster, pink
60. Artemisia, Silver Mound
61. Dianthus, Old Spice
62. Chrysanthemum arcticum
63. Armeria
64. Viola cornuta, Catherine Sharp

replanted in the spring (3″ deep and 6″ apart) they may be properly spaced each spring in relation to the growth of the peony plant. The upright spikes require very little lateral room and are able to take care of themselves.

While the peony maintains its attractive massive foliage throughout the season, to cover spaces left empty by flowering bulbs and such flowers as bleeding-heart (Dicentra spectabilis), Virginia-bluebell (Mertensia virginica), and poppies, annuals may be used to augment and harmonize with the permanent plants in the border. Where space permits annuals such as mallow or gypsophila will branch out and grow right over any flowers past their best and completely hide them.

Edging or border plants which flower with peonies and combine well include coral-bells (Heuchera sanguinea), varying in color from white to deep red with compact tufts of attractive foliage. Snow-in-summer (Cerastium tomentosum) a hardy creeping perennial, has grayish, downy foliage and abundant white flowers. The low evergreen white candytuft (Iberis sempervirens), Gold-Dust, the yellow Alyssum saxatile compactum, the English daisy (Bellis perennis) a dwarf compact perennial with profusion of flowers in all colors except yellow and pansies, make attractive edgings. The various hardy border pinks planted in drifts make mats of blue-green foliage covered with white or pink, sweetly-scented flowers. Cut them back after flowering to encourage new growth. What could be more delightful than the early blooming peony Festiva Maxima's large white flowers, flecked with crimson, displayed above a bed of May blooming Maiden Pink (Dianthus deltoides). The edging adds much and gives a finish to the peony planting.

SEE VARIETIES IN FLOWER

In order to choose wisely one must know what is available. Catalogs are interesting to leaf through and study but one should see varieties in bloom to know them and compare their habits of growth, form and color. As you see the varieties growing, select those with special appeal for you and those suited to your conditions and needs.

If you are really interested in learning about varieties, visit nearby peony gardens open to you when they are in bloom. At that time make notes for fall buying and planting. Visit nearby commercial nurseries when at their height of bloom and public plantings of peonies, if you are fortunate enough to have such a planting nearby. Take advantage of private collections where visitors are welcome and visit peony shows or exhibitions. If you are sincerely interested, most private growers will welcome you as a visitor to their private collections.

Most peony shows have all flowers well labeled and usually feature the newer varieties as well as the old favorites so attend shows to acquaint yourself with the latest introductions. But keep in mind that most show blooms entered for competition have been pampered and given extra special care to attain the perfection of culture they represent. Please see supplement at the back of the book, page 218, for retail sources, public plantings and private plantings you may visit. Be sure and study the supplement. It is full of valuable information.

5

Selecting Varieties

Although new varieties are constantly being offered to the trade, by comparison with some flowers, varieties change slowly and do not vary noticeably from season to season or become quickly out of date. Many still favored, and deservedly so, were introduced years ago. The problem of keeping up with new varieties is simple compared with the iris or rose where many varieties introduced are soon lost in the struggle for survival.

No two people will agree on the same favorites or best varieties since individual tastes differ widely. Some people find it interesting to experiment with novelties and new varieties, others prefer old reliables. In beauty and reliability many of the old kinds are hard to beat and not so expensive but it is also fun and exciting to try some of the new types. By variation and hybridization the garden forms are now fabulous with many hundreds from which to choose.

In regard to lists, our good friend Winthrop Thurlow of Cherry Hill Nurseries writes, "I object to making out a list of the best twelve as I could not make a list of the twelve people whom I like best or which of my children I like best. There are too many variables".

George W. Peyton of the American Peony Society writes, "Many requests are received by the Secretary for lists of vari-

67

Herbaceous Peony Flowers Measure 2" to 10" in Diameter

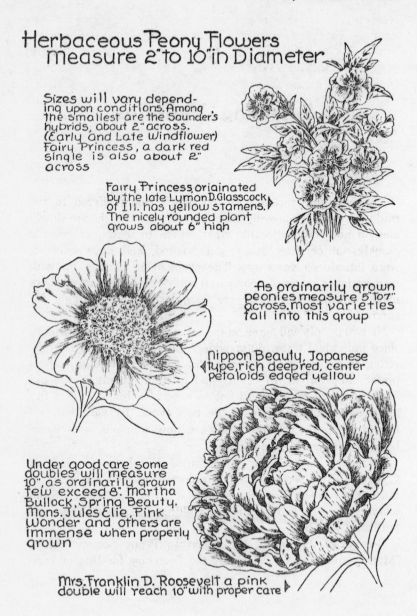

Sizes will vary depend-
ing upon conditions. Among
the smallest are the Saunder's
hybrids, about 2" across.
(Early and Late Windflower)
Fairy Princess, a dark red
single is also about 2"
across

Fairy Princess originated
by the late Lyman D.Glasscock
of Ill. has yellow stamens.
The nicely rounded plant
grows about 6" high

As ordinarily grown
peonies measure 5" to 7"
across. Most varieties
fall into this group

Nippon Beauty, Japanese
type, rich deep red, center
petaloids edged yellow

Under good care some
doubles will measure
10", as ordinarily grown
few exceed 8". Martha
Bullock, Spring Beauty,
Mons. Jules Elie, Pink
Wonder and others are
immense when properly
grown

Mrs. Franklin D. Roosevelt a pink
double will reach 10" with proper care

eties to plant, especially from those who are more or less confused by the glowing descriptions given, not only in catalogs but in articles published in magazines and even in our Bulletin, your Secretary sometimes being the guilty party. The beautiful blooms seen in our shows occasionally add fuel to the fire.

"In answering such requests, it must be remembered that every individual has his own idea of what he wants in his garden and so for another to make the selection is rather dangerous as the varieties chosen may be far from those that will please. For this reason it is always wise to call the attention of the inquirer to this fact. He is also advised that the Society publishes lists of the ones that have been chosen by the members as those most popular.

"If the inquirer still insists that a specific list be recommended, it is done. Then if the ones listed do not please the inquirer, the Secretary's skirts are clear.

"Picking varieties at an exhibition is often not a satisfactory way of doing the job. Flowers shown in exhibitions are there to win prizes and are not shown for garden effect and use. Every lawful device, such as bagging to prevent injury and preserve color, and disbudding and fertilizing to produce size is employed—and it is proper for the exhibitor to do so. For this reason varieties for garden use should be picked, if possible, in a garden, where they are grown as they would be by the ordinary gardener. Then, if a 'lemon' is chosen, the buyer did it with his eyes open".

Variety lists can be helpful, especially for the beginner, to indicate what is available, so we are including several. The fact you do not find a variety on the list in no way condemns it. It may be equally good.

25 TESTED PLANTS FOR THE BEGINNER

Singles
Arcturus, red
Krinkled White, blush
Le Jour, white

Seashell, pink

Japanese
Ama-no-sode, pink

Charm, dark red
Shaylor's Sunburst, blush to
    white

Anemone
Primevere, white and yellow

Semi-Doubles
Silvia Saunders, light pink

Doubles, white or blush
Alice Harding, white tinted
    pink
Elsa Sass, white tinted pink
Festiva Maxima, white red
    spots
James Kelway, blush
Kelway's Glorious, white,

fragrant
La Lorraine, blush

Doubles, light pink
Mrs. F. D. Roosevelt
Nick Shaylor
Reine Hortense
Therese

Doubles, dark pink
Loren Franklin
Mons. Jules Elie
Sarah Bernhardt
Walter Faxon

Doubles, red
Mary Brand, bright red
Philippe Rivoire, dark red,
    fragrant

25 RARE PEONIES FOR THE CONNOISSEUR

Also see growers' lists for many more fine varieties.

Hybrids
Archangel, white, single
Claire de Lune, yellow, single
Red Charm, red double, best

Singles
Champlain, blush
Dawn Pink, bright pink
Pico, white

Japanese
Isani Gidui, white
Mount Palomar, red
Westerner, pink

Semi-Doubles
Mildred May, pure white
White Rose, exquisite

Doubles
Alma Hansen, white tinted pink
Bonanza, red
Dolorodell, light pink
Doris Cooper, light pink
Florence Ellis, light pink
Frances Mains, light pink
Mary E. Nicholls, white
Mattie Lafuze, blush
Moonstone, pale pink
Mother's Choice, white faintly tinted pink
Mrs. Livingston Farrand, purest pink, temperamental
Oriental Gold, yellow. Syns. Yokihi and Golden Dream
Victory, white tinted pink
Yosemite, white tinted yellow

VOTE WINNERS

The following four somewhat shortened lists tabulate results from a poll of the members of the American Peony Society for 1958. It must be kept in mind that not all members voted. One hundred and eight questionnaires were returned to the Secretary.

Forty Most Popular—All Types
(in order of popularity)
Mons. Jules Elie, double, dark pink
Nick Shaylor, double, light pink
    the above two tied
Mrs. Franklin D. Roosevelt, double, light pink
Kansas, double, red
Kelway's Glorious, double white
    the above two tied
Philippe Rivoire, double red

Myrtle Gentry, double, light pink
Elsa Sass, double, white
Festiva Maxima, double, white
Red Charm, hybrid, double, red
  the above two tied
Le Cygne, double, white
Blanche King, double, dark pink
Therese, double, light pink
  the above two tied
Hansina Brand, double, light pink
Victory, double, white
  the above two tied
Solange, double, blush
Karl Rosenfield, double, red
Seashell, single, pink
  the above two tied
Krinkled White, single, blush
Minuet, double, light pink
  the above two tied
Martha Bulloch, double, dark pink
Mary Brand, double, red
Moonstone, double, light pink
Walter Faxon, double, medium pink
  the above three tied
Isani Gidui, Japanese, white
Mrs. Livingston Farrand, double, light pink
Alice Harding, double blush
Mrs. J. V. Edlund, double, white
Tempest, double, red
  the above two tied
Alesia, double, white
Nancy Nicholls, double, blush
Pico, single, white
  the above three tied
Chocolate Soldier, hybrid, semi-double, red
Ella Christiansen, double, light pink

Felix Crousse, double, red
Longfellow, double, red
  the above four tied
La Lorraine, double, blush
Nippon Brilliant, Japanese, red
Ruth Elizabeth, double, red
Sarah Bernhardt, double, dark pink
  the above four tied

You will notice that the doubles won most of the votes. First honors went to two full doubles; Mons. Jules Elie with an immense dark pink flower which looks like a big chrysanthemum and is an excellent keeper, and Nick Shaylor a top-notch variety with light delicate pink petals shaped like a rose.

Mrs. Franklin D. Roosevelt, another double, fragrant, light pink, was voted second place. It has good substance and keeps well cut. In third place the light red Kansas tied with the white Kelway's Glorious which received the most votes in the 1958 poll as the "One Best" peony. It is a fine mid-season, lacy white, rose type, with strong stems and fully deserves its high rating.

The "One" Best
(in order of popularity)
Kelway's Glorious, double, white
Elsa Sass, double, white
Kansas, double, red
Hansina Brand, double, light pink
Le Cygne, double, white
Mons. Jules Elie, double, dark pink
Mrs. F. D. Roosevelt, double, light pink
Red Charm, hybrid, double, red
  the above four tied
Festiva Maxima, double, white
Nick Shaylor, double, light pink
  the above two tied

Ten Most Popular in Each Color and Type
(1-2-3 indicate top three in popularity)

SINGLES

White or Blush	Pink	Red
Albiflora, The Bride	Angelus	Arcturus (1)
Dancing Nymph	Dawn Pink	Flander's Fields
Dunlora	Elfin Pink	Fortune Teller
Exquisite	Helen (2)	Imperial Red (3)
Krinkled White (1)	Josette	Kaskaskia
Le Jour (3)	L'Etincelante	Kewanee
Pico (2)	Mischief (3)	Kickapoo
Rebecca	Pride of Langport	Man O' War
Virginia Dare	Seashell (1)	President Lincoln (2)
Watchman	Sparkling Star	Vera

The singles, if not disbudded, will bloom for almost the entire peony season.

JAPANESE

White or Blush	Pink	Red
Bu-te	Akashigata	Break o' Day
Carrara	Ama-no-sode (3)	Charm
Isani Gidui (1)	Doreen	Dignity
Lotus Queen (2)	Goddess	Hari-ai-nin (3)
Midway Island	Largo	Midnight Sun
Moon of Nippon	Sky Pilot	Mikado
Plainsman	Tamate Boku (2)	Mrs. Wilder Bancroft
Shaylor's Sunburst	Vanity	Nippon Beauty (2)
Toro-no-maki (3)	Westerner (1)	Nippon Brilliant (1)
	Yellow King	Rashoomon

ANEMONE—(Listed in catalogs as either Japanese or Doubles)

Aureolin (Japanese)—Pink guard peteals, yellow center fading to white.

Cathedral (Japanese)—Pink guard petals, yellow center fading to white.

Fancy Nancy (Japanese)—Cerise pink.

Gay Paree (Japanese)—Pink guard petals, white center. (3)

J. C. Legg (Double)—White guard petals, yellow center.

Laura Dessert (Double)—White guard petals, yellow center.

Madame Butterfly (Japanese)—Pink.

Nippon Gold (Japanese)—Pink guard petals, yellow center. (1)

Philomele (Japanese)—Pink guard petals, yellow center.

Prairie Afire (Japanese)—Pink guard petals, red center. (3)

Primevere (Double)—White guard petals, yellow center. (2)

Torpilleur (Japanese)—Red.

Ada Priscilla (Double)—White guard petals and yellow center, mid-season. One of the finest of all but did not appear on any list.

SEMI-DOUBLES

White or Blush	Pink	Red
A. G. Perry	Aerie	Albuquerque
Margaret Lough (3)	Auguste Dessert	Blazing Star
Marie Jacquin	Ave Maria	Chippewa (3)
Mildred May (3)	Banner Bright	Maestro
Minnie Shaylor (2)	Lady Alexandra	Mr. L. Van Leeuwen
Miss America (1)	Duff (1)	Red Goddess (1)
Nanette	Mrs. Deane Funk	Rosalie (3)
Rare China	Prairie Belle	Sinbad
Susan B. White	Phyllis Kelway (3)	The Mighty Mo (2)
White Rose	Silvia Saunders (2)	William F. Turner
	Spring Beauty	

DOUBLES

White	Blush
Alesia, late	A. B. Franklin, late
Dr. J. H. Neeley, mid-season	Alice Harding, mid-season to
Elsa Sass, late (2)	late (3)

DOUBLES (continued)

White

Festiva Maxima, early (2)
Frances Willard, mid-season
Kelway's Glorious, early (1)
Le Cygne, early (3)
Mary E. Nicholls, mid-season
  to late
Mrs. J. V. Edlund, late
Victory, late

Blush

Baroness Schroeder, mid-season
Florence Nicholls, mid-season
Gardenia, mid-season
George W. Peyton, mid-season
  to late*
La Lorraine, mid-season to late
Mattie Lafuze, late
Moonstone, mid-season (2)
Nancy Nicholls, mid-season to
  late
Solange, late (1)
Tourangelle, mid season to late

*George W. Peyton sometimes does not open well and stem is
not of the best but it is one of the most exquisitely colored of
all peonies and its informality gives it added beauty. Loved by
artists.

Light Pink

Auten's Pride, mid-season to
  late
Doris Cooper, late
Ella Christiansen, mid-season
Hansina Brand, late
Minuet, mid-season to late
Mrs. F. D. Roosevelt, early to
  mid-season (2)
Myrtle Gentry, late (3)
Nick Shaylor, late (1)
Reine Hortense, mid-season
Therese, early

Dark Pink

Blanche King, late (3)
Edulis Superba, early, fragrant
Helen Hayes, late
Loren Franklin, mid-season to
  late
Martha Bulloch, mid-season to
  late
Mons. Jules Elie, early (1)
Mrs. Livingston Farrand, mid-
  season to late
Sarah Bernhardt, mid-season to
  late (2)
Souv. de Louis Bigot, mid-season
Walter Faxon, mid-season to late

DOUBLES (continued)

Red	Yellow
Felix Crousse, mid-season to late	Oriental Gold, mid-season
Kansas, mid-season (1)	
Karl Rosenfield, mid-season (2)	
Longfellow, mid-season	
Mary Brand, mid-season (3)	
Mons. Martin Cahusac, mid-season	
Philippe Rivoire, late, fragrant (1)	
Richard Carvel, early	
Ruth Elizabeth, late	
Tempest, mid-season	

ACCORDING TO PURPOSE

1. Good Garden Border Varieties

Suitable garden varieties depend on the individual border. This is a general list of some good garden varieties according to *height* and *time of blooming*. Select those that best fit your situation.

TALL

Extra Early

Any hybrid.

Angelo Cobb Freeborn—strong stems, distinctive red color, sometimes fails.

Garden Peace—good stems, beautiful white single, good bloomer.

Illini Warrior—extra tall, strong plant, red single.

White Innocence—distinctive white flower, single.

Early

Any single tall enough.

Big Ben—strong stems, rather loose globular flower, good red double, dependable.

Festiva Maxima—white double, dependable. If many blooms, stems may bend.

Mons. Jules Elie—stems not so strong, immense globular double flower, pink double.

Mid-season

Kansas—good in every way, light red double.

Sanctuary—similar to Titania (below), but often petals edged with red.

Titania—good stems, outstanding flowers, white semi-double.

Late

Mattie Lafuze—stems, foliage and flowers outstanding, blush double.

Mrs. W. L. Gumm—light pink double, strong stems, good bloomer, large well formed flowers.

MEDIUM HEIGHT—innumerable ones.

Extra Early

Any good hybrid.

Alexander Woollcott—brilliant crimson semi-double. Extra good color. Plant good.

Cardinal's Robe—Scarlet single. Plant good.

Carina—one of the best and most outstanding in color, bright red.

Chocolate Soldier—outstanding almost black, semi-double with brilliant yellow markings. Often Japanese type, single type or almost full double.

Claire de Lune—foliage and flower out of the ordinary, pale yellow. Single.

Flame—glowing color. Plant good. Single.

Helen Matthews—brilliant red, semi-double. Expensive. Stems good.

Sophie—brilliant pink. Plant good. Single.

Many others equally as good.

Early

Any single not tall. Any early Japanese type.

Aerie—pale pink to white semi-double, fine plant. Floriferous.

Kelway's Glorious—white fragrant double. Fair stems. Floriferous.

Mons. Jules Elie—immense globular flower. Should be supported. Pink double.

Mid-season—Hundreds of all types except singles.

Adolphe Rousseau—tallest of medium height, showy crimson flowers sometimes almost single, often semi-double and double.

James Kelway, blush double, good plant, floriferous.

Lady Alexandra Duff—light pink, strong stemmed, semi-double.

Miss America—large flower, blush to white, semi-double. Good stems slightly bending at times.

Late

Elsa Sass—grand in every way.

Mary E. Nicholls—fine plant and foliage, large, white double.

Nick Shaylor—also one of the ten best in every way.

Philippe Rivoire—fragrant red. Fair plant, dark-red double. Fair stems.

DWARF

Extra Early

Tenuifolia and macrophylla hybrids.

Early

Mme. de Verneville—fragrant, white double, stems not so good. Floriferous. Red markings.

Octavie Demay—light pink double, fine stems, floriferous.

Mid-season

Not many outstanding.

Late

Joseph Christie. Grand white double, yellow shaded.

2. For Emphasis or Spectacular Effects

There are also many fine varieties not listed .

Extra Early

Any extra brilliant hybrid.

Early

Champlain, tall strong stems, makes large plant with extra large smooth light green foliage. Opens slightly blush.

Dawn Pink, brilliant pink single. Good plant, also floriferous.

Krinkled White, abundance of medium sized flowers on medium tall upstanding stems.

Pico, white single, large flowers, immense foliage, tall.

Silvia Saunders, rather dwarf grower, compact plant, usually hidden by its charming almost single medium sized flowers of light pink.

Sparkling Star, same effects as Dawn Pink. See above.

Mid-season

The brilliant red and pink Japanese types are excellent.

Break o'Day, Jap.;, contrasting shades of unusual reds. Good plant.

Doreen, brilliant pink guards, bright yellow staminodes. Tall. Fair stems. Japanese.

Dragon's Nest, distinctive coloring and placement of petals and

Garden Princess, splendid plant habit, medium height, beautiful light pink semi-double.

John Howard Wigell, dark brilliant pink of distinctive shade. staminodes. Good plant. Strongly contrasting red and yellow. Rather dwarf and spreading habit.

June Rose, extra bright pink, double, with some stamens showing. Medium height and medium sized flowers.

Largo, large flowers, strong medium tall plants. Good stems. Dark pink.

Mabel L. Gore, brilliant dark pink double. Fine plant.

Nippon Brilliant, extra bright red and brilliant yellow staminodes. Medium sized flowers usually. Tall good stems. Japanese.

Sword Dance, darker red, not so tall. Japanese.

Late

Mattie Lafuze, often immense flowers of blush pink, strong tall stems. Dark green foliage heavily ribbed and large.

Mildred May, may be late midseason. Extra fine plant, covered with medium sized pure white flowers often born in triangular clusters. Circles of stamens intermingled with petals. Tall and upstanding. Foliage medium to large, extra good.

Yosemite, medium tall plant, fine foliage and stem. Exquisitely tinted white, double yellow tints.

The most spectacular of all are the many brilliantly colored hybrids, followed by the brilliant Japanese types. For both foliage and flowers, Laddie, an extra early dwarf hybrid with finely cut foliage and brilliant scarlet single flowers is outstanding.

Annisquam, Champlain, Florence Ellis, Garden Princess, Largo, Mildred May, Minuet and Pico make grand plants and flowers.

3. For Outstanding Foliage

Look over varieties listed under "Spectacular Effects". Many have outstanding foliage. Others with outstanding foliage include:

Amberglow, double, amber tinted white.

Flamingo, early semi-double, light pink.

Lady Aristook, white flowers with some red markings, not so outstanding but has tall, fine, strong stems and showy foliage.

Lowell Thomas, red double with rounded, thickly set foliage, quite distinctive.

Macrophylla, a low spreading plant has extra large uncut foliage. Its hybrids have the same characteristics.

Mlokosewitschi, often hard to grow, has small yellow single flowers with red stems which contrast with its distinctive foliage.

Tenuifolia, dwarf plants with brilliant red flowers, both single and double forms, and cosmos like foliage.

4. For Fragrance

Some people like the strong pollen odor of the singles and semi-doubles, others do not. The following peonies have a pleasing fragrance.

Edulis Superba, double, dark pink, early.

Kelway's Glorious, double, white, early mid-season.

Mandaleen, double, light pink, medium late.

Mrs. R. M. Bacheller, double, white with some stamens, midseason.

Myrtle Gentry, double, light pink, late.
Philippe Rivoire, double, red, mid-season.
Sistie, double pink that fades to white, late mid-season to late.

BY COLOR AND SEASON

It must be noted that color and season of bloom vary
with the climate and situation.

White or Blush

EXTRA EARLY	MID-SEASON	LATE MID-SEASON OR
Camellia, SD.	Alice Harding, D.	LATE
Chalice, S.	Baroness Schroeder,	Alesia, D.
Early Windflower,	D.	Alma Hansen, D.
S.	Dr. J. H. Neeley, D.	Dorothy J., D.
Garden Peace. S.	Florence Nicholls,	Elsa Sass, D.
White Innocence,	D.	Mary E. Nicholls,
S.	Gardenia, D.	D.
	Krinkled White, S.	Mattie Lafuze, D.
	Lotus Queen, J.	Mildred May, SD
	Margaret Lough,	Nancy Nicholls
	SD.	Blush, D.
	Moon of Nippon,	Solange, Blush, D.
	J.	Victory, D.
	White Gold, J.	White Rose, SD.

EARLY
Festiva Maxima, D.
Isani Gidui, J.
James Kelway, D.
Kelway's Glorious, D.
Le Cygne, D.
Le Jour, S.
Minnie Shaylor, SD.
Mrs. Edward Harding, D.
Pico, S.
Shaylor's Sunburst, J.

Yellow

Claire de Lune, S.—Extra Early
Moonrise, S.—Extra Early
Oriental Gold, D.—Mid-Season

White with Yellow Centers (Yellow fades to white with age)

EARLY	MID-SEASON	LATE
Carolina Moon, D.	Ada Priscilla, D.	Couronne d'Or, D.
Duchesse de	Gleam of Gold, D.	Joseph Christie, D.
Nemours, D.	Golden Bracelet, D.	Moonglow, D.
Laura Dessert, D.	Golden Dawn, D.	Yosemite, D.
	Matchless Beauty,	
	D.	
	Primevere, D.	

Light Pink

EXTRA EARLY	MID-SEASON	Annisquam, D.
Arbutus Pink, S.	Auten's Pride, D.	Dolorodell, D.
Birthday, S.	Ella Christiansen,	Doris Cooper, D.
Lovely Rose, SD.	D.	Mandaleen, D.
Madrigal, S.	Mischief, S.	Minuet, D.
Shell Pink, S.	Moonstone, D.	Myrtle Gentry, D.
	Prairie Belle, SD.	Nick Shaylor, D.
	Reine Hortense, D.	Tourangelle, D.
	Seashell, S.	Virginia Lee, D.
	Vanity, J.	LATE MID-SEASON
	Victory Chateau	OR LATE
	Thierry, D.	
	Westerner, J.	

EARLY
Aerie, SD.
Josette, S.
Lady Alexandra Duff, SD.
Madame Calot, D.
Mrs. F. D. Roosevelt, D.

Light Pink, Early (continued)
Pride of Langport, S.
Silvia Saunders, SD.
Therese, D.
Westhill, D.
Yellow King, J.

Dark Pink

EXTRA EARLY	MID-SEASON	LATE MID-SEASON
Flame, S.	Ama-no-sode, J.	OR LATE
Laura Magnuson, SD.	Auguste Dessert, SD.	Anne Bigger, D.
		Blanche King, D.
Ludovica, SD.	Hermione, D.	Ensign Moriarty, D.
Salmon Beauty, D.	June Rose, D.	Helen Hayes, D.
Salmon Glow, S.	Largo, J.	Loren Franklin, D.
	Martha Bulloch, D.	Pres. F. D.
	Mrs. Livingston Farrand, D.	Roosevelt, D.
		Sky Pilot, J.
	Nippon Gold, A.J.	Tamate Boku, J.
	Pink Wonder, D.	Tondeleyo, D.
	Sarah Bernhardt, D.	Walter Faxon, D.

EARLY
Dawn Pink, S.
Edulis Superba, D.
Harriet Olney, S.
Helen, S.
L'Etincelante, S.
Mons. Jules Elie, D.
Off. rosea superba, D.
Prairie Rose, S.

NOTE: Some of the above are sometimes found in light pink lists.

Red

EXTRA EARLY	MID-SEASON	LATE MID-SEASON
Alexander Wooll- cott, SD.	Adolphe Rousseau, D-SD.	OR LATE
		Bonanza, D.

Red (continued)

EXTRA EARLY	MID-SEASON	LATE MID-SEASON
Chocolate Soldier,	Chippewa, SD.	OR LATE
SD.	Dignity, J.	Charm, J.
Golden Glow, S.	Hari-ai-nin, J.	Felix Crousse, D.
Laddie, S.	Kansas, D.	King Midas, D.
Red Charm, D.	Karl Rosenfield, D.	Lowell Thomas, D.
	Longfellow, D.	Philippe Rivoire, D.
	Mary Brand, D.	Ruth Clay, D.
	Nippon Beauty, J.	Ruth Elizabeth, D.
	Red Goddess, SD.	
	Sword Dance, J.	
	Tempest, D.	

EARLY

Arcturus, S.
Big Ben, D.
Cherry Hill, D.
Flander's Fields, S.
Imperial Red, S.
Man O' War, S.
Nippon Brilliant, J.
Officinalis rubra plena, D.
Richard Carvel, D.
President Lincoln, S.
Note: This list
   could be ex-
   panded many
   times.

Other Colors

EXTRA EARLY

Ballerina, SD, greenish yellow.
Carina, SD, scarlet.
Green Ivory, S, light green.
Lavender, SD, lilac.

RECOMMENDED FOR THE SOUTH

George W. Peyton of Rapidan, Virginia, recommends the
following herbaceous varieties for southern gardeners:

For Beginners

Kelway's Glorious	White	Double	Early
Mons. Jules Elie	Pink	Double	Early
Sea Shell	Pink	Single	Mid-season
Karl Rosenfield	Red	Double	Mid-season
Shaylor's Sunburst	Blush	Japanese	Mid-season

For General Garden Use

Elsa Sass	White to Pink	Double	Late
Florence Nicholls	Blush	Double	Mid-season
Therese	Light Pink	Double	Early
Philippe Rivoire	Dark Red	Semi-	
Minnie Shaylor	Blush	Double	Late
		Double	Mid-season
Le Jour	White	Single	Early
Imperial Red	Light Red	Single	Early
Ama-no-sode	Pink	Japanese	Mid-season
Isani Gidui	White	Japanese	Mid-season
Sword Dance	Red	Japanese	Mid-season

RECOMMENDED FOR CANADA

We received the following letter from R. W. Oliver, Horticulturist—Ornamentals, Plant Research Institute, Ottawa, Canada.

"Herbaceous peonies are among the most successful perennials in Canadian gardens because of their hardiness. One of the finest collections in the country was maintained by the late Mr. C. M. Clarke near Beaverlodge, Alberta which is over four hundred miles north of the U. S. border. The deep rich clay loam of that area suited their taste in spite of the —50°F temperatures in winter.

"Likewise in the light sandy garden at the Central Experimental Farm at Ottawa, peonies have been grown with success for the last seventy years. While space limits us to approximately two hundred varieties at one time, something over six hundred different varieties have been tried. Replacements are made whenever a variety is discarded because of disease or inferiority. As the collection is moved from one location to another every ten or twelve years, this operation gives an opportunity for more numerous replacements of varieties.

"So long as we stick to herbaceous varieties, winter does very little damage, as we usually have sufficient snow to provide good insulation. The open winter of 1938, when the collection was covered by a sheet of ice which resulted from mild weather, was the only one to cause much damage in the last twenty-five years. We do not use mulch except over new varieties planted in early September to make sure that they are well established before the ground freezes in early November.

"Our chief battles have been with diseases. Botrytis which seems ever on the alert in cool damp summers, requires constant watching and the removal of affected stems as soon as symptoms are observed. Modern fungicides applied just as foliage is opening and again just after bloom have reduced the damage from this pest. More baffling is a sort of "stunt" that causes the plant to put out numerous thin dwarfed stems with no flower buds. For years we referred to it as Lemoine's disease, which no one seemed clear about. Now being more fashionable, we are inclined to blame it on a virus, but so far have not isolated the culprit. It is quite distinct from the Ring Spot and Leaf Curl viruses that also affect peonies. So far we have no adequate defence but to rogue out and burn affected plants and to sterilize the soil where they have grown before replanting.

"Insects do little damage to peonies directly but aphids and ants may spread the above virus, so we wage war on them with Lindane.

"Unfortunately we cannot devote funds necessary to keep our collection abreast of the newest varieties and have tried very few of the new "hybrids". We hope to make arrangements to obtain "guests" from some of the more generous originators, so that the best of these seedlings can be seen by the three thousand people that go through our display garden each week during the summer months. Peonies are usually one of the chief attractions from June 15-30 though the dates vary from year to year as much as five days on either side.

"Under our conditions many of the older varieties have proven of more value for garden purposes than some recent introductions we have had. The following varieties are recommended most highly for our section of the country."

DOUBLE	SEMI-DOUBLE	SINGLE & JAPANESE
	White	
Festiva Maxima	Couronne d'Or	Isani Gidui, Japanese
Kelway's Glorious	Rare China*	Krinkled White,
Le Cygne		Single
Mrs. Edward Harding		
	Blush	
Baroness Schroeder	Lady Alexandra Duff	Josette, Single*
Blush	Marie Jacquin	Toro-no-maki,
Solange		Japanese
Tourangelle		
	Light Pink	
Georgiana Shaylor	Silvia Saunders	Helen, Single*
Hansina Brand		Kukenijishi,
Milton Hill		Japanese
Myrtle Gentry		
	Medium Pink	
Edulis Superba	Phyllis Kelway	Largo, Japanese*
La France		Tokio, Japanese
Martha Bulloch		
Sarah Bernhardt		
Walter Faxon		
	Dark Pink	
Blanche King	Auguste Dessert	L'Etincelante, Single
	Reine Baronet	Tamate-Boku,
		Japanese

*Newer expensive varieties

Red

Adolphe Rousseau	Instituteur Doriat
Cherry Hill	Anemone (J.)
Felix Crousse	Mikado, red,
Karl Rosenfield	Japanese
Mons. Martin	
Cahuzac	
Mary Brand	
Philippe Rivoire	

SOME PEYTON NOTES ON VARIETIES

The oldest named variety in cultivation: Officinalis rubra plena, about 2,000 years.

The oldest named varieties imported into Europe from China: Fragrans (1805); Whitleyi (Queen Victoria) 1808. Peonies may have been imported into Holland from China, early in the 17th century.

The most beloved and most famous: Festiva Maxima, double white flecked carmine.

The most fragrant: Edulis Superba, double, dark pink.

The "One Best": Kelway's Glorious, beautiful double white flower, good stems, dependable bloomer and fragrant to an unusual degree. So voted by people from New Zealand to the Peace River country of Canada.

The most popular: Mons. Jules Elie, double dark pink and Nick Shaylor, double light pink.

The most perfect flower: Le Cygne, double white.

The most beautifully colored: Mrs. Livingston Farrand, double light pink. Solange, 2nd, double blush. Others: Walter Faxon, double pink; Ramona Lins, double blush pink; Geo. W. Peyton, double blush.

The "loveliest": Japanese type, Isani Gidui and White Rose, a semi-double.

The most charming: Elsa Sass, double white, and Mrs. F. D. Roosevelt, double light pink.

The purest white: Mildred May, semi-double, and Amalia Olson (new double).

The purest pink: Mrs. Livingston Farrand, double light pink, and Walter Faxon, double pink.

The only true yellow double: Oriental Gold also known as Aurea, Golden Dream, Yokihi (Japanese name). Native of Japan.

The blackest: Sable (hybrid.). The bluest: Lavender (hybrid). and Blue Rose (Lins), a double.

HERBACEOUS SPECIES

The species are of extreme importance to the botanist since it is from this source they make their classifications. Many gardeners also find the species of particular interest since a knowledge of species forms a good background for understanding the inter-specific hybrids being developed today. Many catalogs list species for sale and they are sought by both collectors and hybridizers. We are listing some of the more prominent. All the species listed have only one flower to a stem except emodi, lactiflora and veitchi and their varieties. The flowers are always single, however officinalis and tenuifolia both have double forms.

The average American gardener will not be interested in growing the species. You must be a real fan to want to grow anomala. Cambessedesi and wittmanniana are very hard to grow. Many others will be deeply disappointing and equally difficult, so keep this in mind.

ANOMALA—Early, bright scarlet-crimson. Cut leaves. Native of Russia and Central Asia.

ARIETINA—Flowers red, but vary to a soft rose-pink. Native to Italy, Greece and Asia Minor.

BROTERI—Cup-shaped rose flowers with yellow center. Charming shiny-leaved plant. Native to Spain and Portugal.

CAMBESSEDESI—Deep rose, blossoms medium sized. Native to Western Mediterranean Islands.

CLUSI—Cup-shaped white flowers with golden stamens, fine green leaves. Native to Crete.

CORIACEA—Rose red. Used by hybridizers to produce lavender,

violet and light purple hybrids. Its hybrids are the nearest to blue we have. Native to Spain, Morocco and Algeria.

DAURICA—Deep rose-red with yellow center, oval leaves. Native to Crimea, Asia Minor and Caucasus.

EMODI—Handsome fern-like foliage with nodding white flowers. Tallest of all. Native to India.

HUMILIS—Deep red flowers. Native to Spain and France.

JAPONICA—White flowers. Native to Japan.

LACTIFLORA (syns. albiflora, chinensis, edulis and sinensis)— White. Chief source of the Chinese or common peony. Native to Siberia, Manchuria, Mongolia, China and Tibet.

MASCULA—Red-rose, purplish shadings. Native from England to Russia and south to Asia Minor.

MLOKOSEWITSCHI—Lemon sherbet, transparent yellow flowers, light grey-green foliage. Not reliable, often just fades away after a year or two but where it does grow it makes a beautiful plant. Native to region between the Black and Caspian Seas.

MOLLIS—Fine red, also white. Gardens only.

OBOVATA—White to rose-purple. Native to Siberia, Manchuria, China and Japan. Oval leaves.

OBOVATA WILLMOTTIAE—Gorgeous white with immense round leaves. Native to China.

OFFICINALIS—Red. Native to southern Europe.

PEREGRINA—Glistening red. Native to the Balkans.

PEREGRINA LOBATA—A dwarf plant with brilliant vermilion flowers. Blooms early in June in North. Native to the Balkans.

RUSSI—Lovely rose color. Native to the Western Mediterranean Islands.

TENUIFOLIA—Fern-leaved peony. Most finely cut of all peony foliage. Small, gay, deep crimson flowers. Var. rosea is a single pink. Native to Bulgaria, Caucasus. Early.

TENUIFOLIA LATIFOLIA—Very early, rosy-red single, bright and free flowering, very vigorous.

VEITCHI—Magenta blush-pink. Native to China.

VEITCHI WOODWARDI—Magenta blush-pink. Native to Western China.

WITTMANNIANA—The first yellow peony to be discovered. Creamy yellow flowers, pale green carpels. Native to region between the Black and Caspian Seas. Charming species. Blooms early with tall May tulips.

WITTMANNIANA MACROPHYLLA—Vies with P. tenuifolia for the honor of opening the peony season. Flowers around May 12 in the north. Has creamy-white goblet flowers, largest of all peony leaves, highly glossy with odor of boxwood.

6

Hybrids

The hybrid peony has won a place for itself in the average garden, as well as in the fanciers' collection. Every garden should have a few hybrids to supplement lactiflora and officinalis, in this way lengthening the season of bloom and adding new colors and flower forms.

A hybrid peony is produced by crossing a variety of one species with one of another. The scientific breeder or hybridizer makes crosses of known parentage in an effort to work toward a definite goal or objective.

Early in the nineteenth century lactiflora was brought from China to England in three varieties: Fragrans, pink (1805); Whitleyi, white (1808) and Humei, dark pink (1810). One or more of these three varieties were found in nearly all old gardens. These varieties were known for their vigorous constitution and resistance to disease. Most of our peonies are of lactiflora origin. In reading about the peony remember that the words albiflora, chinensis, edulis and sinensis denote the same species as lactiflora, they are synonymous. Early crossings were with lactiflora and officinalis. The majority of officinalis hybrids are notable for a brilliance and purity of color. The early red double found in our grandmother's garden was officinalis rubra plena. Alba plena and rosea plena, with a variation rosea superba, are two other varieties commonly grown.

The great French hybridizer, Victor Lemoine, at the beginning of the century crossed lactiflora with the species wittmanniana, producing for us four new hybrids: Avant Garde, a single pink and Le Printemps, Mai Fleuri and Messagere, three white singles with yellow and green tints.

AMERICAN HYBRIDIZERS

Since 1924 the number of American hybrids have increased by leaps and bounds and now they make a very long list and this undoubtedly is only a beginning in the peony hybridizing field. However, hybridizing is a slow process requiring infinite patience. It takes one year for germination, another three for new hybrids to reach blooming size, and another three to obtain mature performance. In about 1917 in the United States Lyman D. Glassock of Elwood, Illinois, and Prof. A. P. Saunders of Clinton, New York, independently, and a thousand miles apart, started working toward a similar goal, crossing species to prolong the season of bloom, widen and vary the color range, height, form and size and produce better plants. Edward Auten, Jr. of Princeville, Illinois, must have started planting hybrid seed shortly after that time. Mr. Glassock's Legionaire at Des Moines, Iowa, in 1924 was the first showing of a hybrid in this country. Col. Benjamin M. Guppy of Melrose, Massachusetts, began to hybridize about the same time and exhibited some of his hybrids at the Massachusetts Horticultural Society in Boston. He celebrated his ninetieth birthday last May and is still very much interested in the peony, doing some hybridizing in his back yard.

Enthused by the success of these men, others were encouraged to join the group: Mrs. Mary E. G. Freeborn of Proctor, Vermont, W. S. Bockstoce of Pittsburgh, Pennsylvania and Walter Mains of Belle Center, Ohio.

In the beginning these hybridizers used mainly the species lactiflora and officinalis and their varieties, which produced in general shades of pink and red. Prof. Saunders became adventuresome and used almost every available species. Dr. Earle B.

White, formerly of Maryland and now of Florida, followed Prof. Saunders' pattern and made the first known cross between the yellow species, mlokosewitschi, and lactiflora. A pale yellow single, Claire de Lune, was the result after making 4000 crosses.

The extraordinary results already obtained with the hybrid peonies give great promise and hope for the future. Many of the originations of these hybridizers are now on the market. They are scarce, so should be ordered in ample time. They vary in price from $5.00 to $50.00 a root. The wide color range includes every color except a true blue.

With the discovery of the creamy yellow wittmanniana and the light yellow mlokosewitschi hopes mounted that a yellow double would soon be on its way. The greatest success along this line was achieved by Dr. White in his origination of the pale yellow single, Claire de Lune, a variety of charm and distinction. Now with the discovery of the new yellow double "Oriental Gold" we have the only double yellow and the deepest yellow in a herbaceous peony. It was first listed as "Aurea". Certainly the correct name is Yokihi after the most noted of Japanese Geisha girls but since it was sent to this country under a number of different names it was registered as Oriental Gold. It is listed in one catalog as "Golden Dream". No one knows the origin or species from which it came, it is probably a hybrid, perhaps of a species still unknown except in its native habitat.

The pink hybrids embrace all shades including salmons and corals. There are crimsons of all intensities, black-reds, purples, lilacs and lavenders. The coriacea hybrids are a lovely clear pale lilac. Green Ivory is a white with greenish tints. The hybrid "Sable" is the nearest approach to black.

Among the hybrids one finds the earliest to flower, the shortest and tallest, the sturdiest and most graceful of all herbaceous peonies. Mostly singles, many are semi-doubles and some full doubles, with a few of the Japanese type.

Some of the herbaceous hybrids in some locations will die to the ground naturally, often in late July or August, much sooner than the lactifloras which wait for frost. When this happens many think they have lost the plant but it is just its nature. Of course, this does spoil the foliage effect of these hybrids in late season.

Herbaceous hybrids in those 10° to 20° below zero climates (for extended periods) must be protected to prevent severe damage or loss from lack of snow covering.

We are describing just a few of our many favorite hybrids.

We saw Red Charm, a Glasscock introduction, in the Stedman Buttrick garden (Concord, Mass.) this spring. It blooms a week earlier than the regulars, is a bright, rich ruby-red with tall strong stems, a very fine plant and surely one of the finest red doubles in existence.

Chocolate Soldier, an Auten introduction, is early, an exceptionally fine flower with rich black-red petals (almost black) and contrasting yellow dots on the center petals.

Claire de Lune (parentage Mons. Jules Elie x mlokosewitschi) was originated by Dr. White and introduced by Wild and Son in 1954. It is an exquisite pale ivory yellow with crinkled petals, yellow filaments and orange anthers forming an attractive orange center. Its stems are thin but very stiff, a really elegant early single peony.

Five fine semi-double hybrids in the Saunders group of "lobatas" (lactiflora x lobata) which bloom through the first half of June include Lovely Rose, a "creamy" rose pink and all that its name implies. Ludovica, a very large clear rose pink with prettily rounded petals and Nathalie with intense clear rose petals and a magnificent flat bloom, semi-double or more. Alexander Woollcott, a brilliant red and Carina, a shining scarlet, vie for honors in the group of reds.

Please see page 12 for
names of varieties shown in color

I. Luminously lovely tree peony Virginia Irving Pierce

II. Brilliant peonies against a background of snow-in-summer dramatize a garden wall

III. Tree peony Hinode-no-seki

IV. Peonies and bearded iris bloom companionably along a garden path

POPULAR HYBRID VARIETIES ACCORDING TO COLOR

(as voted by members of the American Peony Society—1958)

White
Archangel, single
Campagna, single
Chalice, single
Requiem, single
Starlight, ivory, single
White Innocence, single

Yellow
Claire de Lune, ivory, single
Daystar, single
Mlokosewitschi, single (species)
Moonrise, single
Rushlight, single
Sunlight, single

Pink
Dainty Lass, Japanese
Elizabeth Foster, single
Eros, single
Eventide, single
Janice, single
Laura Magnuson, semi-double
Lotus Bloom, semi-double
Lovely Rose, semi-double
Ludovica, semi-double
May Dawn, single
Nathalie, semi-double
Queen Rose, semi-double
        to double
Roselette, single
Salmon Beauty, double
Salmon Glow, single
Sophie, single
Victoria Lincoln, double

Red
Alexander Woollcott, semi-
   double
Freeborn
Angelo Cobb Freeborn, double
Bright Knight, single
Carina, semi-double
Chocolate Soldier, semi-double
Crusader, double
Flame, single
Gay Cavalier, single
Golden Glow, single
Helen Matthews, semi-double
Illini Belle, semi-double
John Harvard, single
Laddie, single
Mahogany, single
Red Charm, double
Red Red Rose, semi-double
Robert W. Auten, double
Rose Marie, double
Veritas, semi-double
Walter Mains, Japanese

MYRON D. BIGGER HERBACEOUS HYBRID SELECTIONS

Myron D. Bigger of Topeka, Kansas, President of the American Peony Society, lists his choice of herbaceous hybrids and makes some personal comments.

"The time has arrived when every peony lover should plant a few herbaceous hybrid peonies. To my knowledge there is no other group of peonies that contain the wonderful bright reds and pinks the hybrids do. [Ed. Note: Tree peony enthusiasts may disagree.] Most hybrids I have grown are good growers and have been very free from disease.

"A large percentage of the named hybrids are single or semi-double but some are full double and are very lovely indeed. Your peony collection is not complete without some of these new up-to-date peonies.

"As the single hybrid varieties open, most of them are like immense goblets and the colors will dazzle your eyes. Many of them are as bright as the Oriental poppies.

"Because the hybrids are predominantly red, I shall begin with that color. I shall not try to list them as to my preference because I like one variety best this year and liked another one best last year. I shall list only varieties I have grown and shall take them alphabetically. I have omitted some fine ones and I know it. Not because they are not good, but because I have never grown them or have not grown them long enough to risk an opinion.

"Some hybrids are a little difficult to divide while others are very prolific. Only experience will tell you which is which. Like all plants, some varieties will do well in one location, or one soil, and others will do better some place else.

Red

"Alexander Woollcott, semi-double, crimson.
Avelyn, red, bomb.
Cardinal's Robe, very bright single.
Carina, very bright, semi-double to double.
Chocolate Soldier, very dark, bomb type.

Diana Parks, very bright double.
Golden Glow, single, orange-scarlet, large flower.
Jean E. Bockstoce, double.
Marta, double.
Old Main, red, bomb.
Orange Glory, very tall, semi-double with a little orange.
Rosedale, semi-double.
Rose Marie, double.
Red Charm, large, fully double bomb type.
Red Monarch, double with some purple.
Red Signal, small cups, make fine corsages.
Sophie, very bright. On the borderline but really a deep cherry pink.
Tecumseh, very bright single.
Topeka, double.
Veritas, dark semi-double.

Pink
"Angelo Cobb Freeborn, fully double and an extremely pretty plant.
Ceceilia, enormous single.
Janice, single.
Laura Magnuson, semi-double.
Queen of the Dawn, pink single.
Victoria Lincoln, double on established plants.

White, Cream or Yellow
"Chalice, white single.
Claire de Lune, light yellow, ten petaled single.
Daystar, cream, single.
Moonrise, light yellow, single.
Oriental Gold, yellow double. I believe this is a hybrid."

HYBRIDS BLOOM FOR A MONTH OR MORE

In general, the hybrid herbaceous and tree peonies flower at about the same time, continuing over a period of about a month starting, in the north, around May 5th to 15th and blooming for three to four weeks, with the proper selection. The following list will show you how, if you choose carefully, selecting the right parentage, starting with the tenuifolias and ending with the lobatas, you are able to have a sequence of constantly blooming hybrid plants for a period of a month. The lobatas are the last hybrids to bloom and they come with the lactifloras or Chinese peonies in the first two weeks of June in the north.

EARLYBIRD (woodwardi x tenuifolia)—One of the first peonies to bloom. Handsome little plant with finely cut foliage and an abundance of bright crimson flowers.

PLAYMATE (mlokosewitschi x tenuifolia)—Small bright rosy flowers held high above fern-like foliage.

DAYSTAR (tenuifolia x mlokosewitschi)—Third generation. Single goblets of clear pale yellow, about 3 feet tall with red stems and handsomely pointed leaves.

ROSELETTE (lactiflora x second generation tenuifolia x mlokosewitschi)—Prettily-formed large flowers of light rose pink. Blooms just after middle of May.

EARLY WINDFLOWER (veitchi x emodi)—Blooms about May 20. Graceful and unusual plants. Flowers like white anemones, slightly nodding, borne on tall stems. Foliage fern-like and handsome. Sets no seeds.

CHALICE (lactiflora x macrophylla)—Large, pure shimmering white flowers, long silky stamens on good stems, about 3 feet tall. Immense dark glossy leaves. Blooms mid-May in the north.

LATE WINDELOWER (beresowskyi x emodi)—Almost exactly like Early Windflower but blooms one week later.

FIRELIGHT—Pink, combines four species; lactiflora, officinalis, macrophylla and mlokosewitschi. Deep rose pink with deeper flares and crimson stigmas. Gold center.

STARLIGHT—Ivory-yellow, 5″-6″ wide, sometimes faintly blushed. Small creamy center. Fine. Combines 4 species as does Firelight.

EMBLEM (lactiflora x officinalis)—Single deep lusterless red of fine substance. Late May or early June in north.

REWARD (lactiflora x decora)—Good and very early red, dark maroon single, blooms last week in May.

PAGEANT (lactiflora x coriacea)—Fine tall, light rose pink, before the lobata pinks begin. Immense splash of long gold stamens. The heart alone is 4″ across.

GARDEN PEACE (lactiflora x macrophylla)—Great single white flowers, several on a stem, with gold and crimson centers. Its side blooms give it a long season. The dark red stems are so tall they may need a stake. Early June in the north.

REQUIEM (lactiflora x macrophylla)—Another lovely waxy-white single about one week later than Garden Peace. Fine substance and foliage.

JANICE (lactiflora x lobata)—The first of the lobata hybrids to bloom and one of the best, perhaps *the* best. Pale salmon, very vigorous. Tall and erect.

CLAUDIA (lactiflora x lobata)—Semi-double, opens light cherry, becoming pale salmon pink, golden heart. Blooms first half of June in the north.

For bloom during the first two weeks in June there is a long list of wonderful hybrids from which to choose. Following are just a few of the many choice ones on the market today:

ALEXANDER WOOLLCOTT—Brilliant red, semi-double.

BRIGHT KNIGHT—Cherry-red, large semi-double; tall, stiff stems.

CAMELLIA—Large semi-double white with silky luster and flushed peach-pink.

CHOCOLATE SOLDIER—Large semi to full double, maroon almost black with yellow dots on center petals.

CLAIRE DE LUNE—Pale ivory-yellow, single.

CRUSADER—Semi-double bright red with yellow center of golden stamens.

DAINTY LASS—Japanese type, cup-shaped soft coral-pink flowers.

GOLDEN GLOW—Cup-shaped, brilliant orange-scarlet flowers with golden stamens. Single to semi-double. Tall, sturdy stems. Foliage coarse, but an attractive green.

HORIZON—Tall. Very large flesh colored single with enormous center of golden stamens.

JOHN HARVARD—Georgeous ruby-red single that often blooms almost double with attractive golden center.

MONTEZUMA—Bright crimson goblets with shining rounded petals. Tall heavy stems.

NADIA—Deep bright cherry, wide-open blooms.

RED CHARM—Brilliant ruby double.

7

Making New Plantings

BUYING PEONY ROOTS

For the average gardener a standard division is the best root to buy. It is a piece cut from a plant with at least three good roots branching from the crown and 3 to 5 eyes or buds for next year's growth. The roots should be around ½" to 1" in diameter, not too large, and 4" to 6" long. With roots too long

A STANDARD DIVISION ▶
Has 3 To 5 "eyes" for next year's growth. At least 3 good roots ½"-1" in diameter, no longer than 4"-6" with slanting end cut. tip ends facing away from each other, outward and downward. If 2 roots cross each other one should be eliminated

A SMALL DIVISION
Has 1 or 2 "eyes", at least 1 good root. Requires 1 or 2 yrs. longer to develop and very good care first year. About ½ price Standard Division, a nice saving on rare and expensive varieties

and too numerous, little growth will be made for several years. The end cuts should be sloping with the tip ends facing away from each other and outward and downward. If two roots cross each other, one should be eliminated. A one year plant is usually considered equivalent to a standard division.

A small division with 1 or 2 eyes and one good root is sold for about half the price of the standard division. They will do as well, but will require a year or two longer to develop and need very good care the first year, especially during a long, hot dry summer. When buying expensive varieties, this can be a means of quite a saving however.

In southern states a 2 or 3 year old plant gives best results, although carefully cared for small divisions will give good results too. Any plant over 3 years should be divided before planting and then the divisions given a year or two to recover and come back.

Specimen plants can be obtained as tub or pot-grown plants for display on the terrace or planting out but are more costly and require more care. If not to be replanted in the garden in the fall, they should be given large enough containers so they can grow undisturbed for many years. A sixty day or more period of dormancy (freezing or rest period) is also necessary for good results. This hasn't seemed practical to date, but with the great interest in portable or container gardening, someone may experiment and discover a way so it will be practical for city gardens.

Buy peony roots by name from a reliable source so you will get clean, strong, healthy roots, true to name, carefully handled and divided by experts, in other words, quality roots. It is very disappointing to a gardener after growing a root for two or three years to discover it is not the variety ordered. Beware of bargains unless you know the firm. If you select dependable varieties from someone who guarantees the roots as true to name and arrival in good condition, and plant them properly, with occasional feedings and watering during dry seasons, you should have lovely peonies. Small, shrivelled roots, which have been drying out in open baskets in stores, will not make as good a showing as husky, freshly dug roots obtained from peony growers.

It makes absolutely no difference whether a root is grown in the north, east, south or west, if it is from a reliable grower. They all will do equally well for you when properly planted. Customers in Canada have had good success with roots grown in Virginia. Peony roots do not need to be grown nearby.

Place your order early enough so you will have the roots in time for September and October planting. Nurseries that specialize in peonies start shipping freshly dug roots late in August.

CHOOSING THE SITE

You cannot be too careful in deciding the best location for your peonies. Choosing the varieties to plant and the place to plant them are the two most important decisions. They live easily and graciously in an environment suited to their taste and since they represent a lifetime investment, give plenty of consideration to the best location. Once planted a peony will thrive in the same place for twenty-five to fifty years or more.

1. Peonies do require more space than most perennials and do not like to be disturbed, so if possible give 3 feet of space to each plant to allow room for it to grow for years without being moved.
2. Peony roots should not be crowded and resent the intrusion of roots from large trees, shrubs or hedge plants in their ground area, since the roots will rob them of the food and water they need for healthy growth. The strong stems, heavy foliage and masses of large flowers require plenty of food and drink.
3. Peonies need full sun. They can take some shade but should have at least one-half day of sun to do well. A light protection from direct sunlight after the flowers open will save them from fading too rapidly.
4. It is an advantage to have them sheltered from severe winds.

5. Good drainage is essential. This is a point that cannot be too strongly stressed.
6. Never plant where a peony has been planted before unless all soil has been removed to a depth of at least three feet and the same in width.
7. Never plant near a black walnut tree or the plant will, invariably, be killed.

PLANT IN SEPTEMBER AND OCTOBER

Peony tubers or roots are often wrapped in polyethylene for shipment. They should arrive in good condition at the proper planting time. When they arrive look them over carefully and report any damage to the shipper and the transportation company. If very dry, soak them in water several hours. Either heel them in or plant them at once, with as little delay as possible.

The fall planting and transplanting season starts in early September in the north, early October in the south, and continues until the ground freezes. Don't wait too long as it is better to get them in the ground in September in the North, so root growth can start while the soil is still warm and they will have time to become established before the ground freezes. Pot-grown plants may be planted spring or fall, anytime. The only reason peonies should not be planted too early in the south is that a hot, dry, September is not good for newly planted roots.

Roots kept in storage for spring planting, while they will not do as well as fall planted roots the first year, do well planted in the north but not in the south. Never plant them south of Philadelphia in the spring unless they are given extra good care, and even then they often die.

PLAN AMPLE SPACE FOR ROOTS

If peonies are to be planted in beds or borders, the ideal situation would be a space 3 feet wide and a depth of at least 24 inches. Allow an area 2 feet in diameter and 2 feet deep for each peony root, if possible. Some varieties like even more space. For specimen plants dig holes 3 feet in diameter and 3 feet deep. See page 108. Crowded roots or those encroached upon by roots of nearby trees or shrubs will weaken the plant and it may fail to bloom.

PREPARE BEDS AND SOIL CAREFULLY

Preparation of a good, friable garden soil with good drainage is important. Lighten heavy clay with sand or coal ashes and add humus to improve drainage and supply organic matter. To improve a sandy soil, add plenty of humus or organic matter using leafmold (rotted leaves), compost or peat moss. One-fourth humus by volume is a good proportion to good top soil.

To this good top soil with humus added, also use a good garden fertilizer such as 20% superphosphate, bonemeal or one low in nitrogen. Too much nitrogen causes the plants to make tall spindly growth and poor flowers. Bonemeal is slow acting so there is little danger of it burning plants. Use a pound to a plant. With other stronger fertilizers only use one-half pound or follow directions on the package. Mix the fertilizer with the soil thoroughly. Some people use well rotted manure. It should never come in contact with the newly planted roots, as it is thought to bring in disease.

Peonies like a slightly acid soil up to pH 6. If the soil tests higher, and is too acid, mix a generous supply of finely ground limestone into the soil, using 5 lbs. per 100 sq. ft. or 1 qt. for each bushel of soil.

When the beds or holes have been dug, discard the subsoil. Use a few handfuls of pebbles at the bottom of the hole to help drainage. Refill with good garden soil well mixed and enriched with fertilizer, up to 8" or 10" from the surface of the ground. Then fill to the top and mound up a few inches with good garden soil *without* any fertilizer added. Prepare the beds at least two weeks or more before planting time so the soil will have sufficient time to settle properly, then the roots will not sink after

planting. If you must plant immediately, pack the soil with your
feet to prevent roots from settling too deeply.

How To Plant A Peony Root

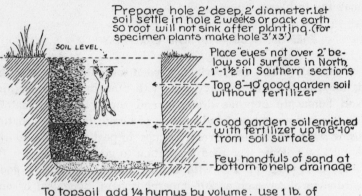

Prepare hole 2' deep, 2' diameter. Let
soil settle in hole 2 weeks or pack earth
so root will not sink after planting. (For
specimen plants make hole 3'x3')

SOIL LEVEL

Place "eyes" not over 2" below soil surface in North,
1"-1½" in Southern sections

Top 8"-10" good garden soil
without fertilizer

Good garden soil enriched
with fertilizer up to 8"-10"
from soil surface

Few handfuls of sand at
bottom to help drainage

To topsoil add ¼ humus by volume. Use 1 lb. of
bonemeal for each plant. With other quick acting
fertilizers use only ½ lb. Mix soil thoroughly.
Water thoroughly and label each plant

HOW TO SET OUT THE ROOTS

Place or set the crown, from which all growth springs and
from which the buds, "eyes", or sprouts arise, not more than 2"
below the ground or soil surface, shallower (1") in southern
sections of the country.

Care should be taken not to plant the roots upside down.
It is truly amazing how many good gardeners do just that and
then wonder why the peony did not come up. Please see sketch
above.

Firm the soil well around the root, working it in with your
fingers until there are no open spaces left. When the root is
completely covered, use your feet if necessary to firm properly
but be careful not to break the root or "eyes" in so doing. Water
each root generously after planting and when the water has
soaked in poke your finger down gently into the soil to make
sure the soil did not settle and pull the root down with it. Peony

specialists are agreed that too deep planting may be the cause of lack of flowers. Roots of all peonies are fleshy, brittle and fragile so handle carefully.

If peony roots are planted late, and do not have time to become anchored before winter, light mulching for the first winter is recommended to prevent heaving. Hill the soil at the time of planting and then after there is frost in the ground apply any loose material like evergreen boughs or straw. Remove the mulch and hilled soil carefully early in the spring, to avoid breaking the new shoots.

Label each plant with a long-lasting label which can be stuck into the soil, or if you have a sketch or blueprint of the garden, mark on it where and what was planted.

8

Caring for Established Plants

FOOD AND WATER

Peonies like fertile loam as they are gross feeders and need plenty of food and moisture to keep them healthy and in full vigor. However, if the soil was properly prepared and enriched at planting time, further fertilization will not be necessary for several years. In good soil little fertilizer will be needed. Porous or sandy soils will, of course, need additional fertilizer oftener than others, as the rains wash it away.

Keep all fertilizers away from the crown of the plants. Spread it over the area where the roots grow, 6″ to 18″ from the crown, thoroughly working it into the soil around the plants.

About the third or fourth year after planting peonies, assuming you started with good fertile loam, use half a handful of bonemeal to a plant each spring and fall. A good garden fertilizer not too rich in nitrogen as 20% superphosphate or rock phosphate is good. Wood ashes containing lime and potash have proven satisfactory. Some peony growers like to use well aged manure in the spring to improve the flowers, others will not use it claiming it brings disease. If you do use manure, do so with discretion, never letting it get over the crown of the plant. Do not overfeed as it encourages soft growth and poor blooms.

110

Although plants need a great deal of water, nature usually supplies enough. However, watering in a very dry season is necessary. If the spring season is dry, the plants should be given a good watering once a week, and if August and September are dry, it is wise to give the peony plants a good watering weekly. Give them a thorough soaking, enough to wet the ground down to the bottom of the roots. Then repeat again when the soil becomes dry.

CULTIVATION TO KEEP DOWN WEEDS

The first warm days, when the ground is no longer frozen, remove any mulch that may have been used, and when the soil is sufficiently dry, loosen or cultivate it sparingly, being careful not to touch or injure the crown or new growth. If you are not certain where the new growth will appear, do not work around the plant until it comes up. From then on weed and loosen the soil as weeds appear, still not cultivating over 2″ near the crown. Some people prefer a mulch to cut down on weed growth and the labor of cultivating, using ground corn cobs, sawdust or a similar mulch. If mulches are used, since mulches use up all the available nitrogen, a good dressing of nitrogen must be supplied. Apply a spoonful or two to a plant.

DISBUDDING FOR LARGER FLOWERS

For maximum show in the garden, do not disbud plants but let all side flowers develop to form a generous display. If you want large flowers for exhibition purposes, pinch off the lateral or side buds as soon as they form, leaving only the terminal or top buds. Another way to get larger flowers is to cut off several of the weaker shoots soon after they appear above the ground, sending more strength into the remaining stems.

For Larger Flowers

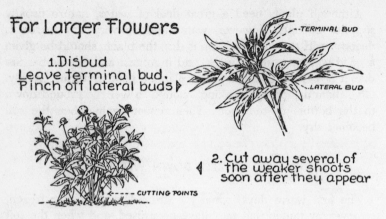

1. Disbud
Leave terminal bud.
Pinch off lateral buds ▶

--- TERMINAL BUD

--- LATERAL BUD

◀ 2. Cut away several of
the weaker shoots
soon after they appear

←---- CUTTING POINTS

SUPPORTS

Some of the fully petaled peony flowers become top heavy and their stems must be supported to bear the weight of the large double flowers, otherwise they will bend to the ground after heavy rains and strong winds. The commonly used circular wire rings are excellent, as they permit plants to maintain their natural and graceful shapes. Stake when plants are about half grown to facilitate the job.

Wire Supports

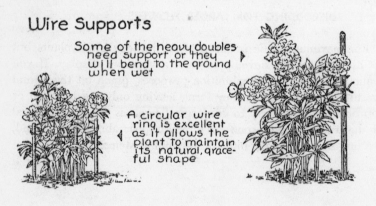

Some of the heavy doubles
need support or they
will bend to the ground
when wet ▶

◀ A circular wire
ring is excellent
as it allows the
plant to maintain
its natural, grace-
ful shape

BURN FOLIAGE AFTER FROST

Some gardeners allow the foliage on an old clump to remain over winter to hold snow and act as a mulch but disease may winter over on the old leaves. It is much safer to cut off the old leaf stalks at ground level, after frost browns the foliage, and then burn them along with hollyhock, iris and other pest-ridden leaves. Never place cut peony foliage and stems on a compost pile because they are susceptible to botrytis disease. As an added precaution, brush away any partially rotted leaves, weed stems, etc., that have collected at the base of the plant and burn or destroy.

TO DIVIDE OLD CLUMPS

If you must divide a clump because of space, or because it is not flowering, dig it up anytime after mid-September. This will allow time for the roots to get well established, after replanting, by the time growth starts in the spring. Cut off all the foliage and stems, then carefully pry up the clump.

Wash away all soil from the roots with a hose and allow them to lie in a shady spot for a few hours to lose their brittleness and avoid root breakage. Cut away any damaged parts and with sharp, heavy shears, lappers or pruning knife cut the clump apart in such a way that each piece will have 3 or 5 dormant "eyes" (never over 8) and several, or a generous proportion, of strong roots. Treat any wound with dusting sulphur. Keep all divisions properly labeled as to varieties.

Shorten the heavy roots back to a maximum of 6", 4" stubs are even better. Divisions from the outer edges of the clump are preferred. If possible, replant each division in a spot where peonies were not formerly grown, never in ground occupied by one that was diseased.

Place the root so that the visible buds or "eyes" are not over 2" below the surface of the soil, 1" in the south. Surround the

To Divide Old Clumps

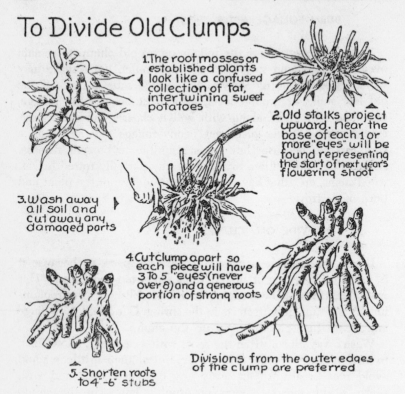

1. The root mosses on established plants look like a confused collection of fat, intertwining sweet potatoes

2. Old stalks project upward. Near the base of each 1 or more "eyes" will be found representing the start of next year's flowering shoot

3. Wash away all soil and cut away any damaged parts

4. Cut clump apart so each piece will have 3 to 5 "eyes" (never over 8) and a generous portion of strong roots

5. Shorten roots to 4"–6" stubs

Divisions from the outer edges of the clump are preferred

root with pure top soil. Never apply any fertilizer or summer mulches over the crown of the plant.

Frequently no blooms are produced the first year after planting and the plant may be somewhat dwarfed. By the third year, however, the plant should produce abundant blooms.

Professional growers who sell peony roots propagate by division usually using three year old stock, since young roots cut up easily, saving time and producing plants which flower freely.

Home gardeners should never divide old clumps which are blooming well, unless there is a special reason or need for it.

SPRAY TO PREVENT DISEASE

Spray or dust with a good fungicide just as the peony plants break through the ground to prevent disease. Repeat again when half grown and a third time just before flowering.

Spraying with fermate or bordeaux mixture, or some similar fungicide, will also prevent leaf spot, so spray several times after the blooming season as well.

9

Diseases and Insects

BOTRYTIS BLIGHT

Fungus diseases are more detrimental to peonies than are insects. Botrytis fungus or blight is the most common and troublesome disease of the peony and may appear during a wet spring, causing the rotting of the stems, buds and leaves in that order. The effects are easily recognized. The young stems rot, there is browning of the buds and discoloration of the flowers and foliage.

Control of botrytis begins with preventive measures, good

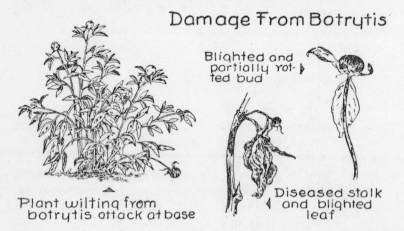

Damage From Botrytis

Blighted and partially rotted bud ▶

Plant wilting from botrytis attack at base

Diseased stalk and blighted leaf

sanitation and good air circulation. Remove all infected parts and burn or destroy them. In the fall, just before frost, cut down the stalks close to the ground and burn or destroy. Dig up and destroy any badly infected plants. As soon as growth starts in the spring, spray or dust with fermate, bordeaux mixture or any good fungicide according to directions on the package, directing the material at the base of the plants and the surface of the soil, repeating at two week intervals until August.

ROOT KNOT OR LEMOINE'S DISEASE

Many varieties bloom in spite of it, others stop blooming. A beadlike swelling appears in infected roots, probably caused by a virus which is difficult to kill. There is evidence it does spread, though slowly. There seems to be no cure so either destroy the plant or replant it in an area by itself.

ROOT ROT

This may be indicated by part of the plant dying down prematurely. Examine the root and if rot is present, dig it up, cut away all diseased parts and then soak the root in a solution of arasan, formaldehyde, semesan or some such chemical for 45 minutes. Replant in soil which has not been exposed to the infection.

NEMAS AND NEMATODES

Occasionally plants are attacked by nemas, microscopic eel-like worms which burrow into the fine roots causing irregular swellings or nodules called nematodes which look like a lot of peas on the ends of the roots. Infested plants are generally stunted, weak in growth and pale green. The roots are unable to take up sufficient nourishment for the plant. Before suspecting nematodes, check other factors for poor growth. If infested, discard the entire plant and do not replant newly purchased plants in the same area.

Several nemacides are now being offered for which the claim is made that they may be used around growing plants and will not harm them. One at least is extremely poisonous to humans and all must be used with the greatest of caution for this reason.

ANTS

Ants crawling over the buds as they begin to open do not eat the buds but feed on the sweet syrup the buds give off. Since they may spread botrytis or aphis, it's best to get rid of them. Treat the soil around the plant with a strong solution of nicotine sulfate or chlordane to take care of them.

THRIPS

Thrips, which are tiny insects, may infest the buds and opening flowers particularly of the late varieties causing failure of buds to open, or a browning of the petals. They are especially bothersome in the south. Lindane or DDT and several sprays on the market may be used to control them. Make three applications ten days apart.

ROSE CHAFERS

Rose chafers or beetles chew the petals. DDT, lindane or chlordane help to control them, if the ground under the plant and surrounding lawn area is treated.

MOLES — RABBITS

If moles are destructive, spray flower beds and adjacent lawn with chlordane. This kills the insects in the soil, the moles' chief food. There are several advertised remedies you can try. If rabbits start to nibble terminal buds as they form protect the plants with some type of wire enclosure.

10

Propagation, Forcing

PROPAGATION

Only species peonies may be propagated, true to name, from seed and only if carefully protected from cross pollination. Seedlings from all other peonies are never true to name but are always new varieties.

Professional peony growers who sell peony roots propagate by root division (see page 103) usually using three year old stock. Root division is the only way to propagate peonies true to name.

The offsprings grown from seed never come true to either parent. It's a fascinating and sometimes heartbreaking pursuit, since one never knows what the seedling will be like and it takes from four to ten years from pollination to get the first flowers.

If peony seeds are allowed to dry out after ripening, they will not germinate under two years so the seeds are gathered and planted immediately, before they dry out, just as they are turning brown. Watch the seed pods from the middle of July on and gather just before the seeds fall from the pod, just as they harden. Seeds may be stratified in peat moss or vermiculite until they sprout, if you wish, for planting. Plant in the open or in boxes set in cold frames,about 2" deep, in good, friable loam. Care must be taken that the seedlings in the cold frames receive sufficient air and moisture and partial shade to prevent drying out. Transplant the seedlings at least 18" apart in a permanent bed and be sure they are properly

119

labeled. After four years the hybridizer may expect to see his much anticipated blooms.

Pollination by bees and insects may produce inferior results so hand pollination, careful cross-breeding, is employed. The two parent flowers are carefully selected, breeding two varieties which have most nearly the characteristics wanted to strengthen certain features.

A covering, as an oiled paper bag, or polyethylene is placed over the two parent flowers. The anthers on the flower to be pollinated are removed to prevent self-pollination. The stigmas are closely watched to see when they are ready to receive the pollen. When they present a waxy, granulated surface they are ready and the pollen is then taken from the ripe anthers of the pollen parent flower and applied to the receptive stigmas of the carpel, the ovule parent flower. The paper bag protection is removed, a label with the parent varieties is fastened to the stem, and from the seeds of the ovule parent flower, young seedlings are grown. The singles and semi-doubles produce seeds freely, the full double varieties seldom bear seeds. If the seedling is not more beautiful, with better form or color and stronger stems ,or a freer bloomer, or more fragrant, or a better yellow or having less blue in its pink, unless it is superior to existing varieties and tests show it will do well in most sections of the country, better discard it.

FORCING BLOOMS AHEAD OF SCHEDULE

Mr. Edward Auten, Jr., of Princeville, Illinois, relates in the second edition of the *Handbook of the Peony* his experience in forcing herbaceous peonies into flower ahead of their normal time, as early as February or March.

"Three or four year old clumps should be dug early in the fall and potted immediately, using a ten-quart pail or larger. Take care to remove as little dirt from the clump as possible. Punch a number of drainage holes in the bottom of the pail. Put an inch or two of gravel or other coarse material over the holes. Shorten the roots no more than necessary to get the clump into the container. Pack new soil around, between the roots, and under the plant, being sure no voids are left unfilled. Water thoroughly to wash the soil down among the roots to be sure this has been done. The eyes should be one inch below the surface.

"Stand the plant outdoors in a cool place until early winter. Freezing is beneficial provided the container has been sunk in the ground. If it freezes while standing above ground, the roots may be damaged.

"After December 20th, bring the plant indoors, first into a cool temperature, later into heat. 60 to 65 degrees F. is best, but 70 is not too high. It is important to water carefully. The time of blooming can be regulated by the time the plant is brought into heat, by temperature, and probably also by amount of light given. This may be done either in home or greenhouse, which will take from six to ten weeks.

"Hybrids can be forced and should bloom earlier than the albiflora (lactiflora) varieties.

Singles, Japanese, semi-doubles and the early, loose doubles will force easier than the full doubles. Some difficulty may be experienced with these, especially the full petaled hybrid doubles which may not respond satisfactorily."

The flowers will not be as large nor the colors quite the same as for normal outdoor blooming but it is possible to have peonies with flowers in February or in March for the large spring flower shows and very special occasions. Forcing peonies in greenhouses for commercial purposes is too costly to be profitable.

11

Peony Questions and Answers

WHY DO PEONIES FAIL TO BLOOM?

1. Plant may be too young. By the third year a plant should bloom freely.
2. Planted too deep. In the north plant "eyes" no more than 2" below soil level, 1" in the south.
3. Moved too often. Peonies do not like to be disturbed. It sets them back.
4. Poor location, too shady or too near voracious shrubs or trees. Peonies need plenty of sun. Their roots should not be crowded or robbed of the food and water they require.
5. Poor drainage, can't tolerate prolonged wet feet. Peony roots will rot or develop a blight or fungus if its roots are kept wet.
6. Soil too acid. Soil should be just slightly acid. If it tests over pH 6 add limestone (see page 107).
7. Failure to divide an old clump when moving it. An old clump must be divided into pieces with only 3 to 5 eyes when moved. If too many eyes are left it will not bloom (see page 114).
8. Too much foliage removed in cutting long stemmed flowers. Some foliage is essential for the health of the plant and to develop a good root system (see page 183).

9. Lack of food. The peony has large leaves and flowers and requires plenty of food, good soil.
10. Not enough moisture. Moisture is necessary for good growth and development.
11. Lack of disease control. Spraying or dusting is a must to keep plants free from disease and vigorous and healthy.

WHY ARE THE FLOWERS POOR?

1. Insufficient nutrients. Flowers will not develop properly or take on their best color unless properly nourished.
2. Overfed with high nitrogen fertilizer. This causes soft growth and poor blooms.
3. Dry weather or a sudden hot spell. A thorough soaking or watering may help. Hope for a better season next year!
4. Wet weather may cause buds to "ball" or fail to open. There isn't too much you can do about this but really good drainage is your salvation.
5. Late frost may kill buds. This is disappointing but gardeners are optimistic and it can't happen twice in succession!

WHERE WILL THEY GROW?

Peonies grow well in all sections of the country except Florida, southern California and the deep south. In dry areas, like northern Arizona and California, there are successful plantings but plenty of water must be supplied every two or three days. In the south two year plants give better results than the smaller ones, unless carefully nursed. Plant the "eyes" only 1" below the surface of the soil, and use a mulch to keep ground cool. To force dormancy in warm sections, withhold water from September through the first half of October and cut the herbaceous varieties back to the ground.

Some peonies bloom better in one part of the country than in others. As a rule easy-opening varieties of loose petalage and the earlier blooming kinds of the single and Japanese types are best for the south or any locality where extreme heat comes quickly. Very late sorts with tight buds and full flowers need cool, somewhat moist weather to make them open best (see page 38). Peonies are hardy and do well in Canada where they are at their best in late June and early July.

Where temperatures get down to 10°-20° below zero for a week at a time, with little snow covering, winter protection as evergreen boughs or straw or soil around the base of the plants to a depth of about 6″ is recommended. Herbaceous hybrids must be protected in such a climate to prevent severe losses.

PART III — THE TREE PEONY

12

General Types and Hybrids

The tree peony, which is a shrub and not a tree, has been cultivated and appreciated in China and Japan for many centuries. It was first exported to England in 1787 where it received much attention and later it was introduced into France and the United States.

Accorded the highest honor in its native China, the tree peony has been known in that country as the "King of Flowers" since time immemorial. It has been the subject of painting and poetry for over 1500 years and is one of the four flowers associated with their four seasons. The white blossomed plum of winter, the peony of springtime, the lotus of summer and the chrysanthemum of fall are well recognized symbols in the Orient.

For several centuries it was decreed by the Chinese rulers that such regal flowers could only be grown in the imperial palaces where they were grown in their natural shape as a bush and also espaliered in many designs. The tree peony was symbolic of high position and wealth as well as being an omen of good fortune.

Introduced into Japan by Buddhist monks sometime between the fifth and eighth centuries, the tree peony became a great favorite, second only to the chrysanthemum and classed with the cherry and lotus as flowers of royal rank. The tree peony and chrysanthemum are generally not used in the landscape proper, their special display being restricted to flower beds arranged in long sheltered areas, usually near the apartments for ladies. In the grounds of the palaces, peonies adorn the open spaces facing the ladies' chambers from which the beauty of the flowers can be readily viewed and enjoyed.

In Japanese art the tree peony is inseparably connected with the peafowl or peacock and they form the constant decoration of temple and palace walls. The affection of the Japanese people for the peony is shown in their legends and folklore, all marked by a charming symbolism. The beauty of texture, color and form of the tree peony through the centuries has made an irresistible appeal and enjoyed great esteem.

There are two general types of tree peonies, the European varieties brought here from China by way of England and favored in the nineteenth century, and the Japanese varieties from Japan, originally from China and Tibet. These later arrivals from Japan, where the tree peony has reached its highest degree of development, are generally more attractive.

The Chinese or European tree peonies are easily recognized for their shaggy, double flowers, usually so heavy they cause the stems to droop. The Japanese varieties have straight stems. The Japanese have selected the more informal single and semi-double flowers from among their seedlings. The plants are graceful, of attractive form, the foliage is beautiful and the usually single to semi-double flowers are generally borne well above the foliage. Not nearly so susceptible to frost damage, they are more reliable in bloom than the European type. They do not need protection from early frost, necessary with the European varieties, and are better suited to our climate.

HYBRIDS

In catalogs you will find three major types of tree peonies to choose from; the Chinese, Japanese and the hybrids. Sir Frederick C. Stern in his "A Study of the Genus Paeonia", published by the Royal Horticultural Society in London in 1946, calls all three tree peonies P. moutan and he groups the garden forms that come from China and Japan as P. suffruticosa. The species delavayi, lutea and potanini he calls the delavayi group, but in catalogs this group is offered to the trade under lutea hybrids. The Chinese and Japanese tree peonies flower first and the lutea and delavayi hybrids follow them about two weeks later. On Long Island, New York, Dr. David Gurin says the flowering time for him lasts from around May 5 to June 5. Around Boston it is about a week or more later. The dates will vary several days according to the season. See supplement, page 218 and note dates gardens are at height of bloom.

P. suffruticosa (syn. P. arborea—P. moutan) has an ancient and interesting history. It has large white flowers with magenta-purple blotches at the base of the petals. The group now includes many varieties of delicate tints and surprising brilliance with a range of colors from purest white and palest pink through rose-pink, vermillion, blazing scarlets, crimson and rich purples, mauves, lilac and a wisteria blue. Some have feathered white petals striped with crimson, others open pale salmon, fading white with age. Since records show only this one species of the tree peony in the Orient before comparatively recent times, it is probable that early varieties resulted from seedling variation or natural mutations.

Of comparatively recent discovery (brought to Paris from China in 1883 and 1884) are P. lutea and P. delavayi, the first known yellow and maroon species.

P. delavayi, the first maroon tree peony to be discovered, is believed to be the oldest and most primitive species of the group. It has single flowers 2″ to 4″ across, dark mahogany in color and is commonly called the maroon or Delavay tree peony. This species probably enters into the parentage of most of all the darker hybrid varieties. Potanini is another deep maroon-red, a native of China and Tibet.

P. lutea has thick, deeply lobed, dark-green leaves and fragrant, single, cup-shaped flowers about 2″ to 3½″ across with waxy, fleshy petals of a wonderful golden yellow, strong and pure. In some blooms the lower half of the filament is red giving the effect of a red ring in the center of the flower. This little peony has great beauty and in addition has a pleasant fragrance. Crossed with P. suffruticosa it has become one of the parents of a long list of hybrids, the origin of the yellow and orange colored flowers. The wide color range in single, semi-double and fully double blossoms starts with a silvery-cream through all the yellows to the color of golden ripe grain.

Interbred with P. suffruticosa, using the pollen of the moutan varieties on the maroon and yellow species, the resultant hybrids have supplied us with a totally new range of impressive colors from white and ivory, pale and golden yellow, blush to dusky rose-pink, to scarlet, crimson and maroon, to almost black. Many varieties are fragrant and they may be had in single, semi-double and double forms. Some varieties are compact, others spreading and some upright in form. There is also a low type. The outstanding hybrids have more vigor, grow better, are more shapely and attractive and easier to handle and transport than the P. suffruticosa varieties. They also bloom about 10 days later extending the peony season by at least 2 weeks.

The tree peony hybrids resulted from the work of Victor Lemoine of France and Prof. A. P. Saunders of Clinton, New York. Lemoine worked in the nineties, Mr. Saunders not until the 1920s and these so far are the only tree peony hybridizers. The one criticism of their hybrids was weak stems. P. lutea and P. delavayi both hide or hang their blooms in the foliage. Lemoine made crosses with the double Chinese varieties producing huge flowers which weighted the stems down so they hung underneath the leaves. In crossing P. delavayi he produced Sang Lorraine, a wonderfully fragrant, single or semi-double, dark crimson. Prof. Saunders in using Japanese varieties produced smaller, single flowers like Argosy, introduced in 1928, which hold themselves up well. One of his introductions, a magnificent semi-double, Age of Gold, came from a Japanese variety and even though its weak stems allow the flowers to hang beneath the leaves, it is undoubtedly the most beautiful yellow peony today.

These early hybridizers made a wonderful start and increased the blooming season and earlier color range of white, pink, red and purple by adding yellow and the darker colored hybrids. We owe them a tremendous debt of gratitude for their foresight and developmment of the peony. Since their time, P. lutea ludlowi with large yellow flowers on strong stems which comes into bloom about two weeks before P. lutea has been introduced.

13

Tree Peonies in the Landscape

Few plants offer the landscape artist the opportunities presented by the tree peony. This beautiful and exotic plant is remarkable in its shrub-like habit, of convenient size, easy to grow, hardy and long-lived. Its woody stems carry attractive soft green foliage above which appear beautifully shaped flowers of supreme beauty which last long on the plant. The shrubs' graceful lines and delicately parted foliage have an Oriental look and older plants bearing scores of blooms make a striking focus. Once established they increase in size and number of blooms from year to year, their wide umbrella of foliage making a delightful plant even after blooming is over. More and more gardeners are making the acquaintance of the tree peony and finding it irresistible. No other bloom can compete with the tree peony when it is in flower and it blooms in advance of most garden perennials.

A show plant, grown primarily for its spectacular display of blooms, the tree peony should be given a place of prominence. Nothing else has quite the glamorous impact of a tree peony in full flower. The ethereal beauty of the plant with its delightful qualities and charm deserves close range inspection and should be planted so one may go up to and walk all around it to enjoy the detail of its beauty to the fullest. Plant it where you will enjoy it most. If possible, where you can enjoy it from indoors as well as out, where a window will frame it for you.

WHERE TO PLANT

Hillside Planting

In its native China the tree peony is found growing in the forest regions on the mountainside, a reasonable amount of high shade from the trees protecting the pale and delicate colors from the intense heat of the afternoon sun. The shade of the trees also keeps the temperature of the soil about the roots cool. Where terrain permits, this type of planting is ideal. At Swarthmore College Dr. John Wister has a hillside planting of tree peonies, a perfect setting and a beautiful sight when in flower. The trees also offer protection from severe wind and storms.

On Level Ground

On level ground where drainage is good, a grouping of tree peonies planted under trees several feet from the trunk to avoid the tree roots and too much shade makes an ideal situation. Dr. David Gurin on Long Island, New York, has such a planting. Picturesque gray birch trees furnish some high shadows, the dappled shade keeping the flowers fresh and playing interesting patterns on the lovely peonies.

Terraced Planting

In China tree peonies are grown on stepped terraces, or planted in high raised beds enclosed with stone or marble, a good idea in any country, supplying good drainage and pleasing landscape effects. The precious plants are also protected in China when in flower with bamboo shades or a cloth screening to keep off wind and sun and to prolong the blooming period.

As A Focus

When in flower the tree peony stands out in all its glory whether planned as a focal area or not. Why not place it to make the most of its natural eye catching beauty to accent the garden design and show off to best advantage. As a focal area on a wide sweep of lawn, in the garden border, in a terrace border, or along the garden path, the tree peony, when in bloom, attracts the major attention. Place it so it complements its companions and the garden as a whole. As specimen plants in front of a

Gardens Featuring Tree Peonies

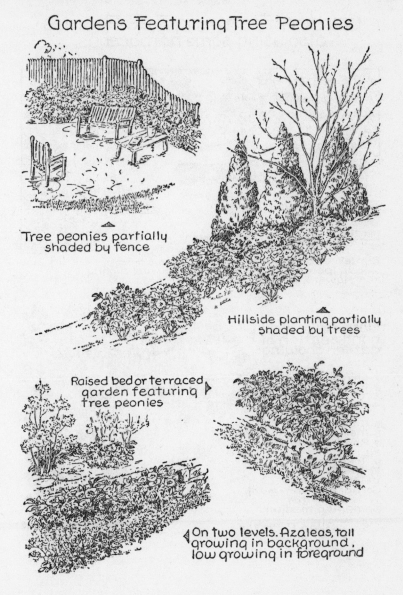

Tree peonies partially
shaded by fence

Hillside planting partially
shaded by trees

Raised bed or terraced
garden featuring ▷
tree peonies

◁ On two levels. Azaleas, tall
growing in background,
low growing in foreground

Garden Featuring Tree Peonies
also using some herbaceous

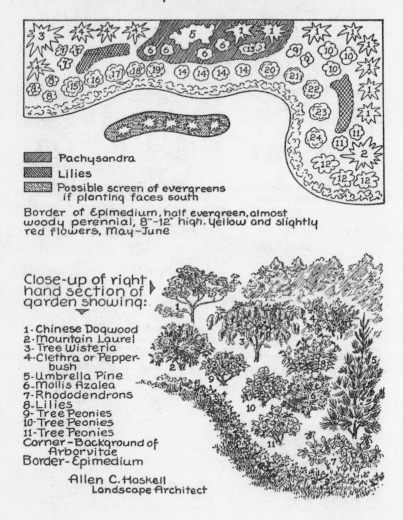

Pachysandra
Lilies
Possible screen of evergreens
  if planting faces south

Border of Epimedium, half evergreen, almost
woody perennial, 8"-12" high. Yellow and slightly
red flowers, May-June

Close-up of right
hand section of
garden showing:

1- Chinese Dogwood
2- Mountain Laurel
3- Tree Wisteria
4- Clethra or Pepper-
     bush
5- Umbrella Pine
6- Mollis Azalea
7- Rhododendrons
8- Lilies
9- Tree Peonies
10- Tree Peonies
11- Tree Peonies
Corner - Background of
     Arborvitae
Border- Epimedium

Allen C. Haskell
  Landscape Architect

This planting featuring peonies has seasonal interest, and is practical and easy to maintain.

Key to materials used in Allen C. Haskell plan.

1. Dark green arbor-vitae.
2. Umbrella pine (Sciadopitys verticillata).
3. Cryptomeria, Japanese evergreen tree of pyramidal habit.
4. Canadian hemlock.
5. Chinese dogwood (Cornus kousa chinensis) to 15 ft., flowers in June, red autumnal foliage.
6. Mountain laurel (Kalmia latifolia) 5 ft. to 6 ft., flowers in late May and early June—blush-pink clustered flowers.
7. Cotoneaster divaricata, 6 ft to 8 ft spreading.
8. Hypericum hidcote, low growing summer-flowering shrub 18 inches tall, bright yellow flowers, late June until frost.
9. Enkianthus campanulatus. Rather erect graceful shrub of narrow outline to 10 ft. or more. Dropping dainty bell-shaped yellow flowers in pendulous clusters on long slender stems in May. Striking orange-scarlet fall foliage.
10. Clethra alnifolia (Sweet Pepperbush)—Spikes of fragrant white flowers from late July through September.
11. Mollis or Chinese azalea, "Directeur Moerelands" to 5 ft., handsome clusters of soft golden yellow flowers in abundance in May and June.
12. Rhododendron hybrid 'Boule de Neige", white flowers, bushy, compact plant.
13. Tree wisteria, pale purplish-blue flowers.
14. Herbaceous peony, white, single, 4 plants.
    TREE PEONIES (15-24)
15. Reine Elizabeth, bright salmon-rose, double.
16. Howzan, bright light pink, double.
17. Gabisan, large white, double.
18. Teikwan, enormous bright red, double.
19. Tama-fuyo, light pink, nearly full double.
20. Alice Harding, yellow, double.
21. Argosy, yellow, single.
22. Flora, immense white flowers slightly blotched violet-carmine in throat.
23. La Lorraine, large soft sulphur yellow with salmon tinge when opening, becomes lighter when expanded.
24. Ubatama, huge satiny black maroon.
25. Lilies for summer color.

backdrop of evergreens or flowering trees and shrubs, the tree
peony shows off to excellent advantage.

To Accent Entrance

As specimen plants to accent the entrance to a home or to a
garden, tree peonies are ideal. Their dignity and beauty when
in flower are unequalled by any other plant, making them excellent specimen plants in the landscape.

A Picturesque Pergola

A pergola letting in plenty of sun yet offering some protection
for the flowers from the afternoon's hottest rays makes an attractive and interesting garden feature.

In Small City Yard

A well drained and slightly high shaded location in a small
city yard can be used successfully for the growing of one or
two specimen plants, which may then be complemented with
several dwarf evergreen azaleas, deutzias, roses, or any one of a
number of plants suitable for such a situation.

Potted Tree Peonies

Potted tree peonies were used in China on a seasonal basis
to grace the courts of the wealthy but in our climate pot culture
for terrace or portable gardens as yet is not practical and is
too costly. Sealed in heat and moisture destroy the roots at a
time when these very roots have a heavy foliage to support.
Then there is the problem of dormancy, which requires cold
storage and handling, increasing labor costs.

JAPANESE INFLUENCE

Japanese influence is seen in many of our gardens today,
especially in tree peony gardens. A well shaped pine, a few
spring flowering trees, a garden bridge spanning a stream of
water are all typical Japanese features. They make an ideal
setting for a planting of tree peonies.

We may well consider some of the practical features of
Japanese landscaping. Since for generations they have had to

make the most of limited space, they have become masters in giving depth and a feeling of size within a small area. Security and privacy with an utter detachment from the outside world is a must in their gardens. The garden is a place for repose, meditation and quiet; a place to induce relaxation and provide seclusion from the hustle and bustle of life. It is not a garden until it is enclosed, although no opportunity is lost to take advantage of, capitalize on, and "borrow" the pleasing views of surrounding scenery, giving the small enclosed private garden a feeling of great space and distance.

A feeling of simplicity, restraint and quiet harmony prevails. The garden must appear natural, weathered and related to the entire setting. The architecture of the area is constructed from materials on hand and always an inconspicuous part of the plan. Symbolism plays an important role. Native rocks or stones, water and moss are basic. Moss is encouraged and cherished to suggest age.

A group of low growing pines located at the stream's edge indicates the symbolic tortoise island, the tortoise signifying a long life. Symbolic shapes of clipped shrubs resembling a tortoise or a crane also signify a long life. The three, five and seven combinations of arranging garden stones or shrubs, so often seen, signify holiness or happiness.

The stone lantern, of purely Japanese origin, illuminates and guides the way by night and also gives the feeling of age. A bamboo screening or thicket of growing trees conveys security and privacy for the owner.

Water is of intrinsic value in the Japanese garden and always featured, a stream or cascade making a pleasing sight. If not available, water is simulated. Carefully selected and carefully placed stones, gravel and sand are used to suggest a running stream. A simple garden bridge is a familiar sight even over a "dry-up" water stream. A simple garden gate and garden house are other typical features.

Primary and secondary paths of native stone are made taking one to a destination by the most interesting route. Along the path in the tea gardens are low type water-filled basins where one may rinse the mouth and hands, symbolic of spiritual cleansing or purifying oneself, before entering the tea room for the tea ceremony. Enough diversity is allowed to suit the needs of the individual owners and the Japanese gardens are as varied as our own even though they all follow a few basic principles. Ease of maintenance is an appealing feature of all Japanese gardens.

COMPANION PLANTS

A picturesque pine; the Japanese maple with its dainty, finely cut leaves; the dwarf Japanese larch, its new growth soft and delicate in texture; late flowering cherries and the plum; the azalea and wisteria all come to mind when thinking of Japanese gardens and tree peonies.

A tree peony garden can be planted with a wide variety of plants useful for both foliage and flowers. With judicious selection, wonderful garden effects may be achieved.

Flowering Trees

A flowering plum or late cherry covered with blossoms makes a fitting setting for the early season display of tree peonies. Pink blossoms of a crabapple somewhere nearby add interest and color. The Washington hawthorn, where space permits (20-30 feet), has profuse white flowers in May and June and lustrous scarlet small fruit in clusters in September and October. The Siberian pea-tree (caragana) grows from 15-20 feet, has bright green leaves and small, bright yellow pea-shaped flowers in June, a good background specimen and the yellow repeats the yellow centers of many of the tree peonies.

Flowering Shrubs

There are many fine shrubs that bloom with the tree peony including azaleas, rhododendrons, and the hybrid lilacs and shrub roses. Viburnum tomentosum grows about 8 feet tall, has creamy-white flowers in June and colorful dull red foliage in the fall. Deutzia kalmiaeflora grows 3 feet in height and is

Companion Plants For The Tree Peony

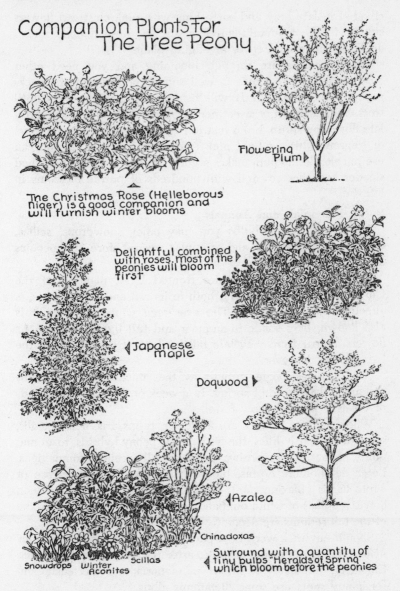

Flowering Plum ▶

The Christmas Rose (Helleborous Niger) is a good companion and will furnish winter blooms

Delightful combined with roses. most of the peonies will bloom first ▶

◀ Japanese maple

Dogwood ▶

◀ Azalea

Chinadoxas

Snowdrops   Winter   Scillas
              Aconites

◀ Surround with a quantity of tiny bulbs "Heralds of Spring" which bloom before the peonies

covered in late May and early June with pink clustered flowers similar to the mountain-laurel or kalmia. Rose daphne makes an excellent ground cover or edging plant.

When peonies are through blooming and you need other color, a shrub like althea is well suited for screening or background in the border. It will furnish blooms from July until frost. Summersweet or sweet pepperbush (clethra) is a delightful late flowering shrub 4 to 5 feet in height with finger-like clusters of fragrant white or light pink (var. rosea) flowers. If you can use purple, desmodium makes a gorgeous display with its arched slender branches covered with hundreds of purple blossoms in late fall.

Bulbs, Perennials and Annuals

Used with spring bulbs you may enjoy snowdrops, scillas, chionodoxas, daffodils and primulas even before the peonies are in flower.

A grouping of tree peonies fronted by a planting of the Christmas rose (helleborus), both in its red and white forms, is effective the year round. The evergreen winter rose, as it is also known, likes shade in summer and full light in winter, its flowers appear from very late fall until April or May when the tree peony takes over.

Tree peonies begin growth as the crocuses and daffodils announce the arrival of spring. In a week or two the flower buds of the tree peonies show form.

When the tree peonies are in flower, tulips, iris, hemerocallis, some of the hardy lilies, the herbaceous peony hybrids, roses and phlox, clematis and morning glories are all excellent companions. Later delphinium, hostas, blue salvia, spikes of purple-rose or white liatris (blazing star); platycodon, blue or white (balloon flower); spikes of white bugbane (cimicifuga simplex) and some of the tall sedums are decorative with the peony plants.

Should any rock work be a part of the garden use some phlox divaricata with alyssum saxatile, aster frikarti with phlox (Miss Lingard); for shady locations pulmonaria and mertensia and for sunny spots use some dictamnus albus.

Edging Plants

There are many excellent edging plants that bloom with the tree peony. With a carpet of garden pinks (Old Spice) and white sweet alyssum at their feet tree peonies make a lovely picture in the spring. Pansies, iberis (candytuft), cerastium (snow-in-summer), arabis (wall cress), and arenaria (sandwort) are also good low, companions.

Heuchera (coral-bells) has slender, tall stems with loose clusters of small, bright-red flowers in May and June but the tufted plant with its well rounded attractive leaves is attractive throughout the season when not in flower and makes an excellent edging plant.

14

Making New Plantings

BUYING THE PLANTS

Although tree peonies are more expensive than herbaceous roots, improved propagating and growing techniques are bringing the price of this choice plant down nearer the reach of most gardeners. The cost should be considered as a long time investment since there are tree peonies in the Philadelphia area known to have been in the gardens of one family for over 100 years.

Tree peonies may be bought 2 or 3 years after they are grafted. Since the early years are the crucial ones, the beginner would do well to buy an older well established plant, one at least 3 years old or older, of blooming age. Results will be more certain and quicker. The plant should have some good new roots to give satisfaction. If immediate results are wanted, by all means buy an older established plant. Plants from seed are sold when they are 5 to 8 years old, when just ready to bloom for the first time.

Commercially most tree peonies are offered bare root. Some specially prepared pot-grown plants are now being offered guaranteed to bloom within the first growing season following planting. Also balled and burlapped specimen plants with 3 and 4 dozen buds on and close to the stem are now available for fall planting. To ball and burlap a tree peony successfully re-

142

quires a knowledge of the type roots of each variety as the roots of some varieties are unsuitable for balling. At no time is spring planting advised for bare root plants. Fall planting of bare roots requires some winter protection the first year.

CHOOSING THE LOCATION

SUNLIGHT. Tree peonies love the sun as herbaceous peonies do, yet as a forest plant in its native China, it likes a reasonable amount of high shade to protect the pale and delicate flower colors from the heat of the afternoon sun and to keep the temperature of the soil about the roots cool.

The plants bloom most freely in full sunlight but a play of shadows intensifies the colors. The pink varieties need more shade, both to show off their sublety of color and texture and to preserve the flower, which by opening too wide in mid-day heat loses its lovely goblet shape so characteristic of the tree peony. Blooms last longer when not exposed to the hot sun all day.

ROOT COMPETITION. Plant at sufficient distance from trees and shrubs so the peony roots will not have to compete for water and food.

PROTECTION. A protected location sheltering the plant from heavy winds, rain and hail is advisable.

DRAINAGE. The limestone, mountainside forest regions from which the tree peony originated suggest good drainage. Although the peony will withstand drought, during a rainy season the water must move downward through the soil and not stand around the peony roots. Adequate drainage is a *must*.

PREPARE BEDS AND SOIL CAREFULLY

SOIL AND HOLE. Tree peonies like a deep sandy loam rich in humus (decayed organic matter: compost, leafmold or peatmoss) and enriched with a fertilizer like bonemeal. Decayed organic matter prevents heavy soils from packing and light sandy soils from rapid drying. Too heavy soil may also be lightened with sand or coal ashes.

Iron in the form of sulphate is of value in producing vigor in the plant and depth of color in the blooms. Too much nitrogen may produce soft growth, abnormally subject to botrytis. Roots should never come in direct contact with manure in any form. If the soil tests pH 5.5 or lower add one-half cup ground limestone or one-quarter cup white lime for each plant, to the soil, to decrease the acidity bringing it up to around pH 6.

Dig the border or holes for the plants 2′ deep and 3′ in diameter if you have the space and fill in with well-prepared soil a month or more before planting time. This will give the soil time to settle. Plants set in freshly dug soil may sink too deep for best results.

Preparation of the hole and soil for each plant is very important since the tree peony lives to such a ripe old age. A bushel of leafmold and a generous supply of bonemeal incorporated with the soil should get the plant off to a good start.

DRAINAGE. Tree peonies need both good air and water drainage and cannot take water standing around their roots as will happen in heavy soil. Excessive moisture encourages a fungus growth to which the tree peony is susceptible.

WHEN AND HOW TO PLANT

Late September or October is a good time to plant, a month later in the south. When planting, always examine the roots carefully for any fungus growth. Cut off any rotted parts and give the roots a soaking in a 5% solution of formalin. Unless the fungus is thoroughly removed, it will spread and eventually cause the death of the peony. This fungus disease can only be prevented not cured.

Set the plants the same depth they were in the nursery. Since most tree peony stock is grafted, the graft junction or union should come well below the ground level (4″) so the scion can

Festiva Maxima, an old favorite, softens the harsh lines of a picket fence

Above, shading flowers from the hot sun keeps them
from fading quickly

Below, Peonies form a pleasant pathway in this handsome gard

ROCHE P

Iris and holly in the background and double peonies in the foreground
are planted in an informal design in the garden of a rustic house

Tulips, boxwood, alyssum and peonies for accent
in the garden of Mrs. Irving C. Wright

Left, Magnolia, a Japanese type peony, has bright rose-pink flowers with
yellow stamens. An outstanding deep pink variety, Mons. Jules Elie,
is on the right

Queen Rose and Constance Spry, semi-double to double, above. Below is the lutea hybrid peony Age of Gold

Two views of the tree peony are shown, one in closeup and below a plant
in full bloom

Pink peonies in a Japanese stoneware usabata placed on two mahogany
scroll stands

Three varieties of peony, mostly Sarah Bernhardt, an apple blossom shell-pink, two blooms of Walter Faxon, a true pink, and rosy-white buds of Myrtle Gentry are arranged in an alabaster compote

Opposite An arrangement in an antique chafing dish features three rose-colored peonies and one white and one green caladium leaf. Golden nine-bark is the foliage used for the back line

Branches of flowering crab and flowers of the single pale pink Japanese
peony Akashigata against a gold background, with a Chinese figurine
and a bronze bird to complete the design

ARRANGED BY MRS. GEORGE GOLDSON   BOUTRELLE PHOTO

Framing an Oriental jade figurine are branches of pine and white peonies
with their own foliage

Dried flowers can be lovely! This design includes pale pink to deep rose-red peonies, pink larkspur for line, pale blue salvia, pink to deep red roses and pressed beach leaves

Opposite, This Kakubana arrangement conforms to the strict rules which govern traditional Japanese designs. The Heaven line is 2½ times the height of the container, the Man line is ⅔ of Heaven, Earth is ⅔ of Man. The material is first arranged in the hand, and subordinating branches added and cut to desired lengths. A fork-shaped branch wedged firmly into the wide mouth of the container holds the material

登面新陽

驪山偃多屋

ARRANGED BY MRS. SEIHO ARAKAWA

Left, pink peonies are combined with coral-bells and fleece· flower in an ivory cherub compote. Below, White Japanese type peony Isani Gidui with blossoms of sweet rocket in a round porcelain container

ARRANGED BY
MRS. ALFRED R. WALPOLE

RIDGE STUDIO PHOTO

ARRANGED AND
PHOTOGRAPHED BY
JEANNETTE GROSSMAN

Tree peony gardens staged by Marinus Vander Pol and designed by
Allen C. Haskell are popular at the New England Spring Flower Show.
The authentic Japanese garden above features exotic tree peonies (ranging in color from pearly white through pinks to deep garnet), dainty cut-
leaved maples, low pine and larch, lavender-pink wisteria and late
flowering cherries. Rock, water and moss, basic to any Japanese garden,
are featured

In the photo which follows, an informal contemporary garden uses tree
peonies, a yew hedge, flowering dogwoods, shad, birch, and pine. The
sitting area is bluestone slate. A pixie, a piece of driftwood, ferns and
epimedium complete the picture

Described on the preceding page

This is a grafted plant on herbaceous peony root. Note new roots developing from the Tree Peony stock. This is 3-year graft.

Same grafted plant pruned and set in planting hole. Soil must be friable for good root growth. Note planting depth.

This seedling plant is about seven years old, as dug from the field.

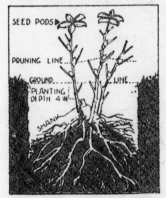

Same seedling set in hole. Note planting depth and pruning line.

How To Plant Tree Peonies
Courtesy of Toichi Domoto Nursery, Hayward, Cal.

develop its own vigorous root system. This in turn means a wealth of subterranean buds and consequently a strong growth above ground.

Space plants at least 4 feet apart. If there is ample room, keep in mind that a tree peony in 6 to 8 years should form a compact bush 2 to 3 feet high and the same across. In the next 10 years it should reach its ultimate height of 4 to 6 feet or more and the same distance across. Once established under favorable conditions a tree peony will live for many, many years and should never be disturbed as long as it is doing well. It, of course, needs enough space to enjoy free air circulation about it.

Planting a pot-grown tree peony is a simple task and it may be planted at any time. Four to five inch pot plants are only one or two years old, so there will be a minimum of root disturbance. If a flower bud has developed on the plant, remove it at the time of planting to insure strong root and top development. Do not cut back the woody growth on young plants except to remove dead or injured parts, since the new growth develops along these woody stems.

15

Caring for Established Plants

FOOD AND WATER

Fertilize as you do for herbaceous peonies (see page 110) applying a small feeding in the spring before the buds start forth, or just before the flowers open, and again in the autumn. If the soil has been properly prepared, very little fertilizer is necessary, perhaps ½ to 1 cup for each established plant in April and again in the fall. Bonemeal is the most effective fertilizer since most tree peonies have high phosphoric acid and potash demands. Wood ashes and superphosphate are good fertilizers. Manure should be avoided (or used with great care) as it may encourage botrytis. Never let it touch the roots.

Since tree peony roots are fairly shallow, in hot, dry weather during the blooming period, a good watering is beneficial.

CULTIVATION TO KEEP DOWN WEEDS

Tree peonies develop a strong system of feeder roots near the surface of the soil so the plant must be cultivated with great care to avoid injury to the shallow roots. Use the hoe with caution in keeping down the weeds.

PRUNING AND STAKING

With the exception of an occasional snipping here and there to shape and the removal of dead ends from the branches, pruning is not necessary. However, when old plants become ungainly or thin after several years, they may be cut to the ground in the fall to rejuvenate them. Strong healthy stems will sprout from below the ground level the following spring.

A fine specimen can also be hurried along by cutting the plant to the ground in early fall, 3 or 4 years after being set out. This gives a completely new set of vigorous, healthy stems. In Japan the plants are pruned rather severely, maybe only leaving 5 stems and flower buds, to increase the size of the flowers. As plants get older the structure may be controlled depending upon whether you want fewer stems with larger flowers or a massive display of smaller flowers.

Some older plants bearing 50 or more flowers may need their weight supported by staking some of the lateral branches.

MULCHING

In a climate like Massachusetts or New York summer mulching is not necessary. However, it has proven valuable in the Middle West and Southern states where the summers are hot and dry. Rather heavy mulching helps keep down ground temperatures and conserves moisture, both conducive to good root growth in tree peonies.

Use straw, hay, ground corncobs, buckwheat hulls, or peat. These mulches do make convenient shelters for mice and other small animals so traps or poison baits may be necessary. Mulches may also harbor spores of fungi, particularly botrytis, so spray mulch with bordeaux mixture or fermate which is an effective control.

The first winter after planting, mulch with a light covering to keep the roots from heaving as a result of frost. Once established, tree peonies are sufficiently hardy to withstand the rigors of the northern climate without protection in winter. Where temperatures are 10°-20° below zero for any length of time, with little snow covering, they do need protection however. In Minneapolis, for example, the Japanese tree peonies have to be boxed in with dry leaves and a wooden box. Even in Clinton, New York, they and the lutea hybrids kill back to the ground in winter and start again like the herbaceous from ground level or below in spring.

DISEASES AND PESTS

The sudden wilting of foliage or branches is an indication of botrytis blight which will not kill but will greatly weaken the plant, the only serious disease problem with tree peonies. This can be guarded against by providing good drainage and good garden sanitation. Botrytis can only be prevented, not cured, so spray plants from early spring at regular 10 day to 2 week intervals with bordeaux mixture, fermate or any good fungicide. Always cut away and burn or destroy any infected or wilted parts. For nematodes, ants and thrips see pages 117-118.

FORCING

Tree peonies may be forced into bloom in advance of their natural flowering time for flower shows or other special occasions. Here is the method employed by Mr. Marinus Vander Pol:

"Select plants at least five years old that have been grown out of doors, properly spaced, never crowded at any time, and well taken care of. They should have been transplanted at least two years and preferably not longer than three years prior to forcing.

"Dig in late fall with as large a ball of earth as possible without disturbing the roots. Place at once in a container large enough to hold the ball of earth without crowding the roots. Be sure there is ample drainage and be sure to fill in underneath the plant and around the edges with the best earth obtainable and pack firmly. Water thoroughly to wash the earth down around the plant. Store out of doors and leave plants to the weather until time to bring them indoors for forcing.

"Bring prepared plants in from six to eight weeks before the date on which they are to be in bloom. Allow three weeks longer for the lutea hybrids. Keep them in good light, but not direct sunlight, at a temperature of not lower than 45° nor higher than 55°. Plants brought along at the lower temperatures do best. Too much heat will cause the buds to come blind. Keep the soil moist, but not wet and never allow water to touch the leaves or flower buds.

"If the flowers come along too fast, they may be delayed by placing the plants in a temperature of not higher than 40° and not lower than 36° and then raising the temperature to 66° a day or two before use.

"Tree peonies may also be held back in order to have good flowers for exhibition at a later date than they normally bloom by following these instructions: dig the plant as soon as frost leaves the ground, pot as above and place immediately in a freezer. Six weeks before the time for the show, bring into a temperature of 40° and allow three days for thawing, then raise the temperature to 55° and keep at that temperature for 20 days, in good light but not brilliant sunshine. Buds will be showing. Again cool off for from six to ten days at 45°, to swell the buds. Return to 55° to 60° to bloom. These times may be slightly varied to suit the circumstances. Be sure to keep all top growth dry and the roots moist.

16

Propagating the Tree Peony

Most tree peonies are propagated by grafting, a slow process. Grafts made in August or September left undisturbed in cold frames, a cold greenhouse or planted in the field are ready for the average garden in 2 or 3 years. This is, however, the quickest, surest, and best method of propagating tree peonies and the method most commonly used.

Propagation by layering, laying a branch down on the ground while still attached to the plant and covering it with a few inches of good soil is not often used. After 2 or 3 years small plants may form somewhere along the branch, grown enough to cut off and transplate in permanent quarters.

Tree peonies are sometimes propagated by root division but this is much more difficult than with herbaceous peonies, since the wood is extremely hard and it is difficult to make the cuts. Root divisions should be set somewhat deeper than the plant from which they are made so the crown of the plant is 4" to 6" below the surface of the ground.

Propagation from seed, except in the species, never produces plants true to name and may require as long as ten years to get a flower. Frequently the percentage of germination is small.

GRAFTING

Here we should like to include a mild warning about mortality in grafting. A nursery that has less than 50% deaths the first year and another 50% the second counts that it is doing pretty well. This is what accounts for part of the expense of a tree peony.

The usual method of propagating the Japanese tree peony is by grafting a shoot or scion of the tree peony upon the fleshy root of a herbaceous peony (P. lactiflora). Choose a scion 2″ to 3″ long bearing 2 or more buds from the current year's growth. Select a good piece of root or understock ½″ to 1″ in diameter, at the large end and shortened to 4″ to 6″ in length.

When grafts are to be placed in the open field, they should be made early enough to allow scion and rootstock to knit before danger of freezing, mid-August in the north, a month later in the south.

The grafts may be left undisturbed in a cold frame or cold

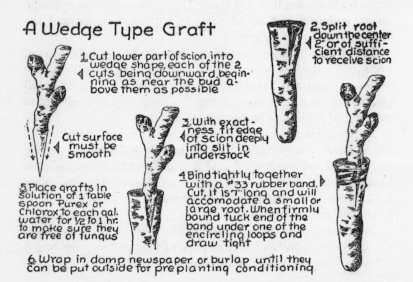

A Wedge Type Graft

1. Cut lower part of scion into wedge shape, each of the 2 cuts being downward beginning as near the bud above them as possible

Cut surface must be smooth

2. Split root down the center 2″ or of sufficient distance to receive scion

3. With exactness fit edge of scion deeply into slit in understock

4. Bind tightly together with a #33 rubber band. Cut, it is 7″ long and will accomodate a small or large root. When firmly bound tuck end of the band under one of the encircling loops and draw tight

5. Place grafts in solution of 1 table spoon Purex or Chlorox to each gal. water for ½ to 1 hr. to make sure they are free of fungus

6. Wrap in damp newspaper or burlap until they can be put outside for preplanting conditioning

greenhouse for 2 or 3 years when they are ready for the average garden. To plant in the open field place the grafts horizontally on a layer of sawdust 2″ deep on the ground, in any well shaded place. Pile 3 or 4 rows deep with sawdust between each layer and cover with a 3" layer. Water occasionally to keep entire bed damp but not wet. Evaporation keeps the sawdust cool. When the union of the scion and understock is well underway (they knit quickly in a cool, moist place) after 3 to 4 weeks, plant grafts in field in rows in a trench the width of a spade. Place vertically on each side of trench 3" to 4" apart with the top bud 2" to 3" below the surface. Level the ground and cover to a depth of 3" with sawdust. If the ground is dry, soak trench before it is completely filled. The grafts need no further attention until they are lifted 2 or 3 years later when the scions should have good roots. The sawdust is a protection from rapid temperature changes and minimizes weed growth. Planted in the open field, grafts should be made early enough to allow union before danger of freezing.

FROM SEED

Tree peonies grown from seed usually require 5 to 7 years to bloom, although the range varies from 3 to 10 years or more. No one can predict just what a seedling will be but the hope and thrill of getting a new and unusual plant spurs many peony lovers on to keep trying, demonstrating a wonderful degree of patience.

To grow seedlings harvest seeds at earliest stage of ripeness, just as they are beginning to turn black. There is no use in planting any soft seed, seeds that give when you pinch them between your fingers. Store in a cool place until you have collected all you want. Soak seeds in Purex or Clorox solution (1 tablespoon to 1 gallon of water) ½ to 1 hour to destroy any fungus. To stratify, choose a clay pot of convenient size. Use a 1" layer of friable, crumbly soil in the bottom of the pot, then a layer of seeds, alternate until pot is filled, being sure each seed is completely covered with soil.

Sink the pot in a well shaded, well drained location deeply into the ground, so the top of the pot rim is 18" below the surface of the ground. If the ground is dry fill the hole with water and let it soak in before placing the pot into it. Soak the pot in water before burying it. In six weeks lift the pot, invert and remove the seed and earth mass. A tiny rootlet will have formed at the open end of each seed that has germinated.

Prepare a trench as wide as your spade and 2½″ deep, in half shade. The soil should be rich and well drained. Scatter sprouted seeds 1″ apart. Refill trench, level ground, cover with 2″ to 3″ sawdust to conserve moisture and keep weeds and grass out when young tree peony shoots make their way up the following spring. In the spring, before growth starts, sprinkle with chlordane dust to discourage cutworms. When tiny plants show, spray with ½ strength solution of bordeaux or fermate. Repeat at 2 week intervals several times the first season. Do not disturb seedlings for two, or better still, three years. Transplant into rows 6″ to 8″ apart and leave until they have flowered. Seedlings perhaps never have the distinction of the fine selected plants but they give a sense of ownership and accomplishment to their grower. The lutea hybrids, being excessively sterile, never set seed, or almost never. If yours does, save and coddle it.

17

Selecting Varieties

EARLY AND LATE VARIETIES

It is possible to extend the blooming season by careful selection of varieties. Start the season with an early bloomer such as Tama-fuyo (Jeweled Lotus) which has very pale pink-blush, cup-shaped flowers of exquisite delicacy. Its semi-double flowers are early and it has deep rose carpels. Gessekai (Moonlit World) is a popular white variety which flowers early. Haku-raku-ten (Poetry of China), a single, has white flowers with reflections in its depth of shell-pink, stamens of gold and a purple pistil, a real beauty.

Shin-tenchi (Between Heaven and Earth) has lovely, semi-double, pink flowers and a dark exciting center. A beautifully shaped and colored flower is Shuchiuka (Flower in Wine). Its delicate pink petals have deep pink splashes at the base. Kintajio (Castle of Kinuta) has lovely pale pink single flowers.

Later comes a deep, dark maroon, Uba-tama, and Hatsu-garashu (First Crow of the Year) which is one of the finest of the dark varieties with crimson-maroon, semi-double flowers.

Usually the Japanese tree peonies are over before lutea hybrids begin though of course, in every season, there is a little overlapping. After the Japanese tree peonies are through blooming the lutea hybrids extend the season. Harvest, a semi-double

Tree Peony Blooms Are From 2" to 12" Across

Sizes differ depending upon culture, weather, etc. Among the smallest are P. lutea, single yellow and P. delavayi, single maroon, resembling the buttercup.

P. lutea about 2" across

Most double flowering European types are of medium size, 5" to 8". Include a wide range of colors, many fragrant, most of superior lasting quality. Foliage broader and less finely cut than Japanese types

P. banksi, double, flesh lavender-pink

Ukaregi-ohi, semi-double, salmon-rose

Tremendous sized flowers among Japanese varieties. Broad petaled, tips crinkled with crepe-paper like texture, central cushion of golden anthers. Gessekai (white) and Haru-no-akebono (white with divided petals shaded with crimson) sometime measure nearly 12" across

lutea hybrid, has bronze gold flowers with petal edges flushed with rose. Age of Gold has a flat rosette flower with ruffled petals of bright gold. And last of all making about three weeks of bloom comes Argosy, one of the last P. lutea hybrids. It has clear sulphur yellow, single flowers 6″-7″ wide, plum-colored flares.

ACCORDING TO COLOR GROUPINGS

The late Dr. A. P. Saunders, beloved Dean and Professor of chemistry at Hamilton College, Clinton, New York, showed his new tree peony "Argosy" in Boston in 1928. It was at a combined American Peony Society and Massachusetts Horticultural Society Peony Show and with it he won the President's cup. He established a special niche for himself in the peony world because of his great contribution in the field of hybridizing, both with herbaceous and tree peonies. Dr. Saunders' daughter Silvia is successfully carrying on his work.

Their choice Japanese tree peonies usually bloom in Clinton the second to the last or last week in May and on into June when the lutea hybrids start, followed by P. lutea itself, the last to flower. The blooming season covers three to four weeks. Two year grafts or older, some nursery grown plants are available at varying prices depending upon the size and quality.

Japanese tree peonies, P. lutea or P. delavayi hybrids bloom through the first half of June, in Clinton, sometimes longer. The above mentioned Argosy is a clear sulphur yellow, single, 6″-7″ wide with plum-colored flares. Silvia Saunders lists her lutea hybrids under six groupings according to color and under each grouping are many fine named varieties. The six groupings are as follows:

1. "Roman Gold" group—Yellow, clear or almost clear, generally single.
2. "Golden Hind" group—Yellow, clear or almost clear. Generally semi- or fully double.

3. "Tea Rose" group—Generally yellow, but tinted and suffused rose. Single to double.
4. "Banquet" group—Generally red in color but with yellow undertones. Single or double.
5. "Black Pirate" group—Six darkest crimson and nine almost black maroon. Single to double.
6. "Mystery" group—Ivories, pearled shades, suffused mauves. Single to double.

EUROPEAN-CHINESE, JAPANESE AND HYBRIDS

European-Chinese

ALBERT CROUSSE—Large double, flesh-pink.

BANKSI—First tree peony variety brought to the new world from China. Large, double, flesh-pink flowers, good bloomer, hardy.

BIJOU DE CHUSAN—Large double, outer petals pure white, center petals cream tipped with green. Good bloomer.

FRAGRANS MAXIMA PLENA—Fine double, salmon-flesh.

OSIRIS—Double, velvety dark red, profuse bloomer. Dwarf grower suitable for rock gardens.

REINE ELIZABETH—A vigorous, free bloomer with large pink, almost rose-red flowers.

SOUVENIR DE DUCHER—Large double, deep violet flower with reddish tinge; outer flat layer of guard petals with a rounded bomb of petals on them.

Japanese Varieties

ANYO-NO-HIKARE (Light in the Dark)—Large double, rich deep crimson with crinkled petals.

FUJI-NO-MORI (Grove of Fuji)—Watermelon pink, deeper in center, crepe-like texture, semi-double.

FUSO-NO-TSUKASA (God of Japan)—Large, ball-shaped double white.

GABISAN (Mountain of the Arched Eyebrow)—Large white, double beautiful center.

GEKKYUDEN (Palace of the Moon Kingdom)—Large double white, shaded yellow.

GENKIMON (Gate of Genki)—Huge white shaded yellow, double.

GESSEKAI (Moonlit World)—Immense double, glistening white crinkled petals.

GODAISHU (Large Globe-like)—White with yellow center, large translucent petals beautifully curved. Double.

HAKU-RAKU-TEN (Poetry of China)—Single, white, reflections in its depth of shell-pink, stamens of gold, purple pistil.

HANA-DAIGIN (Minister of Flowers)—Lustrous deep purple, large full double.

HANA-KISOI (Floral Rivalry)—Large excellent deep cherry-pink, double.

HATSU-GARASHU (First Crow of the Year)—Huge double, rich glowing maroon.

HIGURASHI (Twilight)—Large double, bright pink.

HINODE-SEKAI (World of the Rising Sun)—Large brilliant rosy-red double.

HINO-TSUKASA (Ashes of the Setting Sun)—Big double, glistening fiery scarlet.

HIRA-NO-YUKI (Snow of Hira)—Semi-double white with yellow center.

HOWZAN (Treasure Mountain)—Full double, brilliant light pink, twisted petals.

IMA-CHOW-KOW (Name of Ancient Saint)—Large double, opens lemon-yellow and fades to white.

KAGURA-JISHI (Sacred Lion Dance)—Immense double, rich pink with rose-red center.

KAMADA-FUJI (Wisteria of Kamada)—Double wisteria purple with lavender shadings.

KINTAJIO (Castle of Kinuta)—Full double, blush-pink with fringed petals.

KOKAMON (Gate of Koka)—Double lustrous brilliant maroon.

MOMOYAMA (Mountain of Peach Orchard)—Large full double, fine pink. A favorite.

NISHIKI-NO-TSUYA (Beauty of Brocade)—Double of great size. Scarlet-crimson base.

NISSHO (Sunbeam)—Glistening scarlet, enormous double.

ORIHIME (The Weaving Princess)—Large double, exquisite Chinese-red.

SHIN-MOMO-ZOMA (New Bloom of the Peach Flower Garden)— Immense double, light pink. Coral branches and stems.

SHINTENCHI (New Heaven and Earth)—Large shell-pink, semi-double with thick satiny petals.

SHOGYOMON—One of the largest and best whites, bluish cast. Full double.

SHUCHIUKA (Flower in Wine)—Rose-pink large semi-double. Old favorite.

SUMA-NO-ICHI (Deepest Ink)—Immense satiny deep maroon.

TAMA-FUYO (Jeweled Lotus)—Early blooming blush pink, semi-double to double, establishes easily. Deep rose carpels.

UBA-TAMA (Beautiful Black King)—Huge satiny maroon.

YACHIYO-TSUBAKI (Long Hedge of Camellias)—Brilliant coral-pink double.

YAE-ZAKURA (Very Double Cherry)—Large double, soft cherry-pink.

Lutea (delavayi) Hybrids

French (Lemoine) originations:

ALICE HARDING—Bright lemon yellow, full double but shows stamens in its center when fully open.

SANG LORRAINE—Fragrant, semi-double, deep mahogany-red, black at base.

SATIN ROUGE—Vigorous but not floriferous, large, fragrant, fully double flowers, deep blood-red shade with broad satiny petals.

SOUV. DE MAXIME CORNU—Grows vigorously, large double yellow flowers edged with red.

American (Saunders) originations:

AGE OF GOLD—Like a ruffled camellia. Flat rosette of soft cream gold. Semi- or fully double. Central mass of stamens. Flower stems weak but one of the most beautiful of the yellow tree peonies.

ARGOSY—Single, cup-shaped, clear sulphur-yellow, red blotched at base. Free bloomer.

BANQUET—Shinny flat rosette of cherry red, brilliant dark center.

Single to semi-double.

BLACK PIRATE—Dramatic. Very dark mahogany red single with black flares.

CANARY—Dazzling yellow, one of the brightest, dramatic heart, very fine, single.

GOLDEN HIND—Fluffy 7″-8″ blooms of bright yellow, flared dark. Fine variety. Double.

HARVEST—Color of ripe grain. Petals furled and rosy edged, semi-double. Decorative.

MYSTERY—Large flowers, pearled lavender with darker shading, varied with palest green.

PRINCESS—Semi-double dusky mauve suffused with golden sheen. Pale gold center. Gorgeous.

ROMAN GOLD—Cup-shaped single, brilliant warm yellow, flared dark. Fine form and substance. Seventy-two blooms reported on one plant.

TEA ROSE—Lovely flower of warm light amber.

THUNDERBOLT—Floriferous. Black crimson single streaked scarlet.

There are about seventy-five Saunders hybrid varieties. The flowers are smaller than the Japanese tree peonies but the colors are more unique and magnificent ranging from yellow through orange and blends of yellow and red to almost black. These colors do not exist except for the black maroons, in the European-Chinese and Japanese varieties so are doubly valuable in a collection for they bloom two or three weeks later than most other varieties.

MOST POPULAR TREE PEONY VARIETIES

(As voted by members of the American Peony Society—1958)

White:

Coronal, Rosy tints. S.

Flora, S.

Fuso-no-tsukasa, D.

Gabisan, D.

Genkimon, D.

°Gessekai, D.

Haku-banriu, D.

°Godaishu, D.

Kamikaze, D.

WHITE (continued)
°Renkaku, D.
Suisho-haku, SD.
Tama-sudare, D.
°Tsuki-sekai, D.
Okina-jishi, D.
°Yaso-no-mine, D.
°Yaso-okina, D.

Pink:
Akashigata, D.
Higurashi, D.
Howzan, D.
Momo-yama, D.
Sakura-gasane, D.
Sakura-jishi, D.
°Shintenchi, SD.
Suigan, D.
°Tama-fuyo, D.
°Yachiyo-tsubaki, D.
Yae-zakura, D.
Yomo-zakura, SD.

Cherry:
Beni-chidori, SD.
Hana-kisoi, D.

Rose Red:
Hinode-sekai, D.
Hodai, D.
°Mme. Stuart Low, D.
°Reine Elizabeth, D.
Shin-kagura, D.
°Ukaregi-ohi, SD.

Scarlet:
Impumon, D.
Kin-pukurin, SD.
°Nishiki-no-tsuya, D.
Nissho, D.
Robert Fortune, D.

Taiyo, SD.
Tama-fidori, SD.

Red (Crimson):
Charioteer, S.
Kokamon, D.
Satin Rouge, D.
Shugyo-kuden, SD.
Teikwan, D.

Black Red:
Black Douglas, SD.
Black Panther, SD.
°Black Pirate, S.
Kuro-botan, SD.
Ubatama, D.

Purple:
Hana-daigin, D.
Hatsu-garashu, D.
Hora-kumon, D.
Rimpo, SD.
Souvenir de Ducher, D.

Yellow:
Age of Gold, D.
Alice Harding, D.
Amber Moon, S.
Argosy, S.
Canary, S.
Chromatella, D.
Golden Vanity, S.
Goldfinch, SD.
Harvest, SD.
High Noon, SD.
Kinshi, SD.
La Lorraine, D.
Roman Gold, S.
Silver Sails, S.
Wings of the Morning, S.

Yellow with Reddish Markings:Other Colors:

Banquet, SD.	Aurore, terra cotta, S.
Chinese Dragon, S.	*Kamada-fuji, wisteria, D.
Conquest, SD.	Princess, mauve and gold, SD.
Pastoral, S.	Savage Splendor, ivory, purple,
*Souvenir de Maxime Cornu, D.	and red, S.

Many listed as double (D) are perhaps semi-double (SD). Those * were voted "the best" tree peony. Gessekai received the most votes.

TREE PEONIES that do very well in the south.

Gessekai	White	Double	Early
Tama-fuyo	Blush	Semi-Double to Double	Early
Hana-kisoi	Cherry	Double	Early
Uba-tama	Dark Maroon	Double	Early

PART IV — PEONIES INDOORS

18

An Ancient and Modern
Favorite for the Home

The Chinese in their ancient decorative arts frequently used
two or more arrangements together, flowers in a tall vase with
flowers or fruit beside it in a low basket or cut flowers with pot
plants. The plant material was chosen because of its symbolic or
religious significance or association with the season. The peony
signified spring just as the unfurling leaves or blossoming
branches were a symbol of spring, new strength and virility.
Designs showing a branch of the Japanese plum, a spray of
cymbidium, and the peony are found on screens and panels of
old silk. Magnolia was combined with crabapple and flowers
of the tree peony in seventeenth and eighteenth century woodblock prints. The designs were informal using a few perfect
blossoms and branches of interesting shapes with the emphasis
on the form, texture and color of a few well chosen subjects.

In Japan arranging flowers has long been a recognized art
starting back in the sixth century when the first emissary to
China is said to have brought back to Japan the idea of floral
offerings for Buddhist altars. As in China, much folklore, symbolism and tradition are associated with the art. For centuries
in Japan the peony has been known as the flower of prosperity
and is highly prized by arrangers because of its symbolism and

166

beauty. The Japanese decorative arts seen in paintings, ceramics and textiles, like the Chinese, show frequent pictorial use of the peony. Peach blossoms and sprays of orchids are frequently combined with them. A lacquered cart painted on a sixteenth and seventeenth century Japanese screen shows a basket of wisteria, tree peonies and blossoming fruit branches. In arranging flowers the Japanese have become masters of line design, practicing simplicity and restraint.

In both Europe and America in the eighteenth and nineteenth centuries the peony was a popular garden flower. A study of the Dutch and Flemish flower painters shows the tulip, rose, peony, and iris to be the four favorite flower subjects. The peony was used cut in combination with many other flowers of the day in large, lavish and colorful bouquets.

An abundance of material was used in contrast to the more frugal restraint displayed in the Orient.

Today American arrangers use what is best from the past to fit their present day needs. They use modified mass groupings of the eighteenth and nineteenth centuries, line designs, or a combination of the two, whatever best suits their purpose, depending upon the type home in which they live. If there is a harmony of materials: flowers, container, accessories and setting, a pleasing relationship with the surroundings, the results will be satisfying.

The answers from a couple dozen top arrangers, lecturers and accredited judges when asked how they like to arrange peonies may be summarized by the four following answers.

1. "When peonies are in season I always incorporate them into a lecture, usually in a simple Japanese manner."

2. "I'm not a period or mass arranger and as we have more or less a contemporary home, my choice of containers for peonies is heavy plain glass or pottery. I think they are excellent for practicing in the oriental manner of using just three graduated blossoms. Personally I prefer them with their own foliage but at least they should be in keeping in scale, feeling and visual weight."

3. "I use peonies in arrangements, mostly as a focal point since the large, beautiful flowers are so well suited to that purpose. I do use the tight buds for line in other arrangements. The foliage too is very interesting, especially when it has turned color late in the season."

4. "Peonies are wonderful for weddings or decorating the church, they have excellent carrying power. Use the buds and the full blown ones and don't overlook the tight green buds. Break them up using the various stages. When in the market use them in colorful, lavish bouquets with all the other lovely spring things. Use the foliage and the seed pods too. Tree peonies! Just float one of the exquisite flowers. What could be lovelier!"

19

Peonies In Floral Design

ALONE WITH OWN FOLIAGE

The peony tops the list of flowers that can effectively be arranged alone with its own foliage. Highly decorative it lends itself well to natural groupings which are quick and easy to do. In an arrangement try to capture something of the distinction and spirit of the flower as it grows in the garden, emphasizing its quality of richness and the individual beauty of the flowers, so lovely in both form and texture. Some of the beautiful ruffled white petals are translucent and ethereal in appearance. And the handsome blooms come in colors of surprising brilliance as well as delicate, soft hues. Some fascinating and exciting flowers have undertones of silver in their pink colorings, one lovely white is flecked with carmine and yet another pure white is blotched with purple at the base of the petals. Many have richly marked centers and beautiful stamens, usually of a bright canary yellow.

The fact a bloom may be as big as a saucer need not be a problem. If space is limited use only one, three or five blooms to avoid a bouquet that is too large for the space where it is to be used. Remember five peonies will perhaps equal in bulk a dozen other flowers. Graduate stem lengths letting one or two stand tall, cutting others short, placing each bloom so it can

Peonies Used Alone
With Own Foliage

This simple group-
ing of peonies with
their own attractive
foliage has sparkle
and richness ▶

Peonies of varying heights,
none crowded, the larger
fuller types used at the base

Foliage concentrated ▶
at base adds weight
to support height. Each
bloom is distinct with
a natural charm
and beauty

Their own rich
green foliage con-
trasts and shows
off to best ad-
vantage the
beautiful flowers

Cut to varying stem lengths,
flowers faced in slightly different
directions with largest blooms lowest, design is attractive from all sides

Peonies Used Alone
With Own Foliage

Float a gorgeous flower.
Anchor to holder. Leaves
protect petals from
water soaking

A handsome peony
framed with its own
attractive foliage

The tall bud and two
shorter staggered
stems seem to spring
from one point and
make a pleasing
design

Foliage frames
lower flowers,
accents taller ones,
adds visual weight
at bottom where
needed

Place tallest stem
first. Then arrange
shorter ones below,
using foliage at
base to dramatize
large flowers and
blend arrangement
with container

be appreciated for itself with no crowding. By cutting the stems to different lengths a careful separation of flower heads is obtained so each bloom rises separately from the others. As a general rule the taller, smaller flower forms and those lighter in tone are used to establish the silhouette or basic structure. Then working toward the center and down, the larger and heavier looking blooms, those darker in tone, are used toward the center and at the base for proper balance.

Arrangers aren't particularly interested in huge sizes and often prefer the secondary blooms as a more desirable size to work with. In this case do not disbud. Hybridizers might well consider developing varieties attractive to the arrangers, creating more small versions which are easier to arrange.

Make the maximum use of the natural contrast in texture, form and color between the peony flower and its foliage, concentrating the deeply notched glossy foliage at the base of the arrangement where it will frame and show off the round blooms to best advantage creating the visual weight necessary for proper balance.

Some admirers of the peony feel they should always be used alone and not suffer the distraction of other flowers. At the height of the season massed by themselves in a large bowl they are terrific. The round flower-heads contrast skillfully in form with the deeply cut leaves and glossy leathery texture of the foliage making the translucent petals of the single type flower even more ethereal in appearance although the petals in reality are very tough and strong. The contrast of the bright golden yellow stamens with the color of the satiny petals is fascinating.

As a matter of fact in Japan where the tree peony is of royal rank and regarded as the queen of all flowering plants, in most cases it must be used alone in any indoor arrangement and placed in a position of honor in the room.

WITH SPRING BRANCHES

A minimum of material is required for this type arrangement.

Peonies With A Few Well Chosen Branches

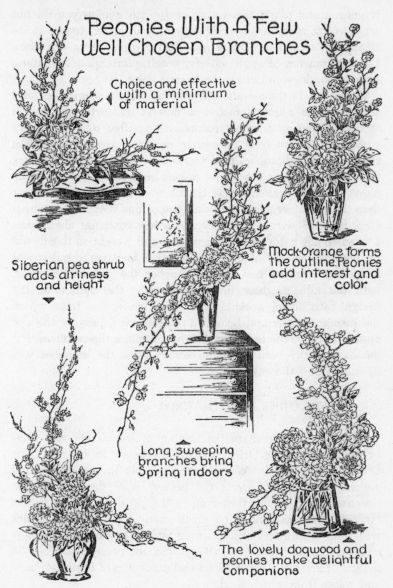

Choice and effective with a minimum of material

Siberian pea shrub adds airiness and height

Mock-Orange forms the outline. Peonies add interest and color

Long, sweeping branches bring Spring indoors

The lovely dogwood and peonies make delightful companions

If your peony plants are young or for any reason you do not want to cut many a very few flowers with short stems can be effectively combined with a few well chosen spring branches. Choose branches of apple, cherry, peach, plum, quince, redbud, spice bush, dogwood or whatever is at hand.

If you cut in the woods, observe the state conservation laws and never for a few branches or flowers do anything to harm or deplete our woodland treasures. If possible select branches with naturally lovely or interesting curves or bend them to the shapes needed. Branches lend themselves well to any size space, since they may be cut as short or long as necessary. If the space requires height branches may be cut three or more times higher than the container since their delicacy of line keeps the arrangement from appearing top heavy. In a low container always use a needlepoint holder of sufficient size and weight so it will not tip with the weight of the branches. Fill an opaque tall receptacle with crushed hen wire to anchor the placements. Start with the taller, lighter branches forming the outline of the design, then fill in, working toward the center and base, where the peonies, larger and heavier in appearance, provide the eye appeal and give the necessary balance. Replace the cut flowers at the base of the branches as necessary since the branches will usually outlast the cut flowers.

WITH OTHER PLANT MATERIAL

Since we do not share the feeling of association and symbolism found in the Orient we use the peony in any way that best suits our needs. We do not maintain an atmosphere of general elegance but dress the peony up or down to fit the situation. After all, in this country the peony is grown in the farm dooryard as well as on great estates. Blooming as it does with both the flowers of late spring and early summer, the most colorful time of the year in the garden, the peony season is the delight of arrangers. There is an endless source of forms, textures and colors from which to choose.

Mass Vertical Groupings

When flowers are abundant in the garden we can afford to be extravagant and use them generously in colorful buxom bouquets. Peonies lend themselves unusually well to this treatment. The big round forms are a natural center of interest. The open blossoms are excellent for emphasis and to focus attention, while the tight buds on longer stems supply line. Eighteenth century Williamsburg arrangements use peonies in mass with a wide variety of other garden flowers.

If one flower is to dominate, it sets the keynote and other flowers are selected to harmonize in color, or contrast, as is desired. Tall pointed or spiked flowers add interest and contrast. Spire-like flowers like the canterbury bell, delphinium, foxglove, lupine and thermopsis furnish height and line. The daylily, iris, madonna and regal lilies and tulips offer contrast in form and color and lend height if needed. Round forms, smaller and different in texture from the round peony, like coreopsis, pyrethrum and the rose add interest. The coral-bell and bleeding heart have graceful lines and add a touch of color.

Greens like ivy or artemisia foliage may be cut from the yard and used for graceful curves to soften any stiffness in the flowers themselves or to soften a severe silhouette. Use the decorative foliage of the peony if your plants are well established and you have enough to cut. It is particularly lovely used in fall arrangements with mums and other fall flowers after turning color late in the season.

Mass Horizontal Groupings

A massed horizontal grouping is practical for the dining, coffee or terrace table. The arrangement should be:

1. low enough not to interfere with the diners' view of one another.

2. attractive from every angle.

3. follow lines of table as round, oblong, square or oval. A longer table requires a longer container and arrangement. A small bouquet is lost on a large table, a large one overpowering on a small one.

4. considered as to total effect: colors, textures, atmosphere, table covering, china, accessories, etc. Must all make a pleasing, unified whole.

For the cocktail, tea or buffet table, plan a design to look down on as people will be standing. Depending on the placement of the table it may or may not be viewed from all sides. Viewed from only three sides it must have a feeling of depth, as though completed on the fourth side.

Generally speaking to arrange, start with the tallest and smallest flowers placing them horizontally in the needle holder, pointing some slightly upward, others downward to the length you want the finished design. Work in toward the center with the partially open blooms to those full blown with foliage or leaves at the base of the container to provide visual weight, interest and transition from flowers to receptacle making a harmonious unit.

For the Modern Setting

Simple uncluttered arrangements fit well in the modern surroundings. Large branches of whatever is available; apple, pear, plum, lilac or dogwood (forced or not) with the round peony blooms used as a focus can produce pleasing results. This is especially true against the large, plain surfaces in the modern home, stressing outline or silhouette, using a selective amount of plant material to obtain dramatic effects through simplicity.

Foliage having strong linear patterns which combine well with peonies for use in modern surroundings include such plants as aspidistra, bamboo, cryptomeria, Japanese holly, hosta, iris, juniper, ligustrum, magnolia, Japanese maple, nandina, narcissus, podocarpus, pothos, willow and wisteria. The hosta leaf is a favorite with peonies because of its strong, broad effects, glaucous sheen and strong veining. The variegated types are especially useful and interesting. Expose both the front and back of leaves for contrast and interest.

FOR LARGE SCALE DECORATIONS
(Platform, Hall, Church and Weddings)

Many of us associate the peony with Decoration Day, graduation or weddings. Because of its size and form it is ideal for large scale decorations. Placed in sturdy containers of pottery, metal or wood and combined with strong companions like the lilac, dogwood or large flowering fruit branches they make excellent pedestal arrangements for the platform or may be used equally well to decorate the church. Special attention must be given to scale in planning flowers for a large hall. Anything too small is out of proportion and ineffective. Cut larger, longer sprays or branches so they will be of sufficient size for the space where they are to be used.

Flowering spring branches are invaluable for large scale peony arrangements as they supply an airy, fairy-like silhouette or basic design for the peonies and add a fragrance, grace and lavishness in keeping with the peony itself. Often a selection of branches from two or three varieties of the same named plant add a subtle interest to the composition. To illustrate use the common, old-fashioned mock-orange or Philadelphus coronarius for the upper and outer branches. Remove the prolific foliage so the fragrant, white, single flowers may be better seen. The branches will last longer with most leaves removed and also appear lighter and less heavy. For the lower branches use P. splendens with its single flowers borne in groups of five and noted for their brilliant yellow stamens echoed in the peonies used in the arrangement and again in the soft gilt of the urn or container used. Cut the branches when ¼ the blossoms along the branch are open using both open flowers and buds.

If room permits and there is ample open space around the arrangement, large designs are effective placed on the floor. Use containers heavy and dark enough in appearance to give a sense of stability. The beauty of the lilac which blooms with the peony is especially lovely and effective viewed from above as is the peony. Cut the lilacs when ¼ to ½ the panicle is open.

Denude each flowering stalk of its leaves. If you want lilac foliage to break up the mass of flowers cut non-flowering branches which may easily be replaced as the leaves drop and wilt rather quickly.

Visibility

An arrangement designed for a large room should have carrying power to be enjoyed and seen by the people at the back. Good visibility is a must. Distinct, clean cut forms devoid of fussiness so the plant material will stand out in simplicity and elegance against a good solid background is important. Restraint is advisable and keep in mind one large arrangement or grouping is much more effective than several, small scattered decorations.

Lighter colors and white flowers show up best. Dark flowers and those in the blue to violet range become invisible at a short distance and look grey in subdued light. Always study the arrangement from the back of the hall or church, from the various entrances, and under artificial light if it is to be seen at night. Yellow loses its intensity under artificial light and becomes almost white. Blues and lavenders are scarcely noticeable and soft pastel shades lose their effectiveness under artificial light.

Flowers show up best with a natural light falling on them, however this is not always possible. A hidden, inconspicuous spotlight can highlight and add to the effectiveness of a decoration.

Church

As in all arrangements suitability and good taste are of first importance. Consider the interior decoration of the church and place the peony arrangements for best effects at the chancel steps or on either side of the altar, where they will enhance the decorations of the church leading the eye to a cross or some similar sacred object.

Plain interiors are easier to handle than the highly decorated as the situation is less complicated. A plain interior makes an excellent background for flowers which add warmth, cheer, color and relieve any bareness. If more than one arrangement is used space and group them so there will be a unity of design and interest using one or two predominant colors to tie the group together and create a unity and harmony.

Appropriate containers should have wide enough openings or tops for graceful arrangements and hold adequate water. Containers for the church are often used in pairs. They should be dignified and suitable, the larger more elaborate churches requiring more elaborate vases. Expensive silver or silver-gilt cups and chalices should have linings to avoid injury to the inside. Some excellent modern reproductions of good shapes and design in stone, lead and marble, carved wood and bronze are available. In a simple country church plain pottery or simple garden baskets are suitable. Peonies can be truly beautiful arranged properly in the chancel of any church. A well done church decoration is particularly rewarding because it is seen and enjoyed by so many people.

Weddings

June is the month of brides and peonies, which are much used and loved for weddings. Practical and lovely for either a home or church wedding with colors to fit any bride's color scheme they may be used in luxuriant decorations or for the simplest type ceremony. Nothing is lovelier than an all-peony wedding.

An arranger friend of ours who plans the flowers for top weddings discovered at the last minute that the bride had invited an extra bridesmaid and not informed her. Short one bouquet she rushed to the garden, cut two open double peonies and three bursting buds, made a collar of peony foliage designing an old-fashioned bouquet, which made an interesting contrast to the other bouquets which were all alike. It was the most admired of the bridesmaids' bouquets.

For mixed combinations featuring peonies there are endless choices, and for home or church decorations there is a wide choice to suit all tastes and pocketbooks.

WHITE. For the traditional white (or green and white) wedding white peonies in any of the five flower types or a combination of the differing forms may be combined with spiked white flowers such as canterbery bells, delphiniums, foxglove or gladiolus, hyacinths, iris, larkspur, lilies, lupines, narcissus, snapdragons, stock and tulips. White roses also combine well with peonies, the round forms contrasting in size, form and texture.

Materials to make up the silhouette or basic design may include any of the many white flowering branches available which supply lightness and a delicacy. Dogwood makes a fairy-tale background ideal for home or church weddings as do white lilacs, spirea or philadelphus. The fragrant, small, white flowers in short broad spikes at the end of branchlets on the fothergilla shrub are interesting and so are the large feathery pinacles of double white filipendula flowers.

Adding a tone of pink, apple blossoms, white lilacs and white peonies are a favorite combination for weddings.

PINK. Apple blossoms or any of the lovely ornamental fruit blossoms, pink dogwood, honeysuckle (Lonicera tatarica), beauty bush (Kolkwitzia) and the lovely magnolia blossoms used with pink or rose peonies and any of the white flowers listed above which come in pink (most of them do) offer a wide choice of materials from which to choose.

WHITE AND YELLOW OR GOLD. There are many possibilities with white and yellow or gold. Use yellow Siberian pea-shrub (caragana) and the more solid heads of white lilacs, to outline the design. Add some pale yellow or gold tulips and narcissus or yellow snapdragons, daylilies, aquilegia or iris using white peonies with yellow or gold centers lower in the arrangement near the base for focus. Use some buds and variegated ivy or pachysandra to soften the lines. Bold hosta leaves showing from behind the tulips will add character and interest to the design.

Possibilities are limitless. The lovely red peonies with yellow stamens have richness and great appeal and could be used with other peonies in all their various shadings from palest pink to deepest red.

HISTORICAL OR PERIOD DESIGNS

The peony was used through all the European historical and period styles as well as in our own Early American and Colonial Williamsburg days. Arrangements in "the spirit of" or characteristic style of these periods must contain the flowers typical of the period, the favored colors, prevailing style of design, preferred containers and accessories and conform in all the elements including plant material, furniture and the fabrics of the time.

For those who live in a period home or wish to enter Flower Show competition there are many fine helpful books available. *The Complete Book of Flowers and Plants for Interior Decoration* by Esther Wheeler and Anabel Combs Lasker is excellent. Visit museums and study the period rooms, paintings and tapestries to acquire knowledge and a feeling for the periods.

20

How to Cut, Condition and Dry

The beauty of the peony is as notable as its hardiness and many varieties are excellent cut for indoor decoration. The decorative flowers and ornamental foliage last well. The lovely satiny petals of the flowers reflect light and hold shadows enhancing their textural beauty. Newer introductions have a wide range of clear colors and intermediate tones and combinations such as a clear white with royal purple blotches at the center, a deep rose edged with silver and delicate lovely blossoms tinged with yellow.

Some of the breathtaking single, open forms add a richness and elegant touch to any arrangement. These forms hold themselves stiffly erect and lend themselves particularly well to Japanese type designs.

There are some almost cabbage-like doubles. These fat and full forms used in buxom bouquets need plenty of space and should be placed low in the arrangement where their apparent weight will focus attention so that balance is achieved. All arrangements must be well balanced or give a sense of stability, never appear lopsided or top heavy.

HOW TO CUT

Peonies may be cut at any time after the color shows in the

182

bud until they reach a fully open stage. Double varieties will
last best however if cut when less than half open. Cut the buds
of the double flowered types just as they are showing the first
signs of color, as the sepals or green covering on the buds have
separated enough to show the true coloring of the flower. This
rule applies to the early varieties such as Edulis Superba, Mons.
Jules Elie and to some late ones which have the so called
"bomb" center. Practically all of these will open from a tight
bud showing only a faint line of color. The late full petalled
varieties usually have to be soft to the touch (like a marsh-
mallow). Press down on them gently and if they feel soft to
pressure they can be cut but if the center is still hard it should
be left until it softens.

Cut tree peonies, single and Japanese types, when the blooms
are just half open. If cut in tight bud they may fail to open in
water. However if you need a tight bud for effect in an arrangement cut it the way you want it. Singles and Japanese often
lock guard petals so tightly they will not open. Give them a
little gentle help if they do.

When cutting peonies leave uncut at least one-third of the
blossoms on the plant. Cut the stems no longer than needed
for the arrangement leaving at least two sets of leaves on each
stalk. If you must cut to the ground for a long stem then leave
one-half the flowers uncut on the plant. In other words if you
cut long stems cut correspondingly fewer blooms.

Remove the dead flowers as they fade to keep the garden
neat and tidy in appearance. Do not cut away an excessive
amount of foliage after flowering is over, some foliage is needed
for good root growth and to aid in storing up the strength for
next year's flower buds or blooms.

CONDITIONING

Observe the following procedure and if picked in the bud
stage peonies will last 7 to 9 days. If newly cut conditioned

blooms show signs of wilting, recut stem ends, place in water hot to the elbow (100°F) and recondition.

1. Cut peonies in the early evening or morning.

2. Take bucket or pail of water, at outdoor temperature, to garden.

3. Cut stems with a sharp knife.

4. Split ends a couple of inches and remove any unnecessary lower leaves.

5. Put directly into the water.

6. Bring indoors and set in a cool place away from drafts. Let condition overnight or at least several hours before arranging.

7. Some people add 3 tablespoons of sugar to each quart of water for better keeping. Chemicals such as Bloomlife and Floralife are quite effective in prolonging the life of cut flowers, but if too much is used the flowers turn brown. So be careful not to exceed directions, maybe a little experimentation is in order.

8. To hold the fragrance, while conditioning, cover the whole bouquet of blossoms loosely with a thin wax paper or cellophane, especially if exhibiting peonies in a class where fragrance counts.

STORAGE

Cut buds of double flowered varieties just as they are showing the first tints of color, pack in a box and put in cold storage. Stored in a cool room or cellar at 45°-50° F. the blooms may be held for several weeks. Bring out in advance of mid-June commencement or wedding and plunge into vessels of water. Keep in as cool a spot as you have, maybe the cellar, for two or three hours before bringing into a warm room, so change in temperature will be gradual. The flowers will explode into full bloom. These stored peonies will not keep very long once placed in warm rooms but long enough for the graduation or wedding for which they were held.

Peonies stored "dry" need at least a day to fill with water. Often when taken from storage "wet" and brought into a room to warm up and open they will wilt slightly but they will recover in an hour or so. If they do not, try hot water. If they do not respond to this they may as well be thrown out. Singles and Japanese are especially liable to flop when first brought out from storage. If they do not revive they were cut too late. As a matter of fact the proper time to cut a peony depends on the variety and is learned best by experience. Also if peonies are cut in the late afternoon, when they have begun to close for the night, as many do, it is almost impossible to tell when they are past the age for cutting. Hence morning is the best time to cut peonies, especially singles and doubles.

Commercially peonies are held for a month or two in cold storage. Thousands of blooms are cut each season and shipped from growers' fields to wholesale centers for sale, through local florists, for Decoration Day and later use. Growing chrysanthemums the year round, which are easier and cheaper to transport, and other changes in the flower industry have reduced the number of wholesale cut peonies in commerce today. However it was a thrill for us to walk into the Ritz in Boston June 1 of this year and see a gorgeous bouquet of Festiva Maxima in the lobby and a few days later to view a superb arrangement of Mons. Jules Elie as we entered a Statler dining room.

DRY FOR WINTER BOUQUETS

Buds and Blossoms

Dry peonies in both bud and blossom for they retain good color and form. The large, round double type flower is excellent in Victorian style winter bouquets and the lovely single Japanese and semi-double are equally effective used in modern designs.

The white, pink and red varieties keep their petal colors well enough to supply color in winter arrangements as do their bright yellow centers. The easiest way to dry buds and double flowers is to hang them upside down, one flower on a string by itself, fastened to a line, hook or coat hanger. In a dark, dry place they should be ready in two or three weeks.

Dried Arrangements Featuring Peonies

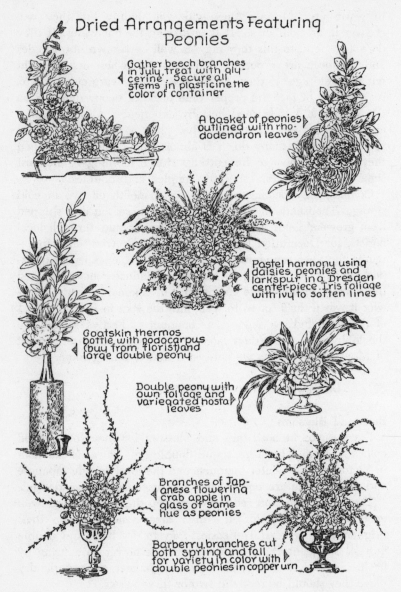

Gather beech branches in July, treat with glycerine. Secure all stems in plasticine the color of container

A basket of peonies outlined with rhododendron leaves

Pastel harmony using daisies, peonies and larkspur in a Dresden center-piece. Iris foliage with ivy to soften lines

Goatskin thermos bottle with podocarpus (buy from florist) and large double peony

Double peony with own foliage and variegated hosta leaves

Branches of Japanese flowering crab apple in glass of same hue as peonies

Barberry branches cut both spring and fall for variety in color with double peonies in copper urn

Drying Techniques
Dry Twice As Much As You Need To Allow For Breakage

◁ Hanging:

Cut buds with foliage at stage you want them. Hang upside down, one to a string, in a dark, dry place. Should dry in 2-3 wks. Cut green foliage in spring, autumn colors in fall. Foliage dried by hanging has form and color

Borax and sand or cornmeal: ▷

Use box deep enough to adequately hold large flower. Place 2" drying mixture in bottom of box

Face Down: Place single or Japanese type with petals smooth, in proper position. Gently cover with mixture.

Face Up: Make hole in center of box just large enough to push through stem of double type peony. Cover flower gently with mixture. Support box at each corner at least height of stem.   Cut flowers at prime, when best color. Do not cover 6-8 days while drying in dark, dry place.

Foliage:

In container with 2" of water. Place stem end of foliage in container with water which will evaporate in week. Let foliage remain until dry. Has depth and form.

Pressing foliage keeps color but has no depth. Lay flat on absorbent paper, adjust to curves or shape desired. Do not overlap. Cover with absorbent paper, weight down, turn weekly until dry

Store all dried materials in covered boxes properly labeled ▷

Better results are obtained with the single, Japanese and semi-doubles if dried in borax with sand or cornmeal, either face-down or face-up. Use fine builder's or thoroughly washed and sifted beach sand, well dried (using 1 cup borax to 2 cups sand), or mix one part of powdered borax with six parts of white corn-meal. Two tablespoons of uniodized salt to each quart of mixture will help maintain the brightness of the color.

Cut buds at stage you want them and flowers when they are at their prime, at their best in color. Never cut for drying after a rain, heavy dew or any extreme dampness. Shake off or get rid of any worms or bugs that might be present as they could destroy the dried flowers.

Use a box deep enough to adequately hold the large flowers placing 2 or more inches of the drying mixture on the bottom of the box.

(FACE-DOWN) Place single or Japanese type flowers, face down on the mixture, making sure the petals are smooth and in proper position. Gently work mixture around, up and over the flowers until they are lightly but completely covered.

(FACE-UP) Punch holes in boxes through which you push the stem with the double flower types remaining face-up, resting on the bottom of the box. Make the holes just large enough for the stems to push through but not large enough so the drying mixture will spill through. Support the boxes in some manner at each corner, high enough so the stems do not rest on the shelf or drying table. The flowers should dry in a week. Do not cover while drying and dry in a dark, dry place. The mixture may be used over and over again. When flowers seem thoroughly dry, gently remove from mixture. Never let them stay too long. With a soft brush carefully wipe away any borax and sand or meal.

If time is important flowers may be dried by laying them on newspapers and placing them in an oven turned to its *lowest* heat. They must be closely watched to retain their color. If left too long they will turn brown. It is the quickest procedure for drying but flowers become brittle and baking is only recommended if speed is essential.

Foliage

Peony foliage may be pressed for making flower pictures or hung upside down to dry. Dried upside down it maintains its form and depth. Decorative in form, dried peony foliage also retains its color well in the various shades of green. Since it turns to such wonderful colors as the season progresses toward autumn it is possible to dry many shades of foliage from May till frost for winter bouquets. Peony foliage may also be dried placed upright standing in a jar. Wash the foliage to remove any dust or dirt. Split the stem about 2″. Then place stem ends in a jar with 2″ of water which will evaporate in about a week. Do not add any more water. Let stand until thoroughly dry.

Peony Seed Pod
Useful in Dried Arrangements

As the seed pod develops the sections split open naturally to emit the seeds looking like the petals of a flower

As the seed cases dry they turn brown

Seed Pods

The sections of the peony seed pod as they develop and split open naturally to emit the seeds, look like the petals of a small flower. As the seed cases dry they turn brown. These exciting flower-like shapes add an interesting variety in form to small winter designs. Although you will remove faded flowers and will not allow all flowers to go to seed never hesitate to let a few develop on well established plants if you are interested in the seed cases for fresh or dried bouquets. The pale greenish-yellow seed pods of the peony are especially beautiful when newly formed.

Dried Petals

Remove petals from flower and spread on absorbent paper in a warm room, never in direct sunlight. Since the petals shrink as they dry start with about twice the volume you want. Carefully shuffle the petals daily. They should be dry in 4 to 5 days. Slightly sprinkle with salt and place the dried petals in a covered container until you wish to use them. Pink dried peony petals add a note of color and interest to potpourri and sachet.

Wax White Peonies

For those who are interested in old fashioned waxed Victorian bouquets, dry peonies at room temperature. With atomizer use a solution of 2 parts floral wax diluted with 1 part water mixed well. Use an egg beater. Let flowers drip to remove any surplus wax. Or peony may be gently but quickly dipped in solution if you have no atomizer.

Storage

Store all dried material in covered boxes, properly labeled, in a dry, cool place until needed. Label properly and keep delicate textures separated from heavy material. Have seed pods together in one box and foliage in another for easy finding.

TIPS FOR THE NOVICE

1. Plan simple, uncomplicated designs with a minimum of material.

2. Cut one, two or three well chosen branches for height and to outline the silhouette.

3. Use some tight green buds, some showing color, flowers half open and others well open for interest and contrast in form and size.

4. Combine various peony types as singles with doubles.

5. Cut varying stem lengths.

6. Avoid facing all flowers front or in one direction. Face some profile, others almost completely reversed as they grow in the garden.

7. Place the heavier looking flowers, those large or dark in

color low, with the lighter appearing buds and blossoms higher in the composition.

8. A congenial leaf or vine will soften harsh lines and at the base make a pleasing unity with the container. Vines are useful for their graceful curves.

9. For some arrangements to obtain proper visual balance a suitable base is necessary. Place the completed design on a small stand, pedestal or one, two or three blocks of wood, whichever number seems necessary. Paint the base a blending color or the color of the container. This often gives a nondescript vase or bowl character and distinction.

10. Use simple, well-proportioned containers in good neutral tones. Have at least two to start with; one a low type for the dining table or mantle and the other a taller urn-shaped, oval or upright rectangular for tall designs in the entrance hall or living room.

11. As a guide to good proportion when using a low container place the tallest stem 1½ to 2 times the length or diameter of the bowl, place the tallest stem in the tall container to extend 1½ to 2 times the height of the vase above its rim.

12. Work with these two pet containers, a good flower holder and a few blossoms until you are satisfied with the results you obtain. Then start to expand.

MECHANICS REQUIRED

To Gather Flowers

Pail, something to hold water and easy to carry.
Sharp knife.
Cigarette lighter or candle to sear stems.

To Make An Arrangement

Container.
Plant material.
Needle or pinpoint holders (assorted sizes and shapes).
Posey clay.
Sharp knife.
Wire cutter.
Florists' sticks, wire and tape.

Proper mechanical aids are essential to hold peony arrangements firmly in place and keep their stem ends always in water. The needle or pinpoint holder comes in assorted sizes and shapes and is excellent because stems may be arranged at an angle in this type holder. They are particularly good in shallow, open containers. The best ones have a heavy substantial base with firm brass points set close together to hold stems firmly.

For tall vases or any arrangement in an opaque container hen wire is especially helpful. The wire comes in a roll and may be purchased at a hardware store in any quantity you wish. Hen wire has larger holes and is softer and more easily crushed than chicken wire. Cut the wire with a wire cutter to the size you need. Crush it and fit it into the container. For a heavy flower like the peony use a needle holder with the hen wire crushed over it for a secondary holder.

Use "posey" clay which is non-hardening and insoluble in water to anchor the holder solidly in place. Apply the clay to the bottom of the holder, press it firmly into position securing it to the bottom of the container. The holder should never be visible and can easily be covered with plant material used in the composition.

In constructing large arrangements, using heavy flowers like the peony, especially for a church or public building, wire a florists' stick to the stem of the first placement and see that it is firmly anchored in the holder. This will help hold the entire design more securely.

Many people today like the plastic sponges in place of pinpoint holders, they are so easily used. You can arrange flowers at any angle and carry the arrangement about, to a friend in the hospital or wherever you wish without danger of it getting too much out of position.

See page 12

VI.

VIII. A fine
semi-double,
Phyllis
Kelway

IX. Old-fash-
ioned Paeonia
officinalis, a
double, is still a
garden favorite

X.
Described
on page 12

21

Varieties Best for Cutting

Early in the season, in May, when peonies are not plentiful or only choice extra-early hybrids and singles or tree peonies are blooming, you may hesitate to cut many because you want them for garden display. Just one attractive flower with a collar of peony foliage is most decorative, since the various parts of the flower are so interestingly and beautifully formed and colored. There is much detail and variation to be observed and enjoyed in a single bloom, a choice centerpiece for a dining room table or a table near a favorite living room chair.

Later, when the June-flowering or so-called Chinese herbaceous peonies (P. lactiflora) come along, the last to bloom, you can cut all you want. They bloom profusely and are so plentiful you don't mind cutting them and taking them from the garden. Picked when in almost the tight bud stage they will open to perfection in water and last a surprisingly long time.

It would be sensible for you to select varieties whose colors, form and foliage suit the interior of your home. Double flowers open easily from tight buds, and commercial peony growers usually confine themselves to doubles. Singles, Japanese and semi-doubles are all attractive in home flower arrangements, but be sure not to cut them too soon because they do not open after cutting if in bud. See page 183.

HERBACEOUS REGULAR

Single

The singles resemble huge anemones in form and open three or five days earlier than the Japanese types. If singles are cut at the stage when they will shed the pollen they will show it and the flowers may be badly discolored. Graceful plants, they hold their blooms up well without support, offering very handsome subjects for flower arrangements. They are good peonies for the south. Following are some outstanding varieties. Also see variety list page 74.

ARCTURUS (Auten)—Extremely rich, clear red single. Tall and early.

HELEN (Thurlow)—Double row of broad, cupped petals of deep shell pink, surround a mass of gold stamens. Plant medium size and spreading. Stems very tall, strong and erect with broad foliage. Early.

IMPERIAL RED (Sass)—Large, single, early red. Won third place in the popularity contest for red singles. Really a dark pink but its effect is light red.

KRINKLED WHITE (Brand)—Small bud that expands into a large flower with great, broad pure white petals, like crinkled crepe paper. One of the best single whites. Mid-season. When first opening petals are blush, which fade white in sunlight but will not fade when cut early and kept in the dark.

LE JOUR (Shaylor)—Long overlapping pure white guard petals with a center of golden yellow, stamens pink tinged. Remarkable substance. Plant large, compact. Early mid-season.

PICO—Early white. Won second place in the popularity contest for white singles. Foliage extra large.

PRESIDENT LINCOLN (Brand)—Single, early red. Won second place in the popularity contest for red singles.

SEASHELL (Sass)—A lively delicate pink, slightly fluted, with a full center of golden stamens. Strong stems hold the large flowers erect. Outstanding variety. Distinctive. Mid-season.

Japanese

The Japanese type peony is graceful in growth and quite different in type of flower with wide flaring petals of exquisite coloring and texture. The centers are usually a more or less compact mass of tiny petalodes if anemone (Japanese) or staminodes if regular Japanese, usually a color contrasting with the main petal color. Very charming color effects are found among them. They are ideal for making striking flower arrangements. For cutting see variety list page 74 as well as the fine varieties listed below.

AMA-NO-SODE (Japan)—Bright rose-pink, cup-shaped guard petals surrounding a center of long, yellow staminodes, edged gold and faced with pink. Large flower, medium height, strong stems, good foliage. Mid-season.

HARI-AI-NIN (Babcock)—Dark maroon-red petals with center of broad stamens color of petals heavily tipped yellow. Late mid-season.

ISANI GIDUI (Japan)—Rounded guard petals of pure white, which surround a compact cushion of golden staminodes. Like a large white poppy. Mid-season. Lovely white and gold effect. Moderately tall.

LOTUS QUEEN—Second only to Isani Gidui in popularity vote for best white or blush, Japanese type. Mid-season bloomer. Stems strong.

NIPPON BEAUTY (Auten)—Rich deep garnet-red, center staminodes are garnet edged with golden yellow. Strong grower, tall and free bloomer. Late. Lovely for cutting.

NIPPON BRILLIANT—One of finest in its class, crimson and gold, tall, late.

TAMATE BOKU (Japan)—Also incorrectly known as Tomtabako. One of the largest of the Japanese type. Bright old rose China pink, center yellow and tipped pink, gold edges. Mid-season.

WESTERNER (Bigger)—Guard petals very large, beautiful shade of light rose-pink. Center filled with yellow staminodes extremely firm and erect. Cup-shaped form is gracefully poised and held rigidly erect. Mid-season.

Anemone

The anemone peony is listed in catalogs either under Japanese or doubles. It has several rows of guard petals, which are usually white or pink, with a center of small narrow petals (petalodes) of yellow or the same color as the guards, sometimes of a different shade. Many of these erroneously, since the yellow always fades to white, are called "yellow" peonies. Interesting and useful for cutting. In addition to the varieties listed below also see pages 74-75.

ADA PRISCILLA (Guille)—White petals with yellow center fading to white. Mid-season. (Listed under Doubles)

LAURA DESSERT (Dessert) (Listed under Doubles)—White guard petals with yellow center, fading to white. Early.

NIPPON GOLD (Auten) (Listed Japanese)—Dark pink guard petals with yellow center. Mid-season.

PRAIRIE AFIRE (Brand)—The guard petals are broad and a soft creamy-rose with good substance. These surround a great ball of brilliant fiery red staminodes. Listed as Japanese.

PRIMEVERE (Lemoine)—A flattish flower, medium size, with creamy white cupped guards rarely splashed with red, with center of deep sulphur-yellow becoming white with age. One of the best and yellowest of the "yellow" herbaceous peonies. Mid-season. Listed as a double. Tall, floriferous, stems lax, good dark green, rather coarse foliage.

Semi-Double

The center of the semi-double is made up of a greater or lesser number of broad petals but it never becomes fully double. Intermixed with the broad petals are many pollen bearing stamens, sometimes grouped together in the center and in other varieties forming rings among the petals, always a prominent and interesting feature of the flower. The group includes some of the most artistic of the peony blooms and are popular with arrangers. See varieties listed page 75 as well as the list that follows.

LADY ALEXANDRA DUFF (Kelway)—Nicely formed flowers with

broad petals of soft pale pink. Tall, robust and delightfully scented. Mid-season.

MARGARET LOUGH (Gumm)—A very fine white coming into bloom at mid-season. The flower shows tints of pink and its golden stamens add interest.

MILDRED MAY, one of the finest whites of all for arrangement where its triangular sprays of bloom can be used.

MINNIE SHAYLOR (Shaylor)—Several rows of fluffy crepe-like petals of clear light pink fading to white. Center of golden yellow. Stamens very attractive.

RED GODDESS—Won first place in the popularity vote for the best red, semi-double. Mid-season bloomer. Medium dark velvety red, about the purest red in the lactifloras.

SILVIA SAUNDERS (Saunders)—Cup-shaped, bright clear rose-pink, fading lighter toward center, which is filled with yellow stamens among which the very bright pink stigmas make a conspicuous pattern. Dwarf, good grower, abundant bloomer, not large. Extra early. The distinctive grey green carpels add greatly to its charm.

WHITE ROSE—Blooms late mid-season to late. Its broad white petals faintly veiled pink with the intermingled stamens make a flower of indescribable charm and lovliness.

Double

Doubles are still the most popular and widely grown and are long lasting and decorative used as cut flowers when properly conditioned. The following varieties are recommended as very fine cut flowers. Also see varieties listed pages 75-77.

Early Blooming
Edulis Superba—Light pink
Festiva Maxima—White
Kansas—Red
Kelway's Glorious (white),
   one of the longest lasting
   of all cut flowers.

Mons. Jules Elie—Pink
Mrs. F. D. Roosevelt—Pink,

Early to mid-season
Pfeiffer's Red Triumph—Red
Richard Carvel—Red, fragrant

Mid-Season

Annisquam—Pink

Karl Rosenfield—Red

La Lorraine—Blush

Le Cygne—Cream-white

Longfellow—Red

Loren Franklin—Dark pink, fragrant

Lottie Dawson Rea—Light pink

Mary Brand—Red

Minuet—Light pink

Myrtle Gentry—Light Pink

Sarah Bernhardt—Pink, fragrant

Souv. de Louis Bigot—Dark pink, mildly fragrant

Late

Avalanche—Creamy-white

Baroness Schroeder—Blush

Felix Crousse—Red

Nick Shaylor—Light pink

HERBACEOUS HYBRIDS

The herbaceous hybrid group includes some of the most striking and beautiful of all the peonies. Brilliant and beautiful in color they are stunning for indoor arrangements. Any of them are good cut. Following is a list of favorites. Also see pages 93-102.

ALEXANDER WOOLLCOTT (Saunders)—Large, flat cups, shining crimson. Brilliant color doesn't fade. Extra early.

CAMPAGNA (Saunders)—Pure white single with gold and green center (no pink tones at all). Blooms just ahead of the lobatas, end of May and first of June.

CHALICE (Saunders)—Large pure shimmering single white, 8"-9", with long silky stamens. On heavy stems 3' tall. Immense dark glossy leaves. Mid-May.

CHOCOLATE SOLDIER (Auten)—Maroon almost black semi- to full double.

CLAIRE DE LUNE (Dr. White)—Pale yellow single variety of great charm and distinction. Greatest success in achieving yellow single, herbaceous peony.

LAURA MAGNUSON (Saunders)—Large cup-shaped clear bright rose, semi-double. Late for this strain. Mid-June.

NATHALIE (Saunders)—Magnificent flat bloom, semi-double or more. Intense clear rose, smooth-edged petals.

ORIENTAL GOLD (Japan)—First true double yellow, origin not known. New, scarce and expensive. Lemon-yellow, fading lighter. Stems medium height, strong bright green with darker foliage.

Blooms with the late Japanese and early lactifloras. Flowers of memdium size. Wonderful for arrangements.

RED CHARM (Glasscock)—Rich ruby-red, bomb shaped double with tall, strong stems. Fine plant. Still scarce.

TREE PEONIES

Cut any of the tree peony blossoms you feel you can spare from the garden for indoor use. They are all highly decorative. A few favorites follow but also see pages 155-163 for others.

ALICE HARDING—Clear yellow, ball-shaped double. Fragrant.

ARGOSY—Clear sulphur-yellow, single, 6"-7" across. Plum colored flares.

CHARIOTEER—Satiny, deep maroon, single with great dark heart, flat, open bloom.

GESSEKAI (Kingdom of the Moon)—A glistening pure white, immense double, with crinkled petals. Vigorous grower. Spectacularly beautiful. Kamikaze is a seedling of Gessekai.

HANA-DAIGIN (Minister of Flowers)—Lustrous, dark purple double.

HANA-KISOI (Floral Rivalry)—Enormous, deep cherry-pink double. A beauty.

HODAI (Reign of Chinese Emperor)—Giant, rose-red double.

KAMADA-FUJI—Large, wisteria colored, double.

RIMPO—Large, deep brilliant purple, semi-double to double, with yellow center.

SHUGYO-KUDEN (Palace of Gems)—Brilliant scarlet-red, semi-double.

SOUVENIR DE MAXIME CORNU—Yellow, full double, with reddish markings (yellow-orange effect). Grows 3' to 4' high. Fragrant.

SUISHO-HAKU (Clear Crystal White)—Semi-double, snow white, incurved petals.

TAIYO (Great Emperor)—Bright-red, enormous, satiny.

TAMA-FUYO (Jeweled Lotus)—Large, exquisite, cup-shaped blush-pink, double.

UBA-TAMA (Brilliant Black King)—Beautiful huge, satiny black-red double, incurved petals. Outstanding.

22

Flower Shows

DATES

Setting dates for peony shows in any locality which will suit all peony growers is impossible for some peonies are early, others late and some gardens are early and others come later. The local show committee should endeavor to set a show date that best suits the majority of peony growers, a time when the most peonies can be brought from the garden to the show without need of holding the blooms in storage.

The peony shows start in the south in early May and gradually move northward, the date varying slightly each year depending upon the type of season. Following are some show dates for this season: Oklahoma May 10-11, Maryland and Nebraska late May, Ohio early June, New York and Massachusetts mid-June, Minneapolis, Minnesota a week later, Ottawa, Canada June 23, North Dakota late June and Duluth, Minnesota and Superior, Wisconsin, mid-July.

MANAGEMENT

No matter how small or large a show a good organization with an efficient director, chairman or manager and capable working committees, each with well defined duties, is essential.

The chairman acts as a coordinator and moderator maintaining a smoothly operating group, with a secretary or assistant keeping accurate records and files of all transactions; the final objective—staging an artistic, educational and successful show. A person who has had organizational experience working with others, who can delegate authority with discretion and then follow through will get the best results. Ability to select the best possible chairman for each committee is important.

The chairman in selecting co-workers must choose some person who knows peonies. He also needs a person with extremely good taste, preferably with a background in art. Sometimes these two qualifications can be found in one person. If there is available someone with show experience, even though in some other field, that will be helpful. Know-how and experience are valuable attributes. The secretary or assistant handling the office work and records must be accurate and dependable.

The number and size of the committees will vary depending upon the type and size show. The chairman should be able to have a voice in choosing his committee associates. Any show chairman will need someone to act as a good dependable secretary to take charge of the records and office work. This may be done from the chairman's home until show time. The secretary will send out all notices of meetings; keep a record of the minutes of each meeting; receive and record all entries in the entry notebook; type and file exhibitors' entry cards alphabetically and distribute them to the exhibitors the day of the show; prepare loose leaf notebook sheets for the judges; type any comments they may want posted with the awards; purchase necessary supplies such as ribbons, stickers, committee badges, etc.; prepare list of awards for the local newspapers; print or have printed labels or signs needed for the show and issue the permits for the exhibitor to remove belongings at the end of the show if this is necessary. In large shows this is important to protect the property of exhibitors. The permit slip must be shown at the door on leaving. At the close of the show the secretary should have a complete record of all transactions.

The show committee is made up of the general chairman, secretary and committee chairmen who are responsible for writing the schedule, staging, judging and hospitality, publicity, tickets and special projects. In a small show combine several of the jobs under one chairman. The show committee should meet from time to time as a group to make decisions, discuss problems, and to be informed on the progress of the show. A good flower show represents a lot of work and thought but it is a known fact that a more lively interest in good gardening, proper landscaping, local parks, conservation of natural resources, removal of unsightly billboards and the general beauty of the community is stimulated in localities where good shows are held annually.

After deciding upon the dates of the show, where it is to be held, and what it is to include the schedule chairman is ready to go to work.

It makes no difference whether the show is large or small. It is the quality of the exhibits and schedule that is important. The schedule should include enough variety in the classes to insure an interesting and worthwhile show.

SCHEDULE

In writing an intelligent schedule for a show, a knowledge of local material and talent is necessary. The schedule should be written to make the best possible use of what is available. You would include a 400 sq. ft. display only if you knew of a large grower with the necessary facilities and talent to set up such an exhibit. You would include an extensive arrangement section only if there were competent people to carry out such a schedule.

Include classes for both amateurs and commercial interests, also open classes for all who grow peonies, amateurs and professionals alike. Plainly indicate whether classes are open or for the amateur or professional so there will be no misunderstanding in making entries. In some cases a distinction between the novice and advanced amateur is made. If so, make sure the two classifications are clearly defined in the show rules.

At peony time it is possible to put on a very interesting and spectacular Flower Show, which in addition to peonies may also include other classes for material which blooms at the same time. Roses, bearded iris, perennials and annuals, rhododendrons and azaleas, other flowering shrubs, flowering house plants, strawberries, cherries and vegetables may all have classes included for entries.

The schedule must clearly state the name of the show, where it is to be held, the dates and hours it will be open, the sponsor of the show and person, with address and telephone number, to whom entry blanks should be mailed or to whom exhibitors may write or call for further information.

RULES

The rules for the show should be clear, concise, simply written and easily understood, to avoid misunderstandings. State the time exhibitors must be finished with their staging in readiness for the judging, removal time, whether the class is for amateurs or professionals. The show management can not be responsible for the property of the exhibitors, whether or not multiple entries are allowed in a class from the same garden by various members of the same family and whether an exhibitor is allowed more than one entry in a class. In other words anticipate any difficulties you may encounter ahead of time and avoid them by a fair, concise set of rules.

Use correct horticultural terms and define such terms as: amateur, novice, professional etc.

CLASSES

Horticultural Classes
The following flower show classes are offered merely as a guide in writing peony show schedules. Any schedule must be adapted to meet local requirements.

Displays

Include displays only if there is talent and material available for such classes. From the scale of points for judging (see page 210) you can see a display is judged both for quality of material and artistic effect with emphasis on the artistic effect. In larger shows classes are sometimes written to cover 100, 200 or 400 sq. ft. using any or all varieties as noted in the class, the number of varieties may or may not be restricted. A fine display is always an asset to any show but a poor one is very disappointing and poor publicity.

Collections

Always specify the number of blooms, square footage if limited, and in some cases length of stem. Include classes for the type peony flowers your exhibitors grow. If possible for a more attractive show provide uniform containers for the cut peonies entered in the collection classes.

Collections may include as few or as many classes as the material available for the show demands.

Small Collections of 3, 5, 6 or 10 may include classes which call for:

1. Specify number, all different varieties, any type, one bloom of each.

2. Specify number, all different varieties, any type, one color, indicate white, light pink, deep pink or red, one bloom of each.

3. Specify number, all different varieties, only one type, indicate double, single, Japanese or hybrids, one bloom of each. (Always show singles for display before the pollen sheds.)

4. Specify number, all different varieties, one type, indicate which; one color, indicate which, one bloom of each.

5. Specify number of blooms, one variety, one type, one color.

Larger Collections of 20, 25 or 50 usually call for a specified number of different varieties, any type, one bloom of each. In some cases in the larger collections the class may be modified to read: 25 different varieties, one bloom of each, not more than 10 blooms may be single and/or Japanese types or: collection of 25 different varieties, one bloom of each, not to exceed 50 sq. ft.

Specimen

Always specify the number of blooms and length of stem in
some cases. If possible supply uniform vases for the specimen
classes. For exhibition purposes cut stems not shorter than 15".

1. Best in a type (specify), any color.
2. Best in a type (specify), one color (specify).
3. Best herbaceous hybrid, any type, any color.
4. Best species.
5. Best miniature, any variety, any color.
6. Best specimen in show.

In advising how best to cut and hold early blooms for specimen competition in shows George Peyton writes "Those who
have extra early locations and those growing the extra early
hybrids will have to resort to refrigeration to hold them till show
time. In order to do this it becomes necessary to cut the peonies
at the proper time and place them in storage. A temperature
of 36 degrees is best but a temperature as high as 50 degrees
is satisfactory if the blooms are to be stored for a week or less.
Blooms can be kept for over a month when stored at 36 degrees.
A very important point to keep in mind is that blooms should
be chilled for several hours before being brought to the show
room. This chilling prevents wilting. Peonies are best stored
with the stems in about eight inches of water.

"Most new exhibitors are also troubled as to what stage of
development buds should be cut. The following types may be
cut when the bud is showing color or when the first petals
begin to unfold: singles, Japanese, semi-doubles. The full double
type such as Hansina Brand should not be cut until almost fully
open. It is important to place in cold storage as soon as possible
after cutting.

"It is a good practice to place the buds in paper bags before
placing in storage. The procedure is this: cut a hole in the bottom
of the bag and slip the stem thru the hole, the open end of the
bag is then closed by twisting. The bag gives protection to the
petals against bruising. The one pound bag is about the right
size for singles, Japanese and semi-doubles while the two pound
bag is more satisfactory for the larger and fuller blooms.

"Cut stems about sixteen inches long and remove all foliage except the top leaf. However the stems should be cut so that at least two leaves are left on the plant. When the buds are brought to the show room, cut off the ends of the stems about a half inch, place in water and carefully remove the paper bag. It's a thrilling sight to see the buds unfold into beautiful blooms and it is even more thrilling to see a ribbon pinned on your exhibit."

New Hybrids and Seedlings

Reserve space for recently introduced and new varieties. These should be judged for Awards of Merit or medals by qualified judges.

Tree Peonies

If you have tree peony exhibitors include specimen and collection classes to fit what they grow as: three blooms, one variety, any type or include an invitational class not for competition encouraging a collection of tree peony flowers from both amateurs and professionals alike.

Arrangement (without definite use being named)

Specify using peonies and peony foliage only or if other material is permissible state what. Also indicate container if you wish and size: not to exceed 6, 12 or 25 blooms, whatever you determine.

Gardens

If there is a nursery nearby or an estate that features peonies contact them and if interested in setting up a garden write a class into the schedule or classes specifying the type gardens they are qualified and equipped to stage. Explore other sources for garden possibilities. They add much to the interest of a show.

Arrangement Classes

Here again plan classes suitable for the talent from which you must draw. It is far better to have a few good, simple arrangements which display the true natural beauty of the peony than to attempt a schedule too difficult for the exhibitors to do well.

For arrangements it is very important to list the conditions under which they will be shown: height at which arrangement will be displayed, background color, size of space and any other pertinent information. It is also very important the exhibitor read the schedule and classes with utmost care. Many a good arrangement has been disqualified because it did not comply with the class requirements. A classification or passing committee or individual checking on entries in this section may catch an error before it is too late.

Some garden clubs include the flower show schedule in their year book. If not, it should be printed, typed or mimeographed and when mailed out to every possible exhibitor it should also contain an entry blank which the exhibitor will return, properly filled out, by a set date, in advance of the show.

Invitational classes can add to the interest and beauty of the show. A simple, well thought out theme will give unity and charm to an arrangement section as a pioneer theme in connection with a centennial celebration or "Peonies Go Modern" or "Fancy Free", themes which give the exhibitor a wide range of freedom in which to work.

Peony classes may be written into the schedule in many ways using peonies with own foliage only, peonies with other foliage allowed or in mixed bouquets. Type peony flower or color to be used may be designated. The following suggest only a few of some of the many possibilities.

"*At Home*" or "*June Glory*". Use some peonies in each arrangement (otherwise free hand or list limitations). State dimensions of niches, shadow boxes or space, height from floor, background color.

1. In a man's den.
2. In a modern room with an oriental influence.
3. In a ranch type house.
4. In an Early American room.
5. In a Victorian room.

"*Around the Clock*"—For table arrangement classes featuring peonies. State whether informal, semi-formal or formal. Indicate number of place settings, size table, in center of room or against wall. List properties show committee will supply, etc.

1. June breakfast on the porch.
2. Noon birthday party for the small fry.
3. Coffee or cocktail hour.
4. Supper at seven.
5. Stag party.
6. Buffet for twenty.

Mantel Arrangement for Home Wedding.

Church Arrangement.

Pedestal Arrangement for the Platform.

Any Design or Motif, peonies predominating.

Junior Classes and Awards

If there is sufficient interest to make it worthwhile a simplified schedule of classes and awards for juniors, in both the horticultural and arrangement classes, is a fine way to interest young folks in the peony and horticulture in general. This often may be done through contact with the schools, scouts or similar organizations.

Educational Exhibits

If possible, especially in a specialized show such as a Peony Show, some member or members should be on duty at all times during the show to answer questions intelligently, explain exhibits, varieties, etc.

Feature books, bulletins and garden magazines that tell about the peony. Explain what the American Peony Society is and what it has to offer and take subscriptions. A mimeographed sheet telling about the peony may be given free to all interested visitors. Encourage the state extension service, arboretums and similar groups to stage exhibits showing propagation, pest control, etc.

Get a landscape architect to demonstrate a simple right and wrong planting design using balled and burlapped plants.

ENTRIES

It is important to have all entries in writing to avoid any misunderstandings or arguments. Do not accept verbal entries. Buy a notebook. Cut up a show schedule pasting each class at the top of a separate page. As the entry blanks come in record them under the proper class in the notebook giving each an entry number and file the entry blanks alphabetically according to name for easy reference. From the notebook you will know just how many entries you have received and how much space to allot to each class. If a cancellation comes in cross it off the page.

The entry blank must include the name and address of the exhibitor with enough space to write or type in the number of entries. As these entry blanks come in the entry chairman can make out the entry cards in advance of the show. The day of the show the exhibitor picks up his entry cards and places them with his exhibits, never with the name showing. Uniform entry cards should be typed for each entry with the name and address of the exhibitor. This information is kept covered until after the judging either by use of an envelope or by placing the card face down. On the envelope or reverse side of the card type the class number and entry number which is all the judges should see.

STAGING

In a large show the chairman should find someone, perhaps a landscape architect, who can draw a floor plan of the hall showing any openings such as doors, windows and stairways or obstructions like posts or partitions, using correct measurements so the person responsible for staging the show can plan and lay it out accurately on paper. In keeping with the theme or type show the staging should be as creative and distinctive as the best talent available can produce. A planned unity or harmony throughout the show is pleasing and effective. With good quality material and the artistic know how the staging committee can do an outstanding job although it does involve a great amount of detail and work. The staging committee is responsible for all the properties necessary in setting up and dismantling the show, the lighting, supplying the necessary water for the exhibitors and for any trees or other decorations necessary in setting up the show. In large shows a decorator may be hired to cover posts with smilac and hang cloth backdrops where needed.

If the staging chairman goes to the hall and can accurately chalk off the exact space for the different classes and number them correctly, before the exhibitors arrive to start working, it will save much time and confusion.

A special clean up committee may be planned. If not the staging group is responsible for cleaning up the hall as well as storing any properties owned by the show committee. Store equipment in proper condition for use another time.

POINT SCALES FOR JUDGING

Suggested scales of points to help in judging flower show classes, especially useful if decisions are very close.

Display
  Scale of points courtesy National Council of State Garden Clubs, Inc.
Arrangement and effect 30
        Grouping of freshly cut peonies so arranged to create an artistic and pleasing overall picture or effect.
Quality, distinctive or excellence of character 30
Variety, diversity 20
Condition, freshness of bloom 10
Correct labeling 10
                                                                                                    ——
                                                                                                   100

Collections
  In collection classes arrangement is considered only in cases of equal scoring.
Courtesy American Peony Society
General Quality 40
    Pleasing appearance. Uniform high quality, harmonious color combinations.

Condition 30
    See "Condition and Freshness" under scale of points below
    for judging Specimen
Conformity to schedule 20
Labeling and display 10
    All labels legible from the aisle preferably written on
    both sides   100
Courtesy National Council of State Garden Clubs, Inc.
Cultural Perfection 45
Types and varieties 30
Staging 20
Correct and suitable labeling 5
                                              100

Specimen

A specimen bloom is judged on its cultural perfection, its merits as a good specimen of the variety it represents.

American Peony Society scale of points

Color 30
    Clear, harmonious, rich; true to variety, outstandingly
    beautiful
    Faults—fading, discoloration, blotches, streaks, defacing
    marks, unpleasant combination, lack of beauty.

Form and pattern 30
    Symmetrical, attractive, graceful, true to type and variety.
    Form of petals, attractive placement, depth of flower,
    form and development of center.
    Faults—lopsided, unattractive, abortive, poorly developed,
    petals notched and crimped, lack of uniformity in place-
    ment of petals, looseness, falling apart, any deviation from
    norm for type or variety. Coarseness.

Texture 10
    Silken sheen, velvety, suede-like, glistening, satiny petals.
    Faults—poor condition, poor sheen; lack of sparkle, irri-

descence, glow; coarse.

Stem and foliage 10

Stem adequate to support flower. One or two leaves.
Faults—No stem, weak, side buds, any damage to stem or
foliage. (Flowers taken from storage not to be penalized
for lack of or damage to foliage.)

Size 5

Normal for variety in the locality or slightly above. No
penalty for oversize except for miniatures and at the
expense of other qualities.
Faults—Undersize for variety and type. Big miniatures.

Distinctiveness 5

Novelty, rarity, difficult of culture, overall charm and
quality. Well staged. Fragrance may be counted an asset.
Faults—Old, commonplace variety and characteristics.
Poor staging.

Condition and freshness 10

Correct degree of maturity, healthy condition, cleanliness,
without insects, spray residue, foreign matter. No pollen
stains or fallen pollen. Turgid.
Faults—Water spotting, soil or spray residue, pollen stains,
over or under age, indications of poor culture, wilted.

                                                                        ———
                                                                        100

Distinguish between single and Japanese types by pollen test.
Japanese nearly or completely void of pollen.

New Hybrids and Seedlings

In judging new introductions the following characteristics
should be studied.

1. Color, is it pure, clear and rich?
2. Form, does it have a pleasing shape and structure?
3. Substance, is it firm in texture?
4. Condition, is it fresh, not fading or shattering?
5. Stem, is it stiff and adequate to hold up the flowers.
6. Distinctiveness, important in a new variety! Does it have

vigor, charm or some other admirable characteristic that makes
it stand out? Is it different from varieties already in the trade.

Only a peony authority with a wide knowledge of existing
varieties is qualified to judge new hybrids and seedlings.

Arrangement without specific purpose or use being named
Courtesy American Peony Society

Conformance to schedule	10
Color	40
Quality of bloom	20
Design	30
	100

Scale of points—Courtesy National Council of State
Garden Clubs Inc.

Design	30
relation of all parts to the whole, all 6 art principles considered	
Color, distinctive use of	20
Suitable relationship of materials	20
Distinction	10
through skillful craftsmanship in how materials are used	
Originality	10
not commonplace	
Condition of all materials	10
	100

Judging a Garden
Scale of points, courtesy Massachusetts Horticultural Society

1. Design and consistency to scale	30
2. Suitability and quality of plant material	25
3. Color harmony	10
4. Seasonability	10
5. Quality and suitability of accessories	10
6. Condition of plant material	10
fresh, fading or falling	
6. Correct and suitable labeling	05
	100

Arrangement Classes

Courtesy National Council of State Garden Clubs Inc.

Arrangement with a theme, title or purpose.

Design, relationship of all parts to the whole, all 6 art principles considered 25

Interpretation, suitability, conformity to schedule 20

Color, distinctive use of 15

Relationship, of suitable materials 15

Distinction, superiority in how materials were used 15

Condition, freshness, freedom from any injury to material 10

                                                                                            ———

                                                                                            100

Table setting for a special occasion or with a title.

Overall design 25

Relation of all materials 20

Color 15

Perfection of arrangement 15

Suitability or interpretation of schedule 15

Condition of all materials 10

                                                                                            ———

                                                                                            100

It goes without saying in a competitive flower show the judging must be honest and fair so great care must be used in selecting competent and qualified judges. If possible out of town judges who do not know the exhibitors are advisable.

JUDGING

It is customary to have three judges work together on the section of classes they are best qualified to judge. Each group of judges should have either an aid or a clerk or in a small show one of the three judges may act as the clerk. The office should supply the clerk with a judge's sheet from a looseleaf note book clamped to a cardboard or board firm enough to write on. This judge's sheet should have the scale of points to be used in judging the class with the class number and the number of entries registered in the class. The clerk should check to see the proper number of entries are in place. On the loose leaf judge's sheet the clerk records the decision of the judges and also records the prize winning entries with the judges comments. Record varieties shown in Specimen classes and in Collections if possible. After this has been completed the sheet must then be signed by the three judges, returned to the office, put in the looseleaf notebook according to the class number and kept there as the permanent official record of the judging of the show.

The office types a list of the awards and may either give the list directly to the local newspapers or to the publicity chairman, depending upon how you decided it should be done.

AWARDS

The question of awards, like report cards, always arises. In general, exhibitors seem to enjoy the competitive spirit and feel it adds to the interest of the show. The exhibitor who learns by his mistakes makes progress. Awards are usually stickers or ribbons with a blue for first, a red for second and yellow for third. An honorable mention may also be given. These stickers and ribbons may be obtained through a State Garden Club Federation Office or from a stationery or specialty shop. Medals may be given for outstanding exhibits; gold representing the highest recognition, silver second and bronze third.

National plant societies, Peony and Rose, have worked out "Point Scales" they use in judging. They also maintain a list of accredited judges who represent their Societies. If you are holding a show under their auspices you must of course use one of their judges to have the award recognized by them. The number of accredited judges in some cases is however limited so you may have to contact the best qualified person you can find to judge the class for you. Many good horticulturists are well qualified to judge in the Horticulture classes. Arrangements should be judged by persons trained and accredited as flower arrangement judges.

SPECIAL AWARDS may be given for special flower show achievements such as:

1. *"Sweepstake Award"* to the person winning the most blue

ribbons in the entire show or the largest number of points.

2. *"Award of Distinction"* to be earned by the highest scoring blue ribbon winner in the horticultural classes or in the arrangement classes or in the entire show.

3. *"Award of Merit"* to go to the exhibit judged the finest in the horticultural classes or in the arrangement classes or in the entire show.

4. *"Trophy"* for the best specimen bloom in the show.

5. A special prize may be offered for the best hybrid or seedling or both, if they are worthy.

A "Tricolor Award" to a top winner, "Cultural Certificates" for material unusually well grown or a "Vote of Thanks" certificate to some one who stepped in the last minute and helped out are all possibilities. Keep the standard for awards sufficiently high so they will have value and be treasured. Interested individuals, groups, organizations or business firms will sometimes offer a special trophy or cash in a specific class if contacted.

PART V — SUPPLEMENT

PRIVATE PLANTINGS

Some of our garden acquaintances who have private peony plantings have given permission for us to list them. They are willing to share the joy of their lovely peonies with others. We are most grateful to them and know you are, too, and know that you will show every consideration for the privilege while visiting their gardens.

California

MR. H. DEAN POISAL, 27 DUTTON AVENUE, SAN LEANDRO.

About 150 tree peonies, the European types do exceptionally well. Season March 1-May 6.

Canada

MR. WILLIAM BROWN, ELORA, ONTARIO.

Three acres, one of largest collections of peonies in Ontario, 250 to 300 varieties, mostly lactifloras, some hybrids and some tree peonies which die down to the ground some winters but come back. At best June 20-25.

MR. CLARE F. WOOD, 130 QUEEN'S QUAY EAST, TORONTO.

On Niagara Parkway, immediately north of Queenston. All types except tree, at best about first week in June. 3 to 4,000 plants and about 300 varieties.

Colorado

MR. F. O. MCKEE, 910 SPRUCE STREET, BOULDER.

240 herbaceous varieties. Best about June 10.

Connecticut

MR. JOHN MAYER, TACONIC AND HOWARD ROADS, GREENWICH.

Has a representative group of Japanese and European varieties of tree peonies, 60 varieties. Specializes in lutea hybrids with 75 varieties. Has 160 varieties of hybrid herbaceous peonies. Samples of all the Saunders hybrids.

The gardens are at their best from May 18th to June 2nd.

Delaware

WINTERTHUR, MR. HENRY F. DUPONT, WILMINGTON.

56 Dr. Saunders tree peony varieties, 31 Japanese tree peony varieties, 21 unnamed Saunders varieties. 94 regular and hybrid herbaceous varieties. At peak first 2 weeks in May. 4 suffruticosa peonies 75 years at Winterthur and 8 Lemoine hybrids, 2 La Lorraine brought from France in 1910 and 2 Maxime Cornu brought from France in 1925. Open to public 5 weeks in spring, around April 21 to May 23. 50 cents garden admission. Naturalized woodland planting on rolling hillside featuring spring blossoms, particularly azaleas.

Illinois

MR. HAROLD E. WOLFE, 24 SOUTH 86TH STREET, BELLEVILLE.

Half acre plot at home has some fine, huge plants. Now devoting energy and time to development of new things in both tree and herbaceous groups, new strains and propagation of chemically induced mutations.

Visitors welcome. Usually last week in April and first week in May.

MR. ELMER A. CLAAR, 617 THORNWOOD LANE, NORTHFIELD.

Most of the herbaceous hybrids introduced; 250 varieties of tree peonies; May 28th at best, however, some bloom as late as June 15th. Nearly all of the lactifloras listed—at best June 8th.

Visitors welcome by appointment.

Kansas

MR. AND MRS. FRANK E. MOOTS, 1127 WEST BROADWAY, NEWTON. WEST SIDE OF NEWTON. HIGHWAY NO. U.S. 50.

Hobby garden of about 400 varieties including 20 hybrids and a fair collection of singles and Japanese. Plants arranged for tractor cultivation. Hybrids bloom first half of May. Season closes Memorial Day or later with the big late doubles. Also 10 acres for cut flower trade.

Massachusetts

MR. STEDMAN BUTTRICK, LIBERTY ST. NEAR OLD NORTH BRIDGE, CONCORD.

200 to 300 named herbaceous varieties. Iris a feature. See National Geographic May 1959.

MRS. ELLERY SEDGWICK, LONG HILL, BEVERLY.

Good collection of tree peonies, named Japanese varieties and their seedlings, also species peonies, not many of the herbaceous hybrids. Lovely through May although at other seasons there are always interesting plants to be seen.

MR. HENRY P. MCKEAN, BEVERLY FARMS.

Some 42 tree peonies which include 27 named varieties. A growing collection. Also iris, roses and hemerocallis of interest.

MRS. GEORGE L. BATCHELDER, JR., MORAINE FARM, NORTH BEVERLY.

Collection of seedling Japanese tree peonies and many of the Saunders hybrid herbaceous peonies.

NOTE: The above three gardens are within ten or fifteen minutes of each other and would make a wonderful expedition for anyone interested in the peony the last week of May.

DR. CHARLES P. SHELDON, 67 DEDHAM STREET, NEWTON HIGHLANDS.

26 regular herbaceous—June 5-20

8 Japanese herbaceous—June 10-25

47 hybrid herbaceous—May 25 to June 10

21 Japanese tree peonies—May 20-June 5

2 European tree peonies—May 30-June 15

11 Lutea hybrids—May 30-June 15

Minnesota

MR. AND MRS. W. E. WIPSON, 903 ARROWHEAD ROAD, DULUTH.

A representative planting of herbaceous peonies, regular and hybrids. They have had to neglect garden recently but visitors are always welcome. Fourth of July best time, although the later, newer varieties come later. Hybrids through blooming early, by the time the others start. Around Duluth, those planted closer to the Lake come later.

Mississippi

MR. MILTON F. RUBEL, 1119 JACKSON STREET, CORINTH.

More than 1,000 varieties, 400 named. Doubles, singles, Japanese. At best around May 10. Also iris, narcissi and hemerocallis.

New Jersey

DR. RUSH C. BAUMAN, 92 HIGH STREET,NUTLEY.

Over 50 tree peonies, some own grafts. At their best in early May.

MR. WILLIAM GOTELLI (GOTELLI ARBORETUM), 66 CREST DRIVE, SOUTH ORANGE.

150 choice varieties of tree peonies which come into bloom around the middle of May. Wonderful collection of conifers.

New York

DR. DAVID GURIN, 4 GROSVENOR PLACE, GREAT NECK, LONG ISLAND.

500 varieties of tree peonies, 200 herbaceous. One tree peony ten feet in diameter. Japanese and European tree peonies at best May 15th. A week or two later lutea hybrids bloom with herbaceous hybrids.

Visitors welcome.

MR. EDWARD HEATHCOTE, 100 COUNTRY CLUB DRIVE, PORT WASHINGTON.

Two acres of formal gardens in which there are about 75 tree peonies, a few lutea and about 75 herbaceous hybrids.

MR. EARL MORSE, 20 SURREY ROAD, GREAT NECK, LONG ISLAND.

Visit by appointment.

Collection of 40 or 50 herbaceous hybrids, mostly Saunders originations. Also 150 Japanese tree peonies and 25 to 30 lutea hybrids. Also unusual range of herbaceous peonies—single, Japanese, semi-double and double as well as some of the species. Visitors welcome but kindly phone or write first to arrange suitable time.

Ohio

MR. WALTER MAINS, BELLE CENTER.

Herbaceous, both regular and hybrids. Two rows of tree seed-lings. Blooming season begins in early May and continues to late June. Seven 200 ft. rows of Alice Harding (late May or early June) lovely in bright moonlight.

MR. A. M. DEWEY, 3 EAST 336TH STREET, WILLOUGHBY.

A dozen tree peonies and 30 herbaceous varieties.

Oregon

MR. PH. HENRY HARTWIG, 3353 SUNNYVIEW AVENUE, N.E., SALEM.

300 varieties of tree peonies, herbaceous hybrids and lactifloras. Also some very fine clematis. Garden always open to visitors.

Tree peonies bloom first and second week of April, hybrids (36 varieties) the first part of May, really beautiful.

Pennsylvania

MR. MORGAN D. REINBOLD, 202 WAVERLY STREET, SHILLINGTON.

20 herbaceous plants, about 60 tree peonies. A number of own hybrids, also lutea and hybrids.. Around May 8.

Texas

MRS. BYRON GIST, 2501 JULIAN BOULEVARD, AMARILLO.

249 plants and 165 varieties (singles, Japanese, semi-doubles and doubles). 229 lactifloras, 15 hybrids, 4 tree peonies, 1 species. Hybrids begin to bloom last of April, continue through May. Best showing May 15-20.

Virginia

MR. FRANK J. GILLIAM, "BELFIELD", WASHINGTON AND LEE UNIVERSITY, LEXINGTON.

24 tree peonies—April 20-May 10. 51 hybrids, largely Saunders introductions—May 1-20. 40 herbaceous—May 10-30. Figures are for different varieties. More than one specimen for many varieties.

Always open to persons interested in peonies.

GEORGE W. PEYTON, WINDY HILL, RAPIDAN. ORANGE COUNTY ROAD 673.

About 1000 herbaceous varieties, a few hybrids and tree

peonies. Best May 15-20, occasionally from April 25-June 1.

MR. AND MRS. WILLIAM GOODE ROBINSON, FAR FIELDS, TIMBER-
LAKE ROAD, LYNCHBURG. (5 miles west of city on left side of
No. 297.)

100 varieties of herbaceous, both regular and hybrid. Early
doubles, Japanese and singles do best, at height May 7-20. 15
varieties of tree peonies which bloom last week in April.

H. F. STOKE, 1436 WATTS AVE., ROANOKE 17.

Many seedling Japanese type tree peonies (some named) in
all the colors from singles to full doubles. About 75 specimen
plants. Top of season, April 20-25. Visitors always welcome.

Washington

MR. AND MRS. J. PAUL MILLER, 304 AVENUE D, GRANDVIEW,
WASHINGTON.

A small garden, one city lot, devoted to the peony. The garden
is a memorial to the father, J. J. Miller, who started the garden,
and is an absorbing hobby for Mr. and Mrs. Miller. More or less
of a test garden limited to Japanese type peonies, 332 varieties.

Readers of this book very welcome. Generally the last week
in May finds the most varieties at their best.

MR. O. B. THORGRIMSON, NORTHERN LIFE TOWER, SEATTLE.

Old favorite herbaceous varieties, singles and doubles; species
and about 50 varieties tree peonies, 2 French hybrids (Maxime
Cornu and La Lorraine). Rhododendrons and peonies at best
in May.

Wyoming

MR. NELSON H. JAMES, 225 FOURTH AVENUE NORTH, GREYBULL.

Several hundred hybrid seedlings, also tree peonies, mostly
seedlings. Blooming season about first week in May with tenuifolia to about June 20 with the moutan and lutea hybrids.
About 400 lactifloras, 50 moutan, 50 tenuifolia, 12 mlokosewitschi,
10 corallinas. Tree peonies bloom about May 20, officinalis
about May 28 to June 5, lactifloras from June 1st. Also grows
iris.

PUBLIC PLANTINGS

If you are fortunate enough to be near a public peony planting, do not miss it at its height of bloom. These gardens are planted for the benefit of the public and even if located at a distance, you will not regret taking the time to visit one of these spectacular dsiplays. We have tried to include sufficient information so you will know what to expect.

Canada

DIVISION OF HORTICULTURE, UNIVERSITY OF ALBERTA,
EDMONTON, ALBERTA.

Collection of the late C. M. Clarke of Teepee Creek, Alberta. Strictly herbaceous, 339 named varieties. Hybrids include 8 P. lactiflora x P. officinalis; 3 P. lactiflora x P. wittmanniana. Six species. June 15-July 15. At best first week in July.

ROYAL BOTANICAL GARDENS, HAMILTON, ONTARIO.

Some species, about 30 varieties of tree peonies and a large number of single, semi-double and double herbaceous varieties contained in a 12 ft. wide border several hundred feet long (about 1200 plants in 250 varieties, both old and recent), arranged according to colors. Normally best second and third week in June. Tree peony collection is planted in the boundary shrub borders with low shrubs in front and taller shrubs forming a background for them. Best from around the end of May until middle of June.

DEPARTMENT OF AGRICULTURE, PLANT RESEARCH INSTITUTE, C.E.F.
OTTAWA.

200 herbaceous varieties, June 15-30, see letter page 86.

Connecticut

HARTFORD PARK DEPARTMENT, ELIZABETH PARK,
HARTFORD.

78 varieties of peonies including 11 hybrids and 22 tree peonies. Tree peonies and hybrids May 16-20. Others June 1-8.

District of Columbia

U. S. NATIONAL ARBORETUM, WASHINGTON, D. C., DR. HENRY T. SKINNER, DIRECTOR.

80 tree peonies, 10 named varieties. At peak about 2½ weeks earlier than herbaceous. 147 named herbaceous varieties. At peak about May 20th.

Illinois

SOUTHERN ILLINOIS UNIVERSITY, CARBONDALE.

In 1958 Harold E. Wolfe gave some 2200 plants of the better varieties of the Japanese type tree peonies to his alma mater. They were mostly 2 year old grafts planted out in the nursery for growing on and later planting on the campus. Such plantings should start in 1960.

NORTHERN ILLINOIS UNIVERSITY, DEKALB.

Planting of hybrid peonies donated by Mrs. Elizabeth Glasscock Falk to her Alma Mater.

MORTON ARBORETUM, ROUTE 53, 1 MILE NORTH OF LISLE.

24 tree peonies, 30 varieties of Saunders hybrids, 25 varieties of Glasscock hybrids, the new yellow double herbaceous peony called both Yokihi and Oriental Gold. Saunders hybrids bloom 3rd week in May, others last of May to first part of June.

DEPARTMENT OF FLORICULTURE AND ORNAMENTAL HORTICULTURE, UNIVERSITY OF ILLINOIS, URBANA.

175 varieties—single, Japanese and double. No varieties added since 1955. Bloom last week in May and first week in June.

Michigan

UNIVERSITY OF MICHIGAN, COLLEGE OF ARCHITECTURE AND DESIGN, DEPARTMENT OF LANDSCAPE ARCHITECTURE, ANN ARBOR.

The peony garden at the Nichols Arboretum has about 360 plants of that many varieties paired for a total of 720. Unplanted spaces allow for an additional 120. They are arranged as follows:

West   *East*
Early   Mid-Season   Late
Whites, Pinks, Reds   Whites, Pinks, Reds   Whites, Pinks, Reds

Thus there is a progression of color durnig the blooming season
from west to east. The regular double peonies, singles and Japanese types, are intermingled on this basis. Tree peonies are not
included in the planting. The peonies are in full bloom starting
the second of June continuing to June 20th.

Missouri

MISSOURI BOTANICAL GARDEN, 2315 TOWER GROVE AVENUE, ST.
LOUIS.

5 varieties of tree peonies. 50 varieties of herbaceous in Lin-
nean Garden. Peak bloom May 11-25.

New Jersey

CEDAR BROOK PARK, PLAINFIELD (UNION COUNTY PARK
COMMISSION)

Peony planting for over 40 years thanks to Mrs. Edward
Harding. Just south of the Japanese iris, planted in fall of 1939.
Paeonia tenuifolia—single and double—with P. emodi, the lovely
species from India, open the season early in May. A half dozen
more varieties of species follow them.

In mid-May the small collection—only eight—of P. suffruticosa
show handsome flowers.

The main collection, about a hundred of the highest rated herbaceous peonies, is usually in full bloom during the last week in
May or very often, the first week in June. These include all types.

This autumn, 1959, there will be planted a sizable new bed,
made especially for a collection of Dr. Saunders hybrids, adding
greatly to the interest and educational value of the Peony Garden.

Harriette R. Halloway, a guiding light in the project, received
the distinguished service medal of the Garden Club of America
for distinguished service in the field of horticulture and as an
outstanding gardener, expert grower and authority on iris, daffodils and peonies.

New York

NEW YORK BOTANICAL GARDEN, BRONX PARK.

35 varieties of tree peonies at best in early May and 178 varieties herbaceous peonies (some hybrids) at height of bloom in late May.

BROOKLYN BOTANIC GARDEN, 1000 WASHINGTON AVENUE, BROOKLYN.

70 varieties of herbaceous peonies which bloom from about May 1 to 15. A few tree peonies just getting started (1959).

CORNELL PLANTATIONS, CORNELL UNIVERSITY, ITHACA.

In the fall of 1959 William Gratwick of Pavilion, New York donated a large planting of tree peonies, to be set out by the Cornell Plantations.

HIGHLAND PARK, ROCHESTER.

Tree peonies, all unnamed seedlings, bloom about May 25. 180 herbaceous varieties acquired from 1905-1940, bloom about June 10-15.

UNION COLLEGE, SCHENECTADY 8.

In Jackson's Garden, cultivated for 125 years, there is a sizeable collection of tree and herbaceous peonies. Some of the tree peonies are 100 years or more old, five to six feet tall and well branched. They were sent to the college by former students who became missionaries located in the Orient. The last several years Saunders hybrids have been added to the tree peony collection. The sizeable herbaceous peony collection is mostly of fairly ancient origin but valuable in the college garden, blooming at Commencement time.

BOYCE THOMPSON INSTITUTE FOR PLANT RESEARCH, INC., YONKERS.

250 hybrid tree peonies produced from seed used in the study of germinating methods.

At best about May 15-20.

North Carolina

BILTMORE ESTATE, ASHEVILLE.

200 varieties herbaceous peonies; singles, doubles, Japanese, etc. Started a collection of tree peonies in 1959 (130 plants).

Ohio

KINGWOOD CENTER, MANSFIELD.

50 tree peony varieties. 400 herbaceous varieties and this number is increasing. Peak bloom dates: June 5-20.

CEMETERY OF SPRING GROVE, WINTON PLACE, CINCINNATI 32.

Border 300 feet long and 6 feet wide devoted to herbaceous peonies, not labeled. Another extensive flower border that includes herbaceous peonies in its border. A number of small plantings of tree peonies, many not labeled, perhaps 300 plants in all, some seedlings, others named varieties.

Tree peonies at peak of bloom latter part of April and first of May. Herbaceous peonies reach peak second and third weeks of May.

Pennsylvania

JOHN J. TYLER ARBORETUM (DR. JOHN C. WISTER, DIRECTOR), LIMA.

25 named moutan tree peonies, 6 yellow hybrids, about 50 varieties of herbaceous hybrids and 100 lactiflora varieties. Height of tree peony season about May 10 and herbaceous varieties last week of May and first week in June.

THE SCOTT HORTICULTURAL FOUNDATION (DR. JOHN C. WISTER, DIRECTOR), SWARTHMORE COLLEGE, SWARTHMORE.

150 or more varieties of tree peonies, at peak around May 10. 100 herbaceous hybrids, which begin on or before May 1 and reach their peak about May 15 or 20. 300 of the late lactiflora varieties. The lactifloras are at their best about Decoration Day, sometimes earlier. One of the finest peony collections in the country.

Washington

UNIVERSITY OF WASHINGTON ARBORETUM, SEATTLE.

43 varieties of tree peonies. Also species P. lutea, P. delavayi, P. potanini, as well as the variety ludlowi of P. lutea. No herbaceous varieties. Peak—second or third week of May.

Akashi-gata	Horakumon	Satin Rouge
Akashi-jishi	Horaizan	Shijoro
Alice Harding	Howzan	Shogomon
Argosy	Hushakukin	Souvenir de Chas.
Aurore	Jules Pirlot	Mechin
Baronne d'Ales	Kamikaze	Souvenir de Ducher
Chiyokagura	Kenreimon	Souvenir de Maxime
Chiyonohana	La Lorraine	Cornu
Daigokuden	Mme. Edouard	Stardust
Flambeau	Seneclause	Sukiden
Funkei	Mme. Fernand	Surprise
Godaishu	Lemaitre	Tamafuyo
Hakugan	Mme. L. Henry	Yachiyo-tsubaki
Hakuo-jishi	Momoyama	Yaesakura
Hatsuhinode	Reine Elizabeth	Yakutsuru
Higurashi	Santa Maria	

West Virginia

OGLEBAY PARK, WHEELING.

Peony garden maintained by the Garden Study Club and contains 10 tree peonies, 25 herbaceous varieties. In bloom about the last week of May. Young material, newly planted.

Wisconsin

ALFRED L. BOERNER BOTANICAL GARDENS, WHITNALL PARK, HALES CORNERS (JUST SOUTH OF MILWAUKEE)

95 varieties of tree peonies. Peak of bloom May 15-30. 172 varieties herbaceous peonies. Peak of bloom June 10-15.

RETAIL SOURCES

Retail nurseries featuring peonies are listed according to states. We have indicated what they sell, if they have a catalog, and when their peony display is at its height. This, of course, depends upon the season, so the dates vary by several days from year to year.

We know that there are many good sources we have not listed, simply because we don't happen to know about them, but we made a special effort to locate as many as we could. We hope you will visit a peony nursery at its height of bloom for the thrill of seeing a spectacular display, and to acquaint yourself with the many beautiful varieties available today.

California

TOICHI DOMOTO NURSERY, 26521 WHITMAN STREET, HAYWARD.
Herbaceous, regular and tree peonies and seeds. Mostly local business. March 15-April 20.

MR. RAYMOND ZIESMER, APPLE TREE FARM, SAN DIEGO COUNTY, JULIAN.
Cut flower business. June 1.

Connecticut

PETER CASCIO NURSERY, 2600 ALBANY AVENUE, WEST HARTFORD.
Herbaceous, regular and tree. Local business. Perennial list. First two weeks in June.

WHITE FLOWER FARM, LITCHFIELD, 14.
Herbaceous, regular and hybrids, and tree. Catalog. Mid June.

Illinois

Herbaceous peonies at best in Chicago area last week in May through first week in June.

CHARLES KLEHM & SON (MR. CARL KLEHM), ROUTE 62, ARLINGTON HEIGHTS.
Herbaceous, regular and hybrids, and tree. Catalog. June 1-20.

MRS. ELIZABETH GLASSCOCK FALK (SUCCESSOR TO LYMAN D. GLASSCOCK) R.F.D. 1, PLAINFIELD.
Herbaceous, regular and hybrids. (Famous hybridizing father, Lyman D. Glasscock produced many wonderful, new hybrids.) Catalog. Hybrids weeks before Decoration Day.

GROVESIDE GARDENS (EDWIN C. FREED, OWNER), 501 SIXTY-THIRD STREET, DOWNER'S GROVE.

Herbaceous, regular and hybrids, and species. Catalog. First two or three weeks in June.

HEBRON PEONY FARM, HEBRON.
Herbaceous, regular and hybrids, and species. Catalog. First week in June.

MISSION GARDENS, HIGHWAY 42A, TECHNY.
Herbaceous, regular and hybrids, and tree. Catalog. May 30-June 15.

RIVER DRIVE PEONY GARDEN, 8740 RIDGE STREET, RIVER GROVE (A. L. MURAWSKA & SONS)
Herbaceous, regular and hybrids. Catalog. May 30-June 10.

VAUGHAN'S NURSERIES, WESTERN SPRINGS.
Herbaceous, regular and some hybrids. Tree peonies. Catalog. Plants not grown here.

Indiana

L. D. BAKER, IRIS AND PEONY FARMS, KENDALLVILLE.
Herbaceous. Catalog. Peonies at best Bloomington, Indiana—May 25-June 1. Corydon, Indiana—May 20-27. Kendallville, Indiana—June 3-10.

TUCKDAWA GARDEN, PERU (R. H. JONES). Highway 19, 1 mile north of Peru.
Herbaceous, regular and hybrids, species. Catalog. May 30-June 15.

SUNDOWN GARDENS, R.F.D. 1, CARMEL (EARL W. AND DOROTHY J. KNAPP). Highway 31, junction with 234.
Herbaceous, regular and hybrids. Catalog. First two weeks in June.

FLOYD BASS PEONY FARM, WEST 62ND STREET, NEW AUGUSTA (MR. RICHARD BASS).
Herbaceous and regular. Local business. Price list. May 30th.

Iowa

INTER-STATE NURSERIES, HAMBURG.
Herbaceous. Catalog. May 27 to June 3.

Kansas

MYRON D. BIGGER, 1147 OAKLAND AVENUE, TOPEKA.
Herbaceous, regular and hybrids. Catalog. May 20th.

HILL IRIS AND PEONY FARM, LAFONTAINE (MR. ROBERT HILL).
Herbaceous, regular and hybrids. Catalog. May 15.

Kentucky

J. A. DRESSMAN, R. 5, BOX 500, LOCUST ROAD, COVINGTON.
Herbaceous, regular and hybrids (Auten's), tree and species.
Catalog. Mid-April. (Visitors with appointment.)

Maryland

CARROLL GARDENS, WESTMINSTER.
Herbaceous, regular and hybrids, tree and species. Catalog.
Early June.

Massachusetts

CHERRY HILL NURSERIES (THURLOWS AND STRANGER, INC.), WEST
NEWBURY.
Herbaceous, regular. Catalog. June 16-20.

GRAY AND COLE, WARD HILL.
Herbaceous, regular and hybrids. Typewritten select list of
better and most successful varieties. Mostly local business. Display planting best about Mid-June.

MARINUS VANDER POL, 755 WASHINGTON STREET (ROUTE 6),
FAIRHAVEN.
Herbaceous, regular and hybrids, and tree. Catalog. May 20th.
WESTON NURSERIES, HOPKINTON (MR. PETER MEZITT).
Herbaceous, regular and hybrids. Catalog.
P. DE JAGER & SONS, INC., SOUTH HAMILTON 72.
Herbaceous, regular. Catalog. No display.

Michigan

AMERICAN PERENNIAL GARDENS, P.O. BOX 37, GARDEN CITY.
Herbaceous, regular and hybrids, tree, species and seeds. Catalog. Early June.

GROWERS' EXCHANGE, INC., P.O. BOX 397, FARMINGTON.
Herbaceous, regular and tree peonies. Catalog.

LIENAU PEONY GARDENS, 25804 JOY ROAD, DETROIT 39.
Herbaceous, regular and some hybrids. June 5-20.

HARRY E. SAIER, DIMONDALE.
Business mainly seeds. Herbaceous, regular and hybrids, tree and species. Catalog. June 1-10.

Minnesota

BRAND PEONY FARMS, BOX 408, 100 E. DIVISION STREET, FARIBAULT.
Herbaceous, regular and hybrids. Catalog. Impressive display any time between June 1-20.

MRS. A. S. GOWEN, ROUTE 5, BOX 105, EXCELSIOR.
Herbaceous, regular and a few hybrids. Display at best June 10-20.

HILLSIDE GARDEN, ROUTE #3, CANNON FALLS
(ADRIAN GIBSON)
Herbaceous, regular and hybrids, tree and species. List. June 5-12.

E. H. LINS, COLOGNE.
Herbaceous, regular and hybrids. Catalog. June 5-20.

SWEDBERG NURSERY, BATTLE LAKE (J. E. SWEDBERG, OWNER).
Herbaceous, regular and hybrids, tree, species and seeds. Catalog, June 15th.

Missouri

ELMER L. BLOCK, ROUTE 1, SARCOXIE.
Herbaceous, regular. List. May 15-25.

SARCOXIE NURSERIES, SARCOXIE (WILD BROS. NURSERY CO.)
Herbaceous, regular. Catalog. May 15-25.

GILBERT H. WILD & SON, SARCOXIE.
Herbaceous, singles, Japanese, doubles and hybrids. Catalog.
Peak bloom—May 20-25, varies, of course, with season.

Nebraska

MR. GILBERT L. CARVER, CARVER PEONY GARDEN, 3115 AVENUE B,
BOX 19, KEARNEY.
Herbaceous, regular and hybrid. Catalog. Display best June
5-15.

New York

CHAUTAUQUA FLOWERFIELD, GREENHURST.
Herbaceous, regular and hybrids, tree, species and seeds.
Mostly wholesale. Catalog. Second week in June. Grow about
35 acres of peonies.

MR. WILLIAM GRATWICK, PAVILION.
Tree peonies. Catalog. Tree Peony Festival last week in May
or first week of June. Mr. Gratwick has one of the finest tree
peony collections in the country. 40,000 blooms.

WALTER J. GUILLE, INC., SYOSSET, LONG ISLAND.
Wholesale but welcome visitors at any time. Flowering season
varies from opening date of May 24 to June 4.

ROSEDALE NURSERIES, INC. SAW MILL RIVER PARKWAY,
HAWTHORNE.
Herbaceous peonies. Mostly local business. Peonies at height
first week in June.

A. P. SAUNDERS, SILVIA SAUNDERS, COLLEGE HILL, CLINTON.
Herbaceous Saunders hybrids, tree peonies, Saunders lutea
hybrids, species and seeds. Catalog. June 8-15 usually. Famous
for Saunders hybrids both herbaceous and tree.

LOUIS SMIRNOW, 85 LINDEN LANE, BROOKVILLE, LONG ISLAND.

Herbaceous, regular and hybrids, tree, species and seeds. Catalog. May 15 to June 10.

MARTIN VIETTE NURSERIES, EAST NORWICH, LONG ISLAND.
Herbaceous, regular and hybrids, tree peonies. Local business. Catalog. June 5-15.

North Dakota

FRANKLIN PAGE, HAMILTON.
Herbaceous, regular. June 25.

Ohio

ATHA GARDENS, WEST LIBERTY 2 (MR. LA VERNE C. ATHA).
Herbaceous, regular and hybrids, tree, species and seeds. Catalog. Tree and hybrids—third week in May. Herbaceous—first week in June.

CURTIS GARDENS (LOUIS MATTFELD), 8810 COLERAIN ROAD, CINCINNATI 39.
Herbaceous, regular, tree and seeds. Tree peony and oriental poppy catalog. End of April.

JOYCELYN GARDENS, 145 EBERLY AVENUE, BOWLING GREEN (W. A. ALEXANDER, PROPRIETOR).
Herbaceous, regular and hybrids. Price list. June 5-10.

WILLIAM H. KREKLER, W. ELKTON ROAD, SOMERVILLE.
Herbaceous, regular and most of the hybrids, species and seeds. Catalog. Memorial Day or just before. 1300 best named varieties (hybrids and lactifloras). Many fine seedlings. Large collection covering 7 acres.

TERRACE GARDENS, 4650 TIPPECANOE ROAD, YOUNGSTOWN.
Herbaceous, regular, tree and species. Catalog. Local business. June 10.

WASSENBERG GARDENS, VAN WERT (MR. RICHARD MILLER, OWNER).
Herbaceous, regular, and species. Catalog. June 3-10.

WAYSIDE GARDENS, MENTOR.
Herbaceous, regular and hybrids, tree. Catalog. June 1st.

Oregon
WALTER MARX GARDENS, BORING.
Herbaceous, regular and hybrids, and tree. Catalog. June 5-15.

Pennsylvania
FAIRVIEW EVERGREEN NURSERY, FAIRVIEW.
Retail list of seedlings, otherwise wholesale. No display.

STYER'S NURSERIES, CONCORDVILLE, U. S. ROUTE #1
(MR. J. FRANKLIN STYER).
Herbaceous, regular and hybrids. Catalog. May 25-June 5.

OBERLIN PEONY GARDENS, 425 PENNSYLVANIA AVENUE,
SINKING SPRING (MORRIS W. JAMES).
Herbaceous, regular and hybrids, tree, species, some seeds.
Catalog. Early May to Mid-June.

FARR NURSERY COMPANY, WOMELSDORF.
A local business. June 1.

Vermont
PUTNEY NURSERY, INC., PUTNEY.
Herbaceous, regular and hybrids. Catalog. Mid and late June.

SHREWSBURY GARDENS, CUTTINGSVILLE (MR. RICHARD JOHNSON).
Herbaceous, regular and hybrids. Catalog. Mid and late June.

Wisconsin
M. C. KARRELS, 3727 SOUTH 46TH STREET, MILWAUKEE 15.
Herbaceous, regular and hybrids. Catalog. June 15. Visitors
by appointment.

DR. CASPER I. NELSON, ROUTE 2, BOX 145, RIVER FALLS.
Local business, herbaceous and hybrids. Show display about
June 14.

REGISTERED VARIETIES

What constitutes a registration? The peonies which have been submitted to the American Peony Society for registration (or which, in the case of varieties originated before the Society was organized, were accepted by the Society as valid names and have been published in bulletins). The following list (for which the library staff of the Massachusetts Horticultural Society deserves full credit) was compiled by going through the complete set of Bulletins published by the Society up to January 1, 1959. It is unfortunate that all hybridizers do not register their new varieties with the Society. Unregistered varieties are not included in this list, although many are mentioned elsewhere in the book.

The names albiflora, chinensis and sinensis are synonyms of lactiflora. They were in common use when many of the varieties were registered and are therefore printed as given in the American Peony Society Bulletins. Most of the varieties listed are lactifloras unless otherwise noted.

KEY

A	— Anemone	L	— Late
AV	— Average	LM	— Late mid-season
D	— Double	M	— Mid-season
DW	— Dwarf	S	— Single
E	— Early	SD	— Semi-double
EM	— Early mid-season	T	— Tall
J	— Japanese	V	— Very (as VL—very late)
		X	— No longer in commerce

A

ABBE (Lewis, 1921), J. Deep rose-pink. AV. M.

A. B. C. NICHOLLS (Nicholls, 1937), D. White, tint of flesh L. AV.

ABEEKINS (Guppy, 1929) D. VE. Ruby red. Albiflora singles x officinalis rubra plena. X.

ABRAHAM LINCOLN (Lanigan, 1935), D. White. X.

ACE (Smith-Krekler, 1954), J. Dark red. E. AV.

ACME (Franklin, 1931), D. Light pink. L. AV.

ADA PRISCILLA (Walter J. Guille, 1948), A. White and yellow. E. T.

ADDIELANCHEA (Brand, 1907), D. Pure white. LM. AV. X.

ADELE SAWYER (Nicholls—Wild & Sons, 1957) (Seedling no. 1177), D. Rose pink. M.

238

ADOLPHE ROUSSEAU (Dessert & Mechin, 1890), D. Dark red. EM. T.

ADONIS (Sass, 1930), D. Pink with yellow collar. L. T.

ADORATION (Lein, 1935), D. Dark red. M. to L. T.. X.

AGLOW (Nicholls-Wild and Son, 1959), D. White. L.

AILEEN BRETHOUR (Brethour, 1935), Pink. AV. M. X.

AKALU (Dessert—reg. before 1926), J. Dark rose-pink. M. AV.

AKBAR (Nicholls, 1941), J. Rose-red. T. Number 202 from Mikado. M.

ALASKA (E. Auten Jr., 1925), A. Salmon red. Fragrant. E.

ALBATRE (Crousse, 1885), Generally considered identical with AVALANCHE.

ALBERT CROUSSE (Crousse, 1893), D. Light rose-pink. L. T.

ALBERTA KELSEY (Kelsey, 1940), SD. Rose pink. Fragrant. EM.

ALBIFLORA, THE BRIDE see THE BRIDE

ALBUQUERQUE (Wild, 1955), SD. Dark red. M. AV.

ALEX. D. VORIES (Vories, 1924), D. American Beauty red. M. T.

ALICE (Krekler, 1955) (seedling no. AQ6), D. Red. LM. AV.

ALICE HARDING (Lemoine, 1922), D. Flesh-pink. M. AV.

ALICE REED BATES (A. B. Franklin, 1939), D. Rose pink. M. T.

ALLINE ROGERS (Nicholls-Wild and Son, 1959), D. Salmon pink. EM.

ALMA (Shaylor, 1916), J. Light pink. M. AV.

ALSACE-LORRAINE (Lemoine, 1906), D. Pure white tinted

with cream and buff in center. LM. AV.

ALSTEAD (E. Auten Jr., 1939), J. Deep pink. Albiflora variety.

ALTAR CANDLES (Pleas, 1908), J. Flesh pink. M. AV.

AMANDA YALE (Brand, 1907), D. Flesh-white. M. AV.

AMA-NO-SODE (Japan), J. Rose pink. M. AV.

AMERICAN LEGION (A. L. Murawska, 1932), D. Rose pink. E. AV. X.

AMOSKEAG (Guppy, 1935), S. White. X.

A. M. SLOCUM (Franklin, 1920), D. Rose-pink. L. DW.

ANDY (E. Auten Jr., 1936), SD. Dark red. EM.

ANETTE CARSON (Risk, 1929), D. Blush pink, creamy white center. Fragrant. L. T.

ANGEL WINGS (R. H. Brant, 1939), "Flat Type". Ivory white. T. LM.

ANGELO COBB FREEBORN (Freeborn, 1943), D. Coral red. VE. T. Officinalis rubra x Madame Jules Dessert

ANGELUS (E. Auten Jr., 1933), S. Light pink. M.

ANNABESSACOOK (Guppy, 1935), J. White. X.

ANNA SASS (Sass, 1930), D. Deep pink. LM. T.

ANN COUSINS (Cousins, 1946), D. White. Rose fragrance. LM. AV.

ANN RUTLEDGE (Lanigan, 1936), D. Cream-white tinted light pink. L. D. X.

ANN ZAHLLER (Mains, 1956), SD. Red. E. officinalis x albiflora

ANNE BIGGER (Bigger, 1945), D. Pink. LM.

ANNE HARGROVE (Nicholls-Wild

and Son, 1959), D. China pink. E. T. Mme. Calot x Nicholls no. 272

APOLLO (Sass, 1930), D. Pink with salmon blush center. L. AV.

A. P. SAUNDERS (Thurlow, 1919), D. Flesh pink, white in center. L. AV.

ARBUTUS PINK (Freeborn, 1951), S. Pink. E. AV. Officinalis rubra plena x Mme. Jules Dessert. VE.

ARCTURUS (E. Auten Jr., 1933), S. Dark red. E.

ARGENTINE (Lemoine, 1924), D. Purest white with creamy tint towards center. Fragrant. L. M. AV.

ARGOSY (Saunders, 1929), SD. Yellow stained deep purple red over small area at base of petals. Lutea x moutan. VE.

ARIEL (Lyman, 1939), J. Pale pink. X.

ARLEQUIN (Dessert, 1921), A. Pale rose-pink. Faintly fragrant. M. AV.

ASA GRAY (Crousse, 1886), D. Pale pink "powdered with minute rosy dots". Fragrant. M. AV.

ASSMANNSHAUSEN (Goos & Koenemann, 1912), D. Light pink, fading white. Fragrant. L.

ATHELSTANE (Brown, 1938), D. Lavender pink. Fragrant. M.

ATLANTA (Franklin, 1931), S. E. AV. White.

ATTAR OF ROSES (Murawska, 1951) (seedling no. 59), D. Dark pink. E. T.

ATTRACTION (Hollis, 1906), J. Red. Fragrant. M. AV.

AUGUSTE DESSERT (Dessert, 1920), D. Pink. Each petal edged with silvery border. M. AV.

AUREOLIN (Shaylor, 1917), A. Light rose-pink. Fragrant. LM. AV.

AURORE (Dessert, 1904), D. Creamy-pink. M. AV.

AUTEN'S PRIDE (E. Auten Jr., 1933), D. Light pink. Rose fragrant. L.

AVALANCHE (Crousse, 1886), D. Blush white. LM. AV.

AVE MARIA (J R. Mann-Van Steen, 1936), D. White. EM. AV.

AVIATEUR REYMOND (Dessert, 1915), D. Light crimson. M. T.

AZTEC (Nicholls, 1941), J. Scarlet rose. Number 200 from Mikado.

B

BABY KELWAY (Kelway, 1929), S. Flesh white. Not sold in U.S.A.

BALL O'COTTON (Franklin, 1920), D. White with wire edge of crimson. Fragrant. LM. AV.

BANDERILLA (Jones, 1957), J. Black-red. M.

BARBARA JEAN ROHE (Napier, 1937), D. White, reverse side blush rose. Fragrant. M. AV. X.

BARBARA UTTERBACK (Winchell, 1948) (seedling no. 91A), D. Red. M.

BARONESS SCHROEDER (Kelway, 1889), D. Flesh-white. Fragrant. LM. T.

BATTLE FLAG (Nicholls, 1941), J. Deep-red. Number 196 from Mikado.

BAYADERE (Lemoine, 1910), D. White. Pink marks on outer petals. Fragrant. M. T.

BEACON HILL (Auten, 1937), S. Dark red. E. T. Officinalis x chinensis

BEATRICE KELWAY (Kelway, 1929),D.Rose. Not sold U.S.A.

BEAUMARCHAIS (Lemoine, 1922), D. Pink-flesh-mauve. L. T.

BELLA DONNA (Nieuwenhuizen, 1935), Rose type. Light mauve pink. D.

BELLE (Field no. 2A3; reg. by Glasscock, 1931), chinensis var. Rose type. Shell pink. Fragrant. L. T.

BELLE CENTER (Mains, 1956), D. Red. E. Officinalis x albiflora

BELLE CHINOISE (Auten, 1935), D. White. Rose fragrance. AV. LM.

BEN HABERMAN (H. P. Sass, 1941), D. Rose type. Bright deep pink. M. AV.

BENJAMIN FRANKLIN (Brand, 1907), D. Dark crimson. Fragrant. M. T.

BERTRADE (Lemoine, 1909), D. White, shaded yellow at base of petals. LM. AV.

BERYL CROCKETT (Nicholls-G. H. Wild & Son, 1954) (Nicholls seedling 442), D. White. M. AV.

BESS BOCKSTOCE (Bockstoce, 1955), D. Light pink. E. AV. Officinalis x lactiflora.

BESSIE (Krekler, 1958), D. Silvery pink. M. T.

BETTY BLOSSOM (Thurlow, 1925), D. White, tinted yellow. LM.

BETTY CALVERT (Nicholls-G. H. Wild & Son, 1950) (Nicholls seedling no. 391), D. Blush. LM.

BETTY GROFF (Krekler, 1958), J. Light pink. M. T.

BETTY J. (Jones, 1957), D. Pink. M. AV.

BETTY MINOR (Nicholls-G. H. Wild & Son, 1954) (Nicholls seedling no. 1372), D. Light pink. L. AV.

BETSEY ROSS (E. Auten, Jr., 1931), D. White. Fragrant. L. T.

BIEBRICH (Goos & Koenemann, 1912), D. Soft pink fading white tinted flesh. Rose fragrance. M. to L. T.

BIG TOP (Jones, 1957), D. White. L. T.

BLACK HAWK (E. Auten, Jr., 1933) S. Dark red. E. AV.

BLACK KNIGHT (Glasscock, 1939), S. Scarlet with orange tint. E. Name changed to Bright Knight. T. Chinensis x Otto Froebel.

BLACK MAGIC (E. Auten, Jr., 1929), S. Black red. AV. E.

BLACK MONARCH (Glasscock, 1939), Rose type. Dark red. Officinalis rubra x Rosy Glow

BLACK PRINCE (Thurlow, 1915), S. Deep crimson. Fragrance not pleasing. M. AV.

BLACK VELVET (Murawska, 1957), D. Bright red. M. AV. Chippewa x Matilda Lewis

BLACK WARRIOR (Nicholls, 1941), D. Red Black. AV. M. Number 3 from M. M. Cahuzac

BLANCHE ELIE (Brethour, 1934), Bomb type. White. Fragrant. E. T.

BLANCHE KING (Brand, 1922), D. Dark pink with silvery sheen. LM. AV.

BLAZING STAR (Auten, 1937), SD. Dark red.

BLONDE (W. A. Dana, 1926), Bomb type. Light pink, bi-colored pink and cream. Fragrant

BLUSH (Nicholls, 1941), D. Rose type. Pink. AV. Number 1 from Othello. M.

BLUSHING BEAUTY (Franklin,

1931), Rose type. Pale pink. Fragrant. L. AV.

BLUSH QUEEN (Hoogendoorn, 1949), D. White. M. AV.

BONNIE BECKER (Sass, 1942), Rose type. Pink. L. AV.

BONNIE WINSLOW (Winslow, 1951) (seedling no. 27), D. Light rose pink. Mildly fragrant. M. T.

BORDER GEM (Hoogendoorn, 1949), D. Red. E. DW.

BOULE DE NEIGE (Calot, 1867), D. White with yellow suffusion and crimson flecks on guards. Fragrance raw and pungent. EM. T.

BOWL OF BEAUTY (Hoogendoorn, 1949), J. Fuchsine rose. E.

BRAND'S MAGNIFICENT (Brand, 1918), D. Crimson with purplish cast. LM. AV.

BRIDESMAID (Kelway, reg. before 1926). The same as Marie Jacquin, which see.

BRIGHT KNIGHT see BLACK NIGHT.

BRIGHTNESS (Glasscock, 1947), albiflora x officinalis Sunbeam. S. Red. VE. AP. V.

BUCKEYE BELLE (Mains, 1956), SD. Red. E. Officinalis x albiflora

BUNCH OF PERFUME (Kelway, 1901), D. Rose. LM. AV.

BURMA RUBY (Glasscock, 1951), S. Red. E. AV. Albiflora x officinalis Sunbeam

BU-TE (Wassenberg, 1954), J. White. M. T. Tamate Boku x Isani Gidui

C

CALUMET (E. Auten, Jr., 1931), S. Red. E. T.

CAMEO (E. Auten, Jr., 1926), Low

bomb type. Blush white. Fragrant. Name changed to Clorinda.

CANDEUR (Dessert, 1920), D. Light rose-pink, flushed darker outside. Faint fragrance. LM. T.

CAPRICCIO see FANTASIA.

CAPTAIN JONES see PINK GLORY.

CAPTAIN KIDD (E. Auten, 1934), SD. Dark red. T.

CARILLON (Richmond, 1951) (seedling no. 51-326), D. Rose pink. LM. T.

CAROL (Bockstoce, 1955), D. Red. E. AV. Officinalis x lactiflora.

CAROLINA MOON (E. Auten, Jr., 1940), Bomb type. White with yellow center, albiflora variety. AV. E.

CAROLYNE MAE NELSON (H. P. Sass, 1937). Dark crimson maroon. L. T.

CARRARA (Bigger, 1952) (seedling no. 59-37), J. White. M. AV.

CASABLANCA (Lins, 1942) (seedling no. R-5-242), D. White. L. T.

CATHEDRAL (Reg., before 1926, origin unknown) (also catalogued as Hana-no-sato), J. Dark rose-pink in combination with pale pink petaloids. Slightly fragrant. M. AV.

CATHERINE CRAIN (Nicholls, 1948), D. Pink. EM. T. Marie Crousse x Spring Beauty

CATHERINE EMMA (Mrs. C. E. Athrop, 1941), D. Strawberry guards, cream-yellow heart. LM. T. X.

CELESTIA LEWIS (Lewis, 1921), D. Clear pink with white petals intermixed. Fragrant. T. X.

CERISE BEAUTY (Risk, 1929), D.

Cerise, darker in center. LM.
AV.
CHALICE (Saunders, 1929), S.
White. E. T. Sinensis x
macrophylla
CHAMINADE (E. Auten, Jr.,
1933), J. Light pink. T.
CHARITY (Saunders, 1929), SD.
Deep cherry crimson. Otto
Froebel x sinensis
CHARLENE (E. F. Kelsey, 1938),
D. White. L. AV.
CHARLES MAINS (Mains, 1956),
seedling no. A18), D. Pink. E.
CHARLES NEIDEL (Wettengel,
1916), D. Rose form. Shaggy
rose-pink. M. AV.
CHARLIE'S WHITE (Klehm,
1951) (seedling no. 69B), D.
White. E. T.
CHARLOT (Doriat, 1924), D.
M. T. Flowers silvery lilac
with carmine base, silvery
borders.
CHARM (Franklin, 1931), J. Dark
red. L. AV.
CHASTITY (Brethour, 1935),
Bomb type. White. Fragrant.
T. X.
CHEROKEE (Franklin, 1931),
Rose type. Pure white. L. AV.
CHERRY HILL (Thurlow, 1915),
D. Dark maroon. Very early.
T.
CHERRY RED (Glasscock, 1939),
Rose type. Pure red. M. DW.
Officinalis rubra x chinensis
CHESTINE GOWDY (Brand,
1913), D. Light rose. Creamy
white collar. Excellent frag-
rance. L. T.
CHESUNCOOK (Guppy, 1935),
J. White. X.
CHIEF (Franklin, 1931), Rose
type. Light pink. Fragrant. L.
CHINA MAID (Murawska, 1943),
J. Medium pink. M.
CHIPPEWA (Murawska, 1943), D.
Dark red. M. T.

CHOCOLATE SOLDIER (E.
Auten, Jr., 1939), J. Bomb
type. Black-red. Officinalis
hybrid
CINDERELLA (R. H. Jones,
1938), S. Apple blossom pink.
EM. AV.
CLAIRE DE LUNE (White,
1954), S. Yellow. E. DW.
Mons. Jules Elie x
mlokosewitschi
CLAIRE DUBOIS (Crousse,
1886), D. Bright rose pink
bordering on mauve-pink.
L. AV.
CLAIRETTE (Dessert, 1905), S.
Pink opening to white. M. T.
CLARA MAY BERNHARDT
(Kummer, 1939), D. Rose
type. Pure white. Fragrant. M.
AV. Pollen parent unknown.
Seed producing this white off-
spring is from Mons. Martin
Cahuzac.
CLEMENCEAU (Dessert, 1920),
D. Globular form. Glowing
rose-pink. Rose fragrance.
LM. T.
CLEOPATRA (E. Auten, Jr.,
1939), albiflora variety, D.
Dark red. Fragrant. L.
CLORINDA see CAMEO.
COATICOOK (Guppy, 1935), J.
Light pink. X.
COBSECOOK (Guppy, 1935), J.
Light pink. X.
COLONEL LINDBERG (A. E.
Kunderd, 1927), D. Dark
red. E. X.
COMMANDO (Glasscock, 1944),
D. Red. E. T. Officinalis x
albiflora
CONQUISTADOR (R. H. Jones,
1938), D. Pale pink with
lavender sheen. Fragrant.
L. T. X.
CONSTANCE MOORE (Mains,
1956), J. Red. E. Officinalis
x abliflora

CONTOOCOOK (Guppy, 1935), J. Deep pink. X.

CONVOY (Glasscock, 1944), D. Red. E. T. Officinalis x albiflora

COPY CAT (Freeborn, 1945), D. Brilliant blood red. E. Officinalis rubra plena x Mme. Jules Dessert

CORAL GLOW (Klehm, 1951), (seedling no. 781 Z), D. Pink. LM. T.

CORAL QUEEN (H. P. Sass, 1937), Γ˙ ᴸᵢ pink. L. T. D.

CORDELIA (submitted by Interstate Nurseries, '37). No description supplied. Name never used.

CORINNE WERSAN (Krekler, 1955) (seedling no. AV4), D. White. M. AV.

CORINTH (Saunders, 1929), D. Light crimson. M. to L. AV. Officinalis x sinensis

CORNELIA SHAYLOR (Shaylor, 1917), D. Globular form. Opens pink becoming white. L. T.

CORNIE MOORE (E. F. Kelsey, 1940), S. Dark red. Fragrant. E T.

CORONATION (Kelway, 1902), D. Pale rose pink flecked with crimson on edges. Fragrant. LM. AV.

COUNTESS MARITZA (Nieuwenhuizen, 1935), Rose type. Pink to white, yellow at base. E. T.

COUNTRY DANCE (E. Auten, Jr., 1931), S. White. E. T.

COURONNE D'OR (Calot, 1873), D. White center. Petals tipped with crimson. L. AV.

CREVE COEUR (E. Auten, Jr., 1929), J. Dark red. Rose fragrance. T. M.

CRIMSON BOMB (Freeborn, 1943), D. Crimson. Officinalis

rubra x Mme. Jules Dessert.

CRIMSON GLORY (submitted by Interstate Nurseries). No description furnished. Name never used.

CRODIE (Krekler, 1958), S. Deep red. EM. T.

CROWN IMPERIAL (Kelway, 1929). J. Imperial pink with large mass of orange-yellow petalodes.

CRUSADER (Glasscock, 1940), SD. Scarlet-red. E. Officinalis rubra x Ruby

CUPID (Glasscock, 1950), S. Pink. E. AV. Otto Froebel x albiflora

CYGNET (Nicholls-G. H. Wild and Son, 1951) (Nicholls seedling no. 35/12), S. White. E. T.

D

DAINTY (Nicholls, 1941), S. Lt. silvery pink. Number 270 from Lady Alexandra Duff. E. AV.

DAINTY LASS (Glasscock, 1935), J. Coral pink. E. Officinalis hybrid

DAISY B. (Nicholls-Wild & Son, 1957) (seedling no. 920), D. White. L.

DANA GARNOCK (Dana, 1920), D. White

DANCE CAPRICE (E. Auten, Jr., 1933), Flesh. SD. T.

DANCING NYMPH (E. Auten, Jr., 1933). S. Pink, crinkled. L.

DANIEL BOONE (E. Auten, Jr., 1931), D. Dark red. T.

DAPHNE (Earnshaw, 1922), D. Pure white. LM. AV.

DARK KNIGHT (Glasscock, 1941), S. Dark red. T. E. Fuyajo x officinalis Jap.

DARKNESS (Brand, 1913), S.

Dark maroon red. Fragrant.
M. AV.

DARWIN (Winslow, 1951) (seedling no. 5), S. Dark red. M.
AV.

DAVID HARUM (Brand, 1920),
D. Clear light red. M. T.

DAWN PINK (H. P. Sass, 1946),
formerly Pink Dawn (seedling
no. 1-34), S. Pink. E. to M.
AV.

DAY DREAM (R. W. Auten,
1939), J. Pink and yellow.
Albiflora variety.

DAYLIGHT (Risk, 1929), J.
White. M. AV.

DEARBORN (E. Auten, Jr., 1929),
SD. Rose type. Dark red. LM.
AV.

DEEDIE MAY (Vories, 1927), D.
White with crimson thread-
line on edges of center petals.
E. T.

DEER CREEK see MID-
AMERICA.

DEFENDER (Saunders, 1929), S.
Dark mahogany crimson. M.
to L. AV. Sinensis x officinalis

DELIGHT (H. P. Sass, 1937), J.
Apple blossom pink

DELPHI (Saunders, 1929), D.
Bright dark crimson. E. Officinalis x sinensis

DENISE (Lemoine, 1924), D. Soft
flesh white center flecked
crimson. Fragrant. LM. AV.

DEPARTING SUN (origin un-
known), J. Dark rose pink,
touched with lilac at tips and
edges. Slightly fragrant.
M. AV.

DESIRE (Brand, 1923), D. Soft
rose-pink. Suggestion of lilac.
M. DW.

DIADEM (Franklin, 1931), Dark
pink. Cup-shape. Fragrant.
L. AV. D.

DIANA (Sass, 1930), D. Pure
white. L. T.

DIANA PARKS (Bockstoce, 1942),
S. Carmine red. Fragrant. T.
Officinalis x chinensis

DIEPPE (Keagey, 1946), D. Pale
lavender pink. LM. AV.

DIEUDONNE (Brethour, 1936),
Pink and white. T.

DIXIE (Franklin, 1931), Bomb
type. Dark red. L. AV.

DOLLY VARDEN (Brethour,
1937), J. Violet pink. T.

DOLORODELL (Lins, 1942)
(seedling no. R-4-49), D.
Pink. LM. AV.

DONALD (E. F. Kelsey, 1936), D.
Rose pink. T. LM.

DONNA BERKLEY (H. P. Sass,
1942), Rose type. White. L.
AV.

DOREEN (Henry E. Sass, 1949)
(seedling no. 35-94), J. Pink.
M. AV.

DORIS (Shaylor, 1920), D. Fresh
pink. M. AV.

DORIS COOPER (Cooper, 1946),
(seedling 35), D. Pink. L. T.

DOROTHY J. (R. H. Jones, 1938),
D. Rose type. Blush white.
L. T.

DOUGLAS MacARTHUR see
GENERAL DOUGLAS
MacARTHUR.

DRAGON'S NEST (E. Auten, Jr.,
1933), J. Bright red guards.
Bright yellow collar. Tuft red
petals in center. M. AV.

DRESDEN PINK (Wild and Son,
1957), D. Pink. L.

DRESS PARADE (Auten, 1937),
J. Light red. E.

DR. F. G. BRETHOUR (H P.
Sass, 1938), Rose type. White.
L. T.

DR. H. BARNSBY (Dessert, 1913),
D. Globular. Dark old-rose,
bordering on magenta. Fairly
fragrant. L. Not sold in
U.S.A.

DR. H. VAN DER TAK (Nieuwenhuyzen, 1916), D. Crimson, lighter sheen on incurved tips. EM. Not sold in U.S.A.

DR. JEKYLL (E. Auten, Jr., 1936), J. Often with SD blooms. Dark red. L.

DUCHESSE DE NEMOURS (Calot, 1856), D. Cupped white guards. Center light canary yellow. E. AV.

DUCHESS OF SUTHERLAND (Kelway, 1929), S. Pure white. Not sold in U. S. A.

DULUTH (Franklin, 1931), Rose type. Pure white. L. AV.

DUNKIRK (Keagey, 1946), D. Pink. T.

DUNLORA (Leyton, 1943), S. White. E. AV.

E

EAU CLAIRE (Dana, 1926), S. Pink. X.

ECSTASY (Brethour, 1926). D. Large flower. White with yellow tone at base of petals. M. T.

ECSTASY (Nieuwenhiuzen, 1935), J. Pink. M.

EDGAR JESSEP (Bockstoce, 1958), D. Brilliant red. E. AV. Officinalis x albiflora

EDITH M. SNOOK (Snook, 1931), Rose type. Soft ivory, tinted coffee brown. Fragrant. L. AV.

EDITH R. STONE (Webb, 1958), SD. Pale pink. T.

EDMOND ABOUT (Crousse, 1885). D. Shell pink with rose tints. Fragrant. LM. AV. Not sold in U.S.A.

EDMOND LEBON (Calot, 1864), D. Dark pink becoming silvery with age at center. M. DW. Not sold in U.S.A.

EDNA (Winchell, 1941) (no. 3C), Light pink. Fragrant. M.

EDULIS SUPERBA (Lemon, 1824), D. Bright old rose pink. Very fragrant. Very E. T.

EDWARD (Lyman, 1939), S. Black-red. X.

EDWARD W. BECKER (Franklin, 1920), SD. Light pink shading to white. Fragrant. M. AV.

EDWIN C. SHAW (Thurlow, 1919), D. Light old rose with flesh pink tones in center and collar. Fragrant. LM. AV.

EEPLES (Guppy, 1922), D. Bright red. Albiflora single x officinalis rubra plena

EEWEE (Guppy, 1932), S. Deep red. T. Albiflora single x officinalis rubra plena. X.

E. G. KENDALL (Nicholls-Wild & Son, 1959), D. Pink. M.

EGLANTINE (Dessert, 1913), S. Flesh pink paling to white. M. AV. Not sold in U.S.A.

EGYPT (Risk, 1929), S. Dark red. E. AV. X.

EGYPTIAN (Brant, 1941), Jap. effect. Rich maroon. Someganoko seed

E. J. SHAYLOR (Shaylor, 1918), D. Dark rose-pink, petals tipped lilac. Globular form. Rose fragrance. LM. AV. X.

EL CAPITAN (Auten, 1937), SD. Light red. LM.

ELEANOR (Winchell, 1946), D. Bomb type. Deep old rose. Fragrant. M.

ELEANOR DANA (W. A. Dana, 1926), Bomb type. Silvery salmon pink. X.

ELFIN PINK (Auten, 1937), S. Pink. E.

ELISA (Dessert-Doriat, 1922), SD. Cup-shaped flower. Carmine-hydrangea pink shaded silvery salmon. AV. M.

ELISE (W. A. Dana, 1926), Rose type. Light clear pink. Fragrant. X.

ELIZABETH BARRETT
BROWNING (Brand, 1907),
D. Creamy blush paling white.
Red marks in center and on
outer petals. Very fragrant.
L. T. X.

ELIZABETH HUNTINGTON
(Sass, 1930), D. Pale pink.
E. T.

ELIZABETH PRICE (Nicholls-
Wild and Son, 1957) seedling
No. 892. D. Pink. LM.

ELLA CHRISTIANSEN (Brand,
1925) D. Medium pink.
Fragrant. M. T.

ELLA CHRISTINE KELWAY
(Kelway, 1899), D. Lavender
flesh color. X.

ELLA WINCHELL (Winchell,
1941), nc 32A. D. Albiflora.
Red. M.

ELLENWILDER (Guppy, 1926),
S. Salmon. Albiflora single x
officinalis rubra plena. X.

ELMER J. WRIGHT (E. Auten,
Jr. 1929), S. Dark red. T.

ELNA (H P. Sass, 1941), D. Rose
type. Bright pink. M. T.

ELOISE (E Auten, Jr., 1934), D
Cr. pink. L. T.

ELSA SASS (Sass, 1930), D.
White. L. AV.

ELVINA (Krekler, 1958), J. Pink.
M. T.

ELWOOD PLEAS (Pleas, 1900),
D. Pale rose pink. Light flesh
pink centers. L. AV. X.

EMALINE (Mrs. W. Wolfe,
1931), Pink. Fragrant. M. T.

EMILE HOSTE (Origin doubtful)
Rated much too high and
suppressed by unanimous
vote of the Directors of the
American Peony Society,
January 1928.

EMILY D. PROCTOR (Freeborn,
1947), J. Old rose. E. AV.

EMMA KLEHM (Klehm, 1951),
DW. Seedling no. 690. D.
Pink. L.

EMPRESS OF BRITAIN (Norton,
1931), D. White. L.

ENCHANTERESSE (Lemoine,
1903), D. White with lemon
tints. Slightly fragrant. Very
L. T.

ENCHANTMENT (Hollis, 1907),
D. Old rose with shell pink
at center. Fragrant. M. AV.

ENGLISH ELEGANCE (Kelway,
1929), S. Flesh pink.

ENTICING (Hruby, 1955), seedling no. 06-C. D. Light pink.
L.

ERIC THE RED (James Pillow,
1923), Dark red. S. X.

EROS (Glasscock, 1940), S.
Salmon pink. E. No. B.5 x
off. Sunbeam.

ESTELLE (Mrs. W. C. Lyman)
S. Pink. X.

ESTHER MITTENDORFF
(Lanigan, 1944), D. Light
rose pink. Mildly fragrant.
M. T. X.

E. ST. HILL (Kelway, 1929), S.
Deep rose pink. E. T.
Not sold in U.S.A.

ETHEL HALSEY (Hans P. Sass,
1952), seedling no. 13-27. D.
Pink. M. T.

ETHEL MARS see MARS.

ETHEREAL (R. H. Jones, 1938),
Rose type. Blush pink. Very
fragrant. T. L.

ETIENNE BRULE (Brethour,
1934), D. Similar to Solange,
white with pink and yellow
tints. L. AV. Cut almost never
opens. X. May be obtainable
in Canada.

ETTA (Terry, 1904), D. Old rose
pink with flesh pink center.
Rose fragrance. L. AV.

EUGENE BIGOT (Dessert, 1894), D. Crimson with violet tinge with silvery tips. Slight fragrance. L. AV.

EUGENIE VERDIER (Calot, 1864), D. Rose pink with crimson near center. DW. L. X. Not a good variety. T.

EUNICE SHAYLOR (Shaylor, 1919), D. Outer petals cupped and wavy. Rosy flesh flushed with rose toward base. Tea rose fragrance. M. AV.

EUPHEMIA (Terry, 1910), Much overated and suppressed by vote of the Directors. X.

EVANGELINE (Lemoine, 1910), D. Dark but bright rose pink. Crimson edges on center petals. Rose fragrance. L. AV.

EVELYN BUECHLY (Buechly, 1923), SD Light pink. AV. X.

EVELYN CLAAR (Glasscock, 1946), D. Cerise. E. AV. Officinalis x sinensis.

EVENING GLOW (Hollis, 1907), SD. Light shell pink, paling to white and old rose. E. T.

EVENING STAR (H. P. Sass, 1937), D. White with crimson edges occasionally. L.

EVENTIDE (Glasscock, 1945), S. Pink. E. T. Officinalis x albiflora.

EVERETT (Simpson, 1929), Crown type. Pink. M. to L. AV. X.

EXCELSA (Franklin, 1931), Rose type. Light pink. L. T.

EXELEE (Krekler, 1958) D. White with pale yellow and and pink petaloids. L. AP.

EXOTIC (E. F. Kelsey, 1940), SD. Deep pink.

EXQUISITE (Kelway, 1912), D. Bright rose pink, paling towards tips of petals. M. AV.

F

FAIR ELAINE (F. W. Auten, 1939), albiflora variety. J. Pink and yellow.

FAIRLEIGH (Brown, 1938), D. Blush Pink. Fragrant. M. T.

FAIRY DANCE (E. Auten, Jr. 1931), S. Pink. E. T.

FAIRY DREAM (Nicholls-Wild and Son, 1959), D. White, tapering to pink. L.

FAIRY PINK (A. B. Franklin, 1939), J. Light pink. M. AV.

FAIRY PRINCESS (Glasscock-Falk, 1955), seedling no. 816. S. Red. E. DW.

FAIRY QUEEN (E. Auten, Jr. 1931), S. Pink. AV. E.

FAITH (Saunders, 1929), D. or S.D. Light rose pink. Season of officinalis. AV. Otto Froebel x sinensis.

FALAISE (Keagey, 1946), This name reserved for future use.

FAMIE (Saunders-Krekler, 1955), D. White. E. Hybrid.

FANNIE HEATH (Cooper, 1946), AV. Seedling no. 1. SD. White. M.

FANNY LEE (Vories, 1924), American Beauty red. M.

FANTASIA (Lyman, 1939), J X. Pale pink. L. Name changed to Capriccio.

FANTASY (Auten, 1925), A. Outer petals deep pink, center yellow. Slight fragrance.

FASCINATION (Brethour, 1936), Rose type. White. Fragrant. T.

FELICIA (Gardner, before 1951), S. Deep pink. M. AV.

FELIX CROUSSE (Crousse, 1881), D. Crimson. LM. AV.

FELIX SUPREME (Kriek, 1955), seedling no. 6. D. Red. M. AV.

FESTIVA (Donkelaer, 1838), D.
LM. DW. White. Much over
rated and suppressed by vote
of the Directors. X.

FESTIVA MAXIMA (Miellez,
1851), D. Globular. White
with prominent crimson
flakes. Fairly fragrant. E. T.

FINE LADY (Kelway, 1909) S.
Cup shape. Blush white.

FIRE CHIEF (Auten, 1934),
Novelty J. Deep red and
yellow.

FIRELIGHT (Brant, 1931), S.
Red. L.

FIREPLACE (E. F. Kelsey, 1940),
D. Mahogany red. EM.

FLAMBOYANT (Origin
unknown)
Correct name Kameno-
kegoromo. J. Dark rose-red or
light crimson. M. T.

FLAME (Glasscock, 1939), S.
Red. E. Chinensis x officinalis
Sunbeam.

FLASH (Glasscock, 1950), S.
Bright red. E. AV. Albiflora
x Sunbeam off.

FLASHLIGHT (Hollis, 1906), J.
Dark rosy red. Pinkish staminodes tipped bright yellow
creates terra-cotta effect to
center of bloom. M. AV.

FLORENCE BRUSS (Franklin,
1953), seedling no. X474. S.
Dark red. LM. AV.

FLORENCE ELLIS (Nicholls,
1948), D. Pink. M. T. Marie
Crousse x Lady Alexandra
Duff.

FLORENCE MACBETH (Sass,
1924), D. Pale shell pink,
deepening toward center.
Slightly fragrant. LM. AV.

FLORENCE NICHOLLS
(Nicholls, 1938), D. Blush
white with a scarlet suffusion.
Very fragrant. EM. AV.

Seedling No. 1 from Mme.
Calot.

FLORIZELL (Brant, 1941), J. Soft
rose. Mikado is seed parent.

FLOWER GIRL (Auten, 1935),
D. Blush, fading to white.
Rose fragrant. DW.

FLOWER OF CHIVALRY
(Kelway, 1928), SD. Rosy
pink. Not sold in U.S.A.

FLOW'RET OF EDEN (Neeley,
1919), D. Light rose pink,
shading to flesh pink at center. EM. AV.

FORTUNE TELLER (E. Auten,
Jr., 1936), S. Light red.

FRAICHEUR (Lemoine, 1914),
D. Pale flesh white with salmon
undertone. Mildly fragrant.
LM. AV. Not sold in U.S.A.

FRANCES MAINS (Mains, 1955),
seedling no. H-3. D. Light
pink. M. AV.

FRANCES SHAYLOR (Shaylor,
1916), D. White. Sometimes
flushed with pink on opening.
Fragrant. M. DW.

FRANCES WILLARD (Brand,
1907), D. Opens pale pink
changing to white with yellow suffusion in collar. Bears
few red lines in center.
Mildly fragrant. LM. T.

FRANCOIS ROUSSEAU (Dessert,
1909), D. Rich crimson.
Fragrant. E. AV. Not sold in
U.S.A.

FRANK E. GOOD (Good & Reese,
1929), Semi-rose type. Flesh
pink. L. T.

FRANKIE CURTIS (Vories, 1924),
D. Delicate flesh changing to
pure white. M. AV.

FRANKLIN'S PRIDE (Franklin,
1931), Rose type. Pink.
Fragrant. L. T.

FRECKLES (Neeley, 1926), Full
rose type. Flesh pink. M.

FRIEND HARRY (Smith-Krekler, 1954), D. Dark red. M. AV.

FRIENDSHIP (Glasscock-Falk, 1955), seedling no. A1-A101. S. Pink. E. AV.

FRONTIER (E F. Kelsey, 1940), D. Pink. L.

FURNACE (W. J. Guille, 1951), D. Red. L. AV.

FURY (Bigger, 1955), seedling no. 9-47. D. Red. M. T.

FUYAJO (Origin unknown. Reg. before 1926), J. Dark purplish crimson. Slightly fragrant. M. T.

G

GAIETY (H. P. Sass, 1937), J. Bright red. L.

GALATHEE (Lemoine, 1900), D. Flesh with pink center. Very fragrant. Very L. T.

GARDEN SENTINEL (Freeborn, 1943), D. Brilliant pink. VE. AV.
Officinalis rubra x Madame Jules Dessert.

GARNET BEAUTY (B. B. Wright, 1935), S. Dark red. EM. to LM. T.

GAYBORDER JUNE (Hoogendoorn, 1949), D. Fuchsine rose. E. AV.

GAY PAREE (E. Auten, Jr., 1933), A. J. Guards deep cerise, center, flushing to white. M. AV.

GEISHA (Sass, 1930), seedling of MIKADO. J. Light pink.

GEISHA GIRL (Richmond, 1952), seedling no. 52-323. J. Rose pink. M. AV.

GENERAL DOUGLAS MacARTHUR (Rosefield, 1942), Semi-rose type. Pink. T. M. General now dropped.

GENERAL GORGAS (Van Leeuwen, 1924), SD. White with rose pink center. Guard petals streaked with red. Fragrant. M. AV.

GENE STRATTON PORTER (Rosefield, 1925), D. White. T. L.

GENE WILD (Cooper, 1956), seedling no. Cooper 6. D. Pink. M.

GEORGE J. NICHOLLS (Nicholls, 1948), D. White. L. T. Marie Crousse x Lady Alexandra Duff.

GEORGE W. PEYTON (Nicholls, 1938), seedling no. 2 from Lady Duff. D. Buff suffused with pink. M. AV. Slightly fragrant.

GEORGIANA SHAYLOR (Shaylor, 1908), D. Light rose pink, paler on backs of petals. Vivid crimson marks on ring of short center petals. Sweet fragrance. LM. AV.

GERMAINE BIGOT (Dessert, 1902), D. Light rose pink. M. AV.

GERTRUDE COX (Krekler, 1958), D. Light pink. LM. AV.

GERTRUDE GIBSON (Reno Rosefield, 1939), Rose type. White. AV. L.

GIANT JAP see JAP. GIANT.

GIGANTEA (Calot, 1860), (original name was Lamartine). D. Rose pink fading to light old rose with silver tipped petals. Fragrant. EM. T.

GILBERT H. WILD (Nicholls-Wild & Son, 1957), seedling No. 392. D. Rose pink. LM.

GINETTE (Dessert, 1915), D. Pale pink with faint old rose shading and crimson marks. Mildly fragrant. LM. DW.

GINNY (Freeborn, 1947), D.
Brilliant red. E. AV. Hybrid.

GISMONDA (Crousse, 1895), D.
Pale creamy pink with rose
pink center. Rose fragrance.
Very L. T. X.

GLAMOUR (Jones, 1957), J. Rose
pink. M.

GLEAM OF GOLD (H. P. Sass,
1937), White with a broad
yellow collar. LM. AV.

GLOBE OF LIGHT (Kelway,
1928), A. Silvery rose.

GLORY OF LANGPORT
(Kelway, 1929), D. Rosy pink.
Not sold in U.S.A.

GLORY OF THE GARDEN
(Toedt, 1929), S. Dark red. X.

GOBLIN (E. Auten Jr., 1931),
J. Bright red. T.

GOLDEN ARROW (Nicholls,
1941), J. Deep red. Number
173 from Mikado. AV. M.

GOLDEN DAWN (Gumm,
1923), A. High yellowish center with guard petals of ivory
white. Fragrant. M.

GOLDEN DREAM see
ORIENTAL GOLD

GOLDEN GLOW (Glasscock,
1935), S. Scarlet red with
orange tint. E. Chinensis x
officinalis Otto Froebel.

GOLDEN LIGHT (Murawska,
1944), J. White. L. T.

GOLDEN SUN (Rosenfield, 1934),
J. Rose pink. AV. L.

GOLD MINE (Hollis, 1907), J.
Dark rose pink. M. AV.

GOLD STANDARD (Rosenfield,
1934), J. White tinted yellow.
T. M.

GOPHER BEAUTY (Franklin,
1933), S. Red. (Seedling no.
R-300, selected 1926.) M. AV.

GRACE BATSON (Sass, 1927), D.
Medium pink. M. to L.

GRACE GEDGE (Kelsey, 1934),
D. Cream white. LM. AV.

GRACE KELSEY (Kelsey, 1940),
D. Pink. M. AV.

GRACE LEWIS (Lewis, 1922), D.
Deep blush, lighter toward
center. Fragrant. M. T. X.

GRACE LOOMIS (Saunders,
1920), D. White with faint
lemon tints in depths of
petals. Mildly fragrant. L.
AV.

GRACE OTT (Gumm, 1923), D.
Brilliant dark crimson. M. T.

GRACE WILLE (Claar, 1955), S.
Pink. E. AV. Albiflora x
lobata

GRADUATION DAY (E. Auten,
Jr., 1939), S. White. Albiflora
var.

GRAND MASTER (Rosenfield,
1934), Rose type. Dark red.
E. AV.

GRANDIFLORA (Richardson,
1883), D. Bright pink shaded
old rose and white. Fragrant.
VL. T.

GRANDIFLORA NIVEA PLENA
(Lemon, 1824), D. Rose type
guards faintly pink fading to
white with prominent red
marks. Sweetly fragrant. VE.
T.

GREER GARSON (Payne, 1945),
D. Pale rosaline purple. Fragrant. LM. AV.

GROVER CLEVELAND (Terry,
1904), D. Bright crimson.
Mildly fragrant. LM. AV.

GUIDON (Nicholls, 1941), D.
Rose type. Rose pink. AV. M.
(Number 5 from Othello.)

GYPSY (Hollis, 1904), J. Guards
dark wine red and cupped.
Petalodes light at base, shading to dark wine red and
creamy white on reverse.
Bordered buff tips. M. AV.

GYPSY ROSE (Franklin, 1939), J.
Rose pink. M. AV.

H

HABANERA (E. Auten, Jr., 1930),
S. Light red. E. T.

H. A. HAGEN (Richardson,
1904), D. Globular. Dark rose
pink. L. AV.

HANSINA BRAND (Brand, 1925),
D. Dark flesh pink shading
darker at base of petals with
a salmon glow. L. AV.

HANS P. SASS (H. P. Sass, 1937),
Blush white, suffused shell
pink. L. AV.

HARBINGER (Saunders, 1929), S.
Pink. E. AV. Otto Froebel x
macrophylla

HARDY GIANT (Freeborn, 1943),
D. Pink. L. T. Officinalis
rubra x Madame Jules Dessert

HARGROVE HUDSON (Wild and
Son, 1949), D. Pink. EM. AV.

HARMON (Smith-Krekler, 1957),
no description. Name never
used.

HARMONY (R. H. Jones, 1938),
Pale rose darker at center.
L. T. X.

HARRIET CORY (Lyman, 1940),
A. J. Deep rose. Fragrant. X.

HARRIET OLNEY (Brand, 1920),
S. Soft rose color. M. AV.

HARRY A. NORTON (Norton,
1939), D. Dark crimson. L.
AV. X.

HARRY F. LITTLE (Nicholls,
1933), Rose type. White. L.
AV.

HARRY L. RICHARDSON
(Rosenfield, 1925), D. Bright
red. Fragrant. VL. AV.

HARRY L. SMITH (Smith-
Krekler, 1953), D. Dark red.
LM. Note: Taller and later
than Monsieur Martin
Cahuzac

HARVARD CRIMSON (Smith,
1928), SD. Crimson. M. X.

HAZEL KINNEY (Brand, 1925),

D. Light flesh pink. M. AV.

HEART OF KNOX (Auten, Jr.,
1939), J. Red. T. Albiflora
var. M. X.

HELEN (Thurlow, 1922), S. Dark
shell pink. E. T.

HELEN DANCER (Dancer, 1935),
S. Cream pink or rose cafe
au-lait. Blooms earlier than
tenuifolia. AV. Parentage
uncertain.

HELEN HAYES (Murawska,
1943), D. Dark pink. L. T.

HELEN MATTHEWS (Saunders-
Krekler, 1953), SD. Brilliant
red. E. AV. Hybrid.

HELEN OF TROY (Pillow, 1923),
S. Light red. X.

HELEN SEARS (Smith-Krekler,
1954), J. Light pink. M. T.

HENNEPIN (Auten, Jr., 1931), S.
Black red. AV. E.

HENRIETTE CLARKE (Mac-
Donald, 1948), D. White
with scarlet splashes. M. AV.

HENRI POTIN (Doriat, 1924), J.
Deep pink tinted carmine filament petals gradually turning
white and vivid yellow at tips.

HENRY AVERY (Brand, 1907),
D. Light pink mixed with
shades of yellow and cream.
Mildly fragrant. L. AV.

HENRY BOCKSTOCE (Bock-
stoce, 1955), D. Dark red.
E. T. Hybrid.

HENRY M. VORIES (Vories,
1924), D. Light pink darker
towards center. L. AV.

HENRY SWINDEN (Swinden,
1941), J. Dark red. M. to L. T.

HERMIONE (Sass, 1932), D.
Pink. L. T.

HIAWATHA (Franklin, 1931), D.
Rose type. Dark red. L. AV.

HIGH JINKS (Auten, Jr., 1929),
A. J. Cerise red. L. T. X.

HIGHLAND LASSIE (Toedt,
1929), S. Center of petals

pink, crimson edges, rolled
and widely ruffled. X.

HIGHLIGHT (Auten-Wild, 1952)
seedling no. 930), D. Red.
LM. AV.

HIS MAJESTY (Kelway, 1929), D.
Maroon crimson surrounding
scarlet central petals.

HOARY (Krekler, 1958), D. White.
LM. T.

HOLLYWOOD (Auten, 1937), J.
Cerise pink. L. AV. X.

HONEYSWEET (A. B. Franklin,
1933) (seedling no. D-103,
selected 1923), Rose type.
White. T. X.

HOPE (Saunders, 1929), SD. Pink
between salmon and cherry.
VE. Otto Froebel x sinensis

HOTTENTOT (Dana, 1926), SD.
Lilac and pink combined with
stamens of various shades. X.

HOWARD R. WATKINS (Bock-
stoce, 1947), D. Red. VE. AV.
Officinalis x chinensis

HUMORESQUE (Auten, 1925), D.
Light pink with unusual
markings of red. X.

I

IDEAL (Franklin, 1931). Rose
type. Dark pink. L. AV.

ILLINI (E. Auten, Jr., 1931), S.
Black red. T. X.

ILLINI BELLE (Glasscock, 1941),
SD. Dark red. VE. AV.
Chinensis x officinalis.

ILLINI WARRIOR (Glasscock-
Falk, 1955) (seedling no.
A1A1), S. Red. E. T.

IMPERIAL PINK (Sass), S. Dark
pink. T. E. Name changed to
Imperial Red, effect is light
red.

IMPERIAL RED
see IMPERIAL PINK

INCA (Nicholls, 1941), S. Scarlet

rose. T. Number 201 from
Mikado. E.

INCA DEITY (McMurray, 1937),
SD. White. E. AV.

INDIANA MOON (Rosenfield,
1933), Bomb type. Pink. T.
AV.

INDIAN HILL (Glasscock, 1950),
D. Black red. E. AV. Otto
Froebel x albiflora

INDIAN MAID (Dana, 1926).
Deep mahogany red. Frag-
rant. M. to L. X.

IN MEMORIAM (Brethour, 1929).
Flesh pink, often a wide ring
of red surrounding the center.
M. Large flower.

INNOCENCE (Hollis, 1904), J.
Light old rose guards. Center
canary yellow fading to
creamy white. LM. T.

INSPECTEUR LAVERGNE
(Doriat, 1924), D. Globular.
Crimson. M. to LM. T.

IROQUOIS (E Auten, Jr., 1931),
J. Dark red. X.

IRVING FLINT (E. F. Kelsey,
1940), D. Rose pink. Fragrant. M.

ISANI GIDUI (Origin unknown),
J. Guard petals pure white.
Center buff-yellow. M. AV.

ISOLINE (Lemoine, 1916), A.
Guards cuplike, cream white
fading lighter. Center tuft
canary-yellow fading almost
white. M. AV.

IWO (Nicholls, 1946). Rose-red.
AV.

J

JACOB STYER (Styer, 1948), D.
White. L. T.

JACQUELINE HANRATTY
(Gardner, before 1951), D.
Red. E.

JAMES BOYD (Thurlow, 1919),

D. Flesh pink. Buff center. very fragrant. L. AV.

JAMES KELWAY (Kelway, 1900), D. Pale pink, paling white. EM. T.

JAMES R. MANN (Thurlow, 1920), D. Rose-type. Dark rose pink. Crimson streaks in center and on outside guards sometimes noted. M. AV.

JAMES WILLIAM KELWAY (Kelway, 1929), SD. Deep purple rose. LM. AV.

JANES OLESON (Oleson, 1926), D. Red. VL. T.

JANET (Auten, 1940), D. Cerise red. T. Off. hyb. E.

JAPANESE BEAUTY (H. P. Sass, 1937). Carmine red. LM. T.

JAPANESE FAIRY (Secor, 1924), S. Pink with yellow center. M. X.

JAP. GIANT (Franklin, 1933), J. Rose pink. T. Seedling no. J-119, selected 1926. M. Often listed as Giant Jap.

J. BEENEY (Nicholls-Wild and Son, 1957) (seedling no. 1374), D. White. Fragrant. LM.

J. BOY (Jones, 1957), D. Bright pink. M.

J. C. LEGG (Wild, 1950), D. White and yellow. M. T.

J. C. NICHOLLS (Nicholls, 1948), D. White. EM. T. Marie Crousse x Spring Beauty

JEAN A. (Alexander, 1955), D. Light pink. LM. AV.

JEAN BRUCE (Chesher, 1941). Delicate pink. Fragrant. D. M. X.

JEAN COOPER (Cooper, 1946) (seedling no. 102), D. White. Very fragrant.

JEAN HARLOW (B. B. Wright, 1938). Pure white. EM. T.

JEANNE GAUDICHAU (Millet,

1902), D. Pale pink paling to white. Crimson edges in center. L. AV. Not sold in U.S.A.

JEANNOT (Dessert, 1918), D. Rose form. Pale rose pink. Old rose center. Overcast of pale violet. Faintly fragrant. L. AV.

JESSIE GIST (Nicholls-Wild and Son, 1953), D. Pink. EM. AV. Marie Crousse x Spring Beauty

JESSIE SHAYLOR (Shaylor, 1916), D. Blush white, darker outside with suffusion of yellow. Slightly fragrant. M. AV.

JEWEL (Glasscock, 1927), S. Red. E. AV. Officinalis hybrid.

J. N. DARLING (Reno Rosefield, 1939). Semi-rose type. Bright pink. T.

JOCELYN (Lemoine, 1923), D. Cup shape. Waved outer petals rose pink. Mildly fragrant. M. AV. Not sold in U.S.A.

JOEHANNA (Mrs. W. Wolfe, 1931). Rose type. Pink, tinged with lavender. X.

JOE HANRATTY (Gardner, before 1951), D. Deep pink. LM. T.

JOHANNA (Mrs. Wm. Karth, 1941), D. Soft rose ivory. LM. Name changed to Mary Jo.

JOHN ALDEN (W. A. Dana, 1926), Rose type. Rose pink. Fragrant. L. T. X.

JOHN GARDNER (Gardner, before 1951), J. Bright red. LM. AV.

JOHN HARVARD (E. Auten, Jr., 1939), S. Dark red. E. T. Officinalis hybrid

JOHN HOWARD WIGELL (H. E. Wigell, 1942), Rose type. Deep pink. EM. AV.

JOHN M. GOOD (Welsh, 1921), D. Outer petals pale pink shading to ivory white center — sometimes pure white. Yellow tint in depth of flower. Very fragrant. LM. T.

JOHN M. LEWIS (Lewis, 1921), D. Rose pink. Center flesh pink. Mild fragrance. LM. X.

JOHN RICHARDSON (Richardson, 1904), D. Flesh pink. Darker center. Pale tips. Fragrant. L. T. X.

JOHN SAYLOR (Krekler, 1958), S. Dark red. M. AV.

JOHN STARK (Freeborn, 1953), S. Deep crimson. E. T. Nippon Beauty x unknown

JOSEPH CHRISTIE (Rosefield, 1939), Rose type. White. AV. L.

JOSEPHELUS (Guppy), D. Bright red. X.

JOSETTE (Brethour, 1937), S. Pink with white centers. AV. E.

JOY (Saunders, 1928), S. Rose pink. T. Sinensis (Venus) x Otto Froebel. X.

JOYCE (Auten, 1938), D. Pink. L. AV.

JUBILEE (Pleas, 1908), D. White with greenish tinge. M. T.

JUDGE BERRY (Brand, 1907), D. Light rose pink of delicate shade. Slight fragrance. E. AV.

JUDGE ORR (Edlund, 1929), Pink. M. X.

JUDY BECKER (H. P. Sass, 1941), D. Rose type. Dark red. M. to L. AV.

JULIA (Auten, 1926), D. Pink. L. X.

JULIA (Glasscock, 1927), D. Pale pink. L. X.

JUNE BRIDE (Glasscock, 1939), Rose type. White. Fragrant. L. T.

JUNE BRILLIANT (Auten, 1938), D. Dark red. T. L.

JUNE DAY (Franklin, 1920), D. Light old rose pink. White outer petals. Crimson line in center of flower. Sweet fragrance. M. AV.

JUNE MOON (E. Auten, Jr., 1931), S. White. L. AV.

JUNE ROSE (R. H. Jones, 1938), D. Deep rose. E. AV.

JUNE WELCOME (Dana, 1926), S. Dark red. Yellow stamens. X.

K

KAHOKIA (E. Auten, Jr., 1931), S. Almost black. AV. E. X.

KAMENO-KEGOROMO see FLAMBOYANT

KANKAKEE (Auten, Jr., 1931), S. Dark red. L. AV.

KANSAS (Bigger, 1940), D. Red. AV. M.

KARL ROSENFIELD (Rosenfield, 1908), D. Bright crimson. M. T.

KASKASKIA (E. Auten, Jr., 1931), S. Dark red. E. DW.

KATE BARRY (Nicholls, 1938), D. Salmon pink. M. T. Seedling no. 214 from Ama-no-sode.

KATHALO (Kelsey, 1940), J. Pink-yellow. M. AV.

KATHARINE HAVEMEYER (Thurlow, 1921), D. Light rose-pink. Tinge of old rose. Mild rose fragrance. M. AV.

KATHRYN E. MANUEL (Phillips, 1953), S. Blush. E. AV.

KATE SMITH (Murawska, 1950), D. Dark pink. Fragrant. LM. AV. Seedling no. 53

KAW VALLEY (Bigger, 1944), D. Dark red. M. AV.

KELWAY'S BEAUTIFUL (Kelway, 1929), D. Silvery lavender. X.

KELWAY'S CRIMSON BANNER (Kelway, 1929), D. Dark red.

KELWAY'S FAIRY QUEEN (Kelway, 1928), SD. Pink. Fragrant. DW. Not sold in U.S.A.

KELWAY'S GLORIOUS (Kelway, 1909), D. White, creamy suffusion in depths. Crimson on outside of guard petals, faint crimson edges in center. Strong rose fragrance. M. AV.

KELWAY'S GLORY OF JUNE (Kelway, 1928), SD. Pink. DW. Not sold in U.S.A.

KELWAY'S GORGEOUS (Kelway, 1929), S. Salmon rose. Not sold in U.S.A.

KELWAY'S LOVELY (Kelway, 1929), D. Light rosy red. Not sold in U.S.A.

KELWAY'S MAJESTIC (Kelway, 1929). J. Carmine. E. Not sold in U.S.A.

KELWAY'S PEACE (Kelway, 1929), D. Creamy white, almost a yellow tint. Not sold in U.S.A.

KELWAY'S PEERLESS (Kelway, 1928), S. Deep pink with large gold center. T. Not sold in U.S.A.

KELWAY'S QUEEN (Kelway, 1909), D. Bright rose pink, few red flakes. Strong rose fragrance. LM. AV.

KELWAY'S ROSE OF DELIGHT (Kelway, 1929), S. Rose pink. L. Not sold in U.S.A.

KELWAY'S UNIQUE (Kelway, 1917), D. Pink with golden petaloids. Not sold in U.S.A.

KEMANKEAG (Guppy, 1935), S. White. X.

KENDUSKEAG (Guppy, 1935), S. Light pink. X.

KEWANEE (E. Auten, Jr., 1930), S. Dark red. Long blooming season. E. AV.

KICKAPOO (E. Auten, Jr., 1931), S. Dark red. L. AV.

KILLINGTON (Freeborn, 1934), D. White. Tea-rose fragrance. L. AV. X.

KING (Krekler, 1958), D. Deep pink. LM. AV.

KING ALBERT (Kelway, 1929), S. Rosy violet.

KING BEE (B. B. Wright, 1935), D. Bomb type. Dark red. M. to LM. AV.

KING BOREAS (Wilkus, 1948) (seedling no. 1), D. White. LM. T.

KING GUSTAV (Rosenfield, 1934), Semi-rose type. Maroon. E. T.

KING MIDAS (Lins, 1942), D. Red. AV. M.

KING OF ENGLAND (Kelway, 1902), J. Dark red center. Buff staminodes streaked with dark rose-pink. EM. T.

KINNEY (Winchell, 1941) D. (no. K.2.A.). Red. M. D.

KINO-KIMO (Origin unknown), J. Dark rose pink petals. M. AV.

KIOWA (E. Auten, Jr., 1931), S. Light red. E. X.

KISSIMMEE (Jones, 1957), J. Rose. M.

KLONDIKE (Franklin, 1939), J. White. M. T.

KUKENI JISHI (Origin unknown), J. Delicate pink guard petals have pale rose shading on outside. Fragrant. E. M.

KURI (Jones, 1957), J. Rose. M. L.

L

LA CANADIENNE (Brethour, 1936), White. L. T. X. Note: form resembles Kelway's Glorious.

LADDIE (Glasscock, 1941), S. Bright red. E. DW. Officinalis Otto Froebel x tenuifolia

LADY ALEXANDRA DUFF

(Kelway, 1902), D. Pale
blush pink, almost white.
Slight fragrance. M. AV.

LADY BERESFORD (Kelway,
1893), A. Guards bright rose
pink. Creamy white petaloids,
edged crimson. Sweetly fragrant. M. X.

LADY EMILY (Pleas, 1907), D.
Light rose pink, deep fringed
shaggy flower. Fragrant. M.
AV. X.

LADY KATE (Vories, 1924), D.
Solid light pink. L. T.

LADY OF THE WEST (Kelway,
1912), D. Soft rose and
creamy white. Light center.
Not sold in U.S.A.

LADY ORCHID (Bigger, 1942),
D. Lavender pink. LM. AV.

LA FEE (Lemoine, 1906), D.
Light old rose pink. Creamy
pink collar. Rose fragrance.
EM. T.

LA FIANCEE (Dessert, 1902).
Considered same as THE
BRIDE, which see.

LA FONTAINE (Lemoine, 1904),
D. Light old rose pink with
pale violet tone. Notably fragrant. LM. T. X.

LA FRAICHEUR (Dessert, 1905),
S. Light rose pink. Faintly
fragrant. T. E. Not obtainable in this country.

LA FRANCE (Lemoine, 1901), D.
Rose type. Light pink. Richer
in center. Crimson splashes
on outer petals. Fragrant.
VL. T.

LAKE O'SILVER (Franklin,
1920), D. Light pink, silver
tipped central petals dark
pink. M.

LA LORRAINE (Lemoine, 1901),
D. Cream white, tinted dark
pink center. M. T.

LAMARTINE (Lemoine, 1908), D.

Mixture of dark old rose pink
and violet shades. Fragrant.
L. AV. X.

LAMARTINE (Calot, 1860). The
original name of GIGANTEA,
which see.

LANGLEY (Bockstoce, 1955), SD.
Pink. E. AV. Hybrid.

LANGPORT CROSS (Kelway,
1929), S. Rose turning to
lavender. X.

LA PERLE (Crousse, 1886), D.
Light old rose. Pink guards
and collar. Center slightly
darker, flaked with red giving whole flower lavender
tone. Spicy fragrance. M. AV.

LA ROSIERE (Crousse, 1888),
SD. White petals, yellow
stamens. M. AV.

LA SALLE (E. Auten, Jr., 1931),
S. Dark red. E. AV.

LASSIE (Glasscock-Falk, 1955)
(seedling no. 10R1), S. Pink.
E. AV. Hybrid.

LAST ROSE (Sass, 1930), D. Pale
pink. L. AV.

LA TENDRESSE (Crousse, 1896),
D. Almost white with slight
lavender tone edged and
flaked with crimson. Fragrant.
M. T. Not listed in this
country.

LA TULIPE (Calot, 1872), D.
Flesh pink. Center creamy
and often streaked with crimson. EM. T.

LAURA DESSERT (Dessert,
1913), A. Guards pale pink in
bud—opening cream or pale
lemon and becoming white.
Moderately fragrant. EM. AV.

LAURA KELSEY (Kelsey, 1940),
D. Blush white. LM. T.

LAURA MARCHES (Smith-
Krekler, 1954), S. Deep pink.
M. AV.

LAURA VORIES (Vories, 1924),

D. White with blush pink center. Mild fragrance. LM. AV.

LAVENDER PINK (Franklin, 1931), Rose type. Lilac. L. AV.

LAVERNE CHRISTMAN (Brand, 1925), D. Deep pink of varied shadings. T. LM.

LEADING LADY (Bigger, 1955), (seedling no. 16-47), D. White. M. AV.

LE CYGNE (Lemoine, 1907), D. White, tinged ivory, becoming pure white without markings as it develops. Moderately fragrant. E. AV.

LEE YOUNGBERG (Claar, 1955), S. Rose pink. E. AV. Albiflora x lobata

LEGEND (Jones, 1957), D. Deep rose. M.

LE JOUR (Shaylor, 1915), S. White with 2 rows of overlapping petals. Center a broad ring of golden yellow stamens. EM. AV.

LEONE GARDNER (Gardner, before 1951), D. Red. M.

L'ETINCELANTE (Dessert, 1905), S. Bright pink petals having a lighter border. Stamens bright golden yellow. M. T.

LETTIE (Nicholls-Wild & Son, 1957) (seedling no. 940), D. Pink. M.

LEWIS' AMERICAN BEAUTY (Lewis, 1921), D. Blood red. LM. T. X.

LIBELLULE (Dessert, 1922), D. Flesh colored flower, marked crimson. Fragrant. T. X.

LIGHTS OUT (Kelsey, 1934), D. Rose pink. L. AV.

LILLIAN GUMM (Gumm, 1921), D. Deep even rose pink suffused by chamois from the base of the petals. Fragrant. LM. T.

LILLIAN WILD (Wild Bros., 1930), D. Flesh color. LM. T. Marie Jacquin x albiflora

LITTLE GEM (Glasscock, 1940), J. Black-red. E. Fuyajo x officinalis Jap.

LIVINGSTONE (Crousse, 1879), D. Old rose pink, flaked on a lighter base. Few petals marked with crimson. Delicate spicy fragrance. L. AV.

LOIS (H. P. Sass, 1941), D. Bomb type. Chinensis. Medium pink. Fragrant. VE. DW.

LOIS Q. GAYLE (Wigell, 1944), D. Flesh. Mild fragrance. L. AV.

LONGFELLOW (Brand, 1907), D. Bright crimson. Fadeless. Fragrance is pleasing. M. DW.

LONG ISLAND (Guille, 1952), D. White. E. AV.

LORA DEXHEIMER (Brand, 1913), D. Bright crimson. M. AV.

LORCH (Goos & Koenemann), D. Outer petals snow-white incurving over a center of pale lemon and cream. Crimson lines on edges of petals near center. Rose fragrance. M. AV.

LORD AVEBURY (Kelway, 1929), D. Crimson maroon. X.

LORD KITCHENER (Kelway, 1929), S. Maroon crimson. E.

LOREN FRANKLIN (Franklin, 1931), Rose type. Dark pink. Fragrant. L. AV.

LORETTA FRANK (Franklin, 1953) (seedling no. H2), S. Dark pink. E. AV.

LOTHARIO (Wettengel, 1923), J. Bright violaceous pink. M. AV.

LOUIS JOLIET (E. Auten, Jr.,
1929), SD. Dark red. AV.
EM.

LOUISE M. Murawska, 1943), D.
White. M. AV.

LOUISVILLE (E. Auten, Jr.,
1940), S. Cerise pink. E.
Officinalis hybrid.

LOVANCIA (Lyman, 1933), SD.
or J. Pink. Fragrant. M. X.

LOVELINESS (Hollis, 1907), D.
Pale flesh pink, center flesh
white with few red markings.
Mild fragrance. VL. AV.

LOVER'S DREAM (Rosenfield,
1934), Rose type. Bright pink.

LOWELL THOMAS (Rosenfield,
1934), Semi-rose type. Dark
crimson. M. T.

LUCILE HARTMAN (Franklin,
1931), Rose type. Light pink.
L. T.

LUCKY DAY (Auten, 1934), S.
Deep pink. E. AV.

LUCKY STAR (Auten, 1938), D.
Dark red. L. T.

LUCKY STRIKE (B. B. Wright,
1935), D. Rose pink. LM.
to L. AV.

LUCY DUNN (Wettengel, 1924),
D. Pink. X.

LUCY INEZ (Nicholls-Wild and
Son, 1954) (Nicholls sedling
no. 1305), D. Light pink. EM.
AV.

LUCY SHAYLOR (Shaylor, 1920),
D. Pure white outer petals.
Many stamens in collar and
center give it a pale yellow
suffusion. M. AV.

LUCY WILLIAMS (Krekler,
1958), D. Light pink. LM. T.

LUETTA PFEIFFER (Brand,
1916), D. Pale pink paling
to near white. Crimson fleck
appears on center petals occasionally. Fragrant. E. T.

LULU CLIFFE (B. B. Wright,

1935), J A. Yellow petaloids,
carpels bright green with
pink stigmas. E. to EM. T. X.

LUXOR (Sass, 1933), D. White.
EM. AV.

M

MABEL L. FRANKLIN (Franklin,
1920), D. Guards and center
rose pink. Collar flesh pink
or pale salmon. Strong lemon
fragrance. M. AV.

MADAME BUTTERFLY (A. B.
Franklin, 1933), J. Rose pink.
M. AV.

MADAME CHIANG KAI-SHEK
(Payne, 1943), A. White and
yellow. E. T.

MAD CAP (Auten, 1931), S. Red,
Flushed to white. L. T. X.

MADELEINE GAUTHIER
(Dessert, 1908), S. Light flesh
pink. EM. AV.

MADELON (Dessert, 1922), D.
Silvery pink, flushed carmine.
L. T.

MAFEKING (Kelway, 1929), S.
Scarlet crimson.

MAHAL (Sass, 1934), Rose type.
White. E. AV.

MAHOGANY (Glasscock, 1937), S.
Deep mahogany. E. Chinensis
x officinalis Otto Froebel

MAID OF ATHENS (Pillow,
1923), J. Pink. X.

MAID OF HONOR (Pillow, 1923),
Semi-rose. Pink. X.

MAJESTIC ROSE (Franklin,
1953) (seedling no. A209P),
D. Rose pink. L. AV.

MAJOR A. M. KREKLER
(Johnson-Krekler, 1957), D.
White. LM. T.

MANCHU PRINCESS (Harding,
1929), S. White tinged with
coffee. E. Never in
comerce.

MANDALEEN (Lins, 1942) (seedling no. R-4-7), D. Light pink. Rose fragrant. AV. M.

MANDARIN (E. Auten, Jr., 1933), Bomb type. Dark red. E. X.

MANOAH (E. Auten, Jr., 1933), D. Lavender. M.

MAN OF WAR (Saunders, 1929), S. Crimson. Season of officinalis. T. Sinensis x officinalis. X.

MARANACOCK (Guppy, 1935), J. Deep pink. X.

MARCELLA (Lins, 1952) (seedling no. A-6-25), D. White. M. AV.

MARCELLE DESSERT (Dessert, 1899), D Pale pink. M. T.

MARCHIONESS OF LANSDOWNE (Kelway, 1899), D. Brilliant rose pink. M. AV. X.

MARCIA (Lyman, 1933), D. Black-red. Fragrant. Never in commerce. Renamed Marcia Dewey.

MARDI GRAS (Winslow, 1951) (seedling no. 16), J. Dark red. M. T.

MARGARET (Sass, 1952), D. Blush white. L. T. (Note: formerly HANS' BLUSH WHITE)

MARGARET ATWOOD (Origin uncertain. Farr found this with no label in a shipment of roots from Holland.) J. White. M. AV.

MARGARET CLARK (Mains, 1956) (seedling no. A18), D. Dark pink. L.

MARGARET HAGERMAN (Hagerman, 1935), D. White, fairly fragrant. M. T. Never in commerce.

MARGARET VIERHELLER (Wettengel, 1920), D. Salmon pink. T. M.

MARGUERITE DESSERT (Dessert, 1913), S. White. Faint fragrance. M. T.

MARGUERITE GAUDICHAU (Millet, 1903), D. Light rose pink. Sweet fragrance. L. T. Not available in this country.

MARGUERITE GERARD (Crousse, 1892), D. Pale flesh pink to dark rose pink. M. AV.

MARIE (Calot, 1868), D. Pale old rose pink, changing to white. VL. VT. Not available in this country.

MARIE CROUSSE (Crousse, 1892), D. Pale pink. M. AV.

MARIE DEROUX (Crousse, 1881), D. Flesh pink, paling to white. L.

MARIE ELIZABETH (Guille, 1959), D. Red. M.

MARIE JACQUIN (Verdier), SD. Pale pink. M. AV.

MARIE LEMOINE (Calot, 1869), D. Lemon white. L. DW.

MARIELLEN (Guppy), S. White. X.

MARIETTA SISSON (Sass, 1933), D. Light pink. M. AV.

MARILLA BEAUTY (Kelsey, 1940), D. Blush white. L. T.

MARION CRAN (Kelway, 1929), SD. Flesh pink. Fragrant. T. X.

MARION PFEIFFER (Pfeiffer, 1929), D. Red. Rose geranium fragrance. T.

MARION TALLEY (Simpson, 1929), D. Rose type. Pink. D. X.

MARJORIE ALLISON (Shaylor, 1918), S. White. M. AV. X.

MARK TWAIN (Franklin, 1939), D. Crimson. M. T.

MARS (Murawska, 1943), SD. White. M. AV. Name changed to Ethel Mars.

MARTHA A. TWYMAN (Wetten-

260

PEONIES, OUTDOORS AND IN

gel, 1920), D. Pink. X.

MARTHA BULLOCH (Brand, 1907), D. Blend of bright old rose pink to pink. Rose fragrance. L. T.

MARTHA V. LANE (Wettengel, 1924), D. White. X.

MARTHA SHARP (Nicholls, 1949), D. Pink. M. AV. Marie Crousse x Lady Alexandra Duff

MARTHA WASHINGTON (Hollis, 1909). Suppressed by vote of Directors. X.

MARVEL (Secor, 1924), D. Light rose pink. Fragrant. L. T.

MARY AUTEN (E. Auten, Jr., 1933), D. White. Fragrant. L. AV.

MARY BRAND (Brand, 1907), Rose type. Crimson. Fragrant. M. AV.

MARY B. VORIES (Vories, 1924), D. Blush pink. Sweet fragrance. L. AV.

MARY C. WEDGE (Secor, 1924), D. Red. Fragrant. M. X.

MARY ELLEN (Franklin, 1931), Semi-rose type. Blush white. L. AV. LM.

MARY E. NICHOLLS (Nicholls, 1941), D. White. AV. Number 210 from Ama-no-sode

MARYGOLD (Mrs. Freeborn, 1931), J. Rose pink. Gold staminodes. X.

MARY J. HAWKE (Hawke, 1946), D. Dark red. M. T.

MARY JOAN CUMMINGS (Guppy, 1940), S. Pale pink. E. Solfatare x James Kelway. X.

MARY JO see JOHANNA

MARY LENA (Lyman, 1936), A. Pale pink with white center. Never in commerce.

MARY L. HOLLIS (Hollis, 1907),

SD. Bright pink. M. AV. X.

MARY LOUISE (Lyman, 1940), S. Pink. T. X.

MARY LOU KIMMEY (Edlund, 1929), Rose type. Light pink with splashes of carmine on center petals. Fragrant. T. X.

MARY M. FISCHER (Croix Farms, 1957) (seedling no. 15C), D. Light pink. LM. T.

MARY P. KING (Franklin, 1920), D. Flesh pink. Mild fragrance. M. AV.

MARY WOODBURY SHAYLOR (Shaylor, 1916), D. Flesh white. Fragrant. LM. DW.

MASSASOIT (White, 1954), S. Dark red. E. AV. Richard Carvel x officinalis anemone-flora aurea ligulata

MATADOR (Jones, 1957), J. Ruby red. M.

MATILDA LEWIS (Saunders, 1921), D. Dark maroon. M. AV.

MATTAWAMKEAG (Guppy, 1935), S. Deep pink. X.

MATTIE LAFUZE (Johnson, 1942), D. White. Fragrant. LM. AV.

MAUD E. TICKNOR (Ticknor, 1940), D. Pale rose pink. E. X.

MAUD L. RICHARDSON (Hollis, 1904), D. Light rose pink. Fragrance strong. VL. T. X.

MAURICE LOWE (Kelway, 1929), D. Rosy pink. Not for sale in this country.

MAURINE (Haupt, 1935), D. Light lavender. E. AV. X.

MAVOURNEEN (Lanigan, 1944), SD. Light rose pink. M. DW. X.

MAXINE ARMSTRONG (Sass, 1952) (seedling no. 21.29), D. White. M. T.

MAY DAWN (Glasscock, 1947), S.

Red. VE. Tokio x officinalis Sunbeam

MAY DELIGHT (Glasscock, 1941), S. Coral pink. E. D. White chinensis x officinalis Sunbeam

MAY MORN (Nicholls, 1952), D. Blush pink. M. T. Mme. Calot x unknown.

MAY OLESON (Oleson, 1924), S. Appleblossom pink. M. AV.

MEDICINE HAT (Auten, Jr., 1936), S. Dark red. AV. E.

MELLOW MOON (Jones, 1938), D. White. Very fragrant. M. AV.

MELODY (Auten, 1925), A. Pale pink. Pleasing fragrance. X.

MEMORIAL QUEEN (Rosenfield, 1934), D. Clear pink. E. T. A sport of Edulis Superba.

MEMORY (Jones, 1938), D. Blush pink with trace of tan at center. Slightly fragrant. L. AV. X.

MENTOR GRAHAM (Lanigan, 1938), D. Pale pink to white. LM. AV.

MENDOTA (Auten, 1937), SD. Red. T.

MERCEDES (Lins, 1956) (seedling no. M-L-96-B), D. Blush pink. LM.

MERRIGOLD (Wright, 1932), J. Violet pink. X.

METEOR (E. Auten, Jr., 1933), J. Red. M. AV.

MID-AMERICA (Bigger, 1952) (seedling no. 52-37), D. Pink. M. Renamed Deer Creek.

MIDNIGHT SUN (Murawska, 1954), J. Dark red. M. AV. Dignity x unknown

MIDSUMMER NIGHT'S DREAM (Pleas, 1906), D. Blush white. Fragrant. LM. AV. X.

MIGNON (Lemoine, 1908), D. Light flesh pink, paling to flesh white. Rose fragrance. M. AV. X.

MIKADO (Japan, 1893), J. Dark crimson. M. T.

MILDRED MAY (Murawska, 1943), SD. White. M. T. Note: changed from MRS. L. E. MAY

MILTON HILL (Richardson, 1891), D. Light shell pink. Faint fragrance. L. AV.

MINE (Krekler, 1958), S. Purplish red. E. T.

MINERVA (Sass, 1930), D. White. L. T.

MINNEAPOLIS (Dana, 1926), S. Pink. Fragrant. E. X.

MINNIE GERTRUDE (Glasscock, 1931), Rose type. Red. M. Officinalis hybrid. X.

MINNIE SHAYLOR (Shaylor, 1919), SD. Light pink. M. AV.

MINUET (Franklin, 1931), Rose type. Light pink. L. T.

MIRIAM MARSH (Freeborn, 1931), J. White with pale yellow center of stamenoids. X.

MIRIAM NAPIER ROHE (Sass-Napier, 1940), D. White. M. AV. Formerly Sass no. 42½. X.

MISCHIEF (E. Auten, Jr., 1925), S. Appleblossom pink. L. T.

MISS AMERICA (J. R. Mann-Van Steen, 1936), SD. White. E. AV.

MISS IDA CHAMBERLAIN (Kelway, 1929), S. Light rose. T. Not for sale in this country.

MISS MINNEAPOLIS (Franklin, 1931), Rose type. Pale pink. L. AV.

MLLE. JEANNE RIVIERE (Riviere, 1908), D. Blush white. Mild fragrance. M. T.

MLLE. LEONIE CALOT (Calot, 1861), D. Flesh pink. Sweet fragrance. LM. AV. X.

MLLE. ROUSSEAU (Calot, 1886), D. Pale creamy pink. Faint fragrance. M. AV. X.

MME. AUGUSTE DESSERT (Dessert, 1899), D. Old rose pink. Elderberry fragrance. E.M. AV. X.

MME. BENOIT RIVIERE (Riviere, 1911). Suppressed by vote of the Directors. X.

MME. CALOT (Miellez, 1856), D. Light old rose pink. Fragrant. E. T.

MME. DE VATRY (Guerin, 1863), D. Light pink. Fragrant. M. AV. X.

MME. DE VERNEVILLE (Crousse, 1885), D. White guard petals. Rose fragrance. Best in cooler climates. E. AV.

MME. D. TREYERAN (Dessert, 1889), D. Flesh pink. Pleasing fragrance. M. DW. X.

MME. DUCEL (Mechin, 1880), D. Pale old rose. M. DW.

MME. EDOUARD DORIAT (Dessert-Doriat, 1924), D. White, tipped crimson. T. LM.

MME. EMILE DUPRAZ (Riviere, 1911), D. Old rose pink. Rose fragrance. M. X.

MME. EMILE GALLE (Crousse, 1881), D. Light rose pink. Rose fragrance. L. AV.

MME. EMILE LEMOINE (Lemoine, 1899), D. White streaks on outer petals. Mildly fragrant. M. T.

MME. ESCARY (Lemoine, 1922), D. White. M. X.

MME. FOREL (Crousse, 1887), D. Pinkish-lavender. Fragrant. LM. AV. X.

MME. GAUDICHAU (Millet,

1902), D. Dark crimson, blackish sheen. LM. T. X.

MME. GEISSLER (Crousse, 1880), D. Light old rose pink. Crinkled petals. LM.

MME. JULES CALOT (Calot, 1868), D. Pinkish white, paling to white. M. DW. X.

MME. JULES DESSERT (Dessert, 1909), D. Flesh-white. Mild fragrance. LM. T.

MME. JULES ELIE (Calot, 1873), D. Old rose guards, cream white collar, pinkish crown. Mild fragrance. M. AV.

MME. LEMOINIER (Calot, 1865), D. Pale old rose pink, lavender tinge. Fair fragrance. M. T. X.

MME. MANCHET (Dessert, 1913), D. Pale old rose pink, distinct purple shading at base. VL. T. X.

MODELE DE PERFECTION (Crousse, 1875), D. Light old rose, tipped with silver. L. DW.

MODELLA (Betscher, 1920), D. Light pink guards. Creamy suffusion in the collar. Sweet fragrance. M. AV.

MODESTE GUERIN (Guerin, 1845), D. Dark rose-pink, slight violet tint. Rose fragrance. E. AV.

MOLLY STARK (Auten, 1927), D. Cream white, pink with red splashes. E. AV.

MONS. CHARLES LEVEQUE (Calot, 1861). Same as Mlle. Leonie Calot, which see. X.

MONS. DUPONT (Calot, 1872), D. White, with crimson blotches on central petals. Fragrant. LM. T.

MONS. JULES ELIE (Crousse, 1888), D. Light rose pink. E. T.

MONS. MARTIN CAHUZAC

(Dessert, 1899), D. Maroon-crimson. EM. AV.

MONT BLANC (Lemoine, 1899), D. White. Fragrant. EM. AV.

MONTEREY (E. Auten, Jr., 1930), J. Light red, cerise and golden tints in center. M. AV.

MONTICELLO (E. Auten, Jr., 1931), S. White. T. X.

MOONGLOW (Rosefield, 1939), Rose type. Pale yellow. AV. L.

MOON MAGIC (E. Auten, Jr., 1939), A. Pink with yellow center. Albiflora var. M. AV.

MOON MIST (E. Auten, Jr., 1929), S. Pale pink. AV. M.

MOON OF NIPPON (R. W. Auten, 1936), J. White. T. LM.

MOONSTONE (Murawska, 1943), D. Blush pink. M. AV.

MORNING SONG (E. Auten, Jr., 1933), S. White. Crinkled. E. AV

MOROCCO (E. Auten, Jr., 1933), D. Red. VE. T.

MOSES HULL (Brand, 1907), D. Old rose pink. M. AV. X.

MOTHER'S CHOICE (Glasscock, 1950), D. White. M. AV.

MOULD OF FORM (Kelway, 1928). Cherry red. Not listed in this country.

MOUNT EVEREST (Sass, 1937), D. White. L. DW.

MOUNT PALOMAR (E. Auten, Jr., 1939), J. Dark red. E. T. Albiflora var.

MR. L. VAN LEEUWEN (Nieuwenhuyzen, 1916), D. Light crimson. LM. AV.

MRS. A. G. RUGGLES (Brand, 1913), D. Light pink, paling lighter. L. T. X.

MRS. A. M. BRAND (Brand, 1925), D. White. Fragrant. L. AV.

MRS. COL. LINDBERGH

(Simpson, 1929), Rose type. Pink. Fragrant. M. T. X.

MRS. C. S MINOT (Minot, 1914), D Flesh pink, coppery tints. L. DW.

MRS. EDWARD BROMET (Kelway, 1929), D. White. Fragrant E. Not listed in this country.

MRS. EDWARD HARDING (Shaylor, 1918), D. White. M. AV.

MRS. E. J. SHAYLOR (Shaylor, 1920), D. Delicate pink. LM. X.

MRS. E. J. STREICHERT (Murawska, 1942), D. Deep pink. M. T. X.

MRS. EUGENE SECOR (Secor, 1924), D. White. Fragrant. L. T. X.

MRS. EVA BARRON (Glasscock, 1932), Rose type. Shell pink. Rose fragrance. M. T. Jules Elie x Georgiana Shaylor. X.

MRS. F. A. GOODRICH (Brand, 1925), D. Dark deep bright pink. LM. AV.

MRS. FRANK BEACH (Brand, 1925), D. Creamy white. L. DW.

MRS. FRANKLIN D. ROOSEVELT (Franklin, 1933) (seedling no. E-6 selected 1924), D. Rose pink. EM. AV.

MRS. FRED ATHROP (Athrop, 1941), D. White, sometimes edged with carmine. LM. T.

MRS. GEORGE BUNYARD (Kelway, 1898), D. Bright rose pink. Fragrant. M. T.

MRS. GEORGE RAWSON (Allison, 1931). Light pink. Fragrant. L. T.

MRS. HARRIET GENTRY (Brand, 1925), D. Pure white. L. AV.

MRS. HARRY A. NORTON (Norton, 1939), Semi-rose

type. Cochineal carmine. M.
AV. X.

MRS. J. F. ROSENFIELD
(Rosenfield, 1934), Rose type.
White. E. T. X.

MRS. J. H. NEELEY (Neeley,
1931), Rose type. White. L.
T.

MRS. JAMES KELWAY (Kelway,
1926), D. Flesh white. EM.
AV. Almost identical with
Kelway's Glorious.

MRS. JOHN M. GOOD (Good &
Reese, 1929), Rose type.
White. M. T.

MRS. JOHN M. KLEITSCH
(Brand, 1925), D. Light violet
rose. AV. L.

MRS. JOHN M. LEWIS (Lewis,
1920), D. Dark crimson, fragrant. M. AV.

MRS. JOHN SMYTHE FOGG
(Hollis, 1907), D. Pale rose
pink. M. T. X.

MRS. J. V. EDLUND (Edlund,
1929). White. Fragrant. L. T.

MRS. LIVINGSTON FARRAND
(Nicholls, 1935), D. Rose type.
Pink. T. LM.

MRS. PHILIP RUNCIMAN
(Kelway, 1928), D. Rose.
Not listed here.

MRS. R. M. BACHELLER
(Vories, 1930), D. Pink. M.
AV.

MRS ROMAINE B. WARE
(Brand, 1925), D. Light flesh
pink, shading lighter. Rose
fragrance. T. L. M.

MRS. R. T. WHITAKER (Reineke,
1936), D. Light pink. Fragrant. M. AV. X.

MRS. SHAYLOR FORCE
(Shaylor, 1919), D. Creamy
white, tinge of lemon. M. AV.

MRS. SPRINGER BROOKS
(Edlund, 1934), SD. White.
M. AV.

MRS. TELFER MAC ARTHUR

(Murawska, 1940), D. Blush
fading to white. M. AV. X.

MRS. WILDER BANCROFT
(Nicholls, 1935), J. Deep red.
AV. M.

MUSKOGEE (Jones, 1957), J.
Dark red. M.

MYRTLE GENTRY (Brand,
1925), D. Rose white, tints
of flesh and salmon. Fragrant.
LM. AV.

MYRTLE ROSENFIELD
(Rosenfield, 1934), Rose type.
Pink. AV. X.

MYRTLE REINEKE (Reineke,
1936), D. White, with cast
of pink. M. AV. X.

N

NANCY (White, 1954), S. Peach
pink. E. DW. Officinalis rubra
plena x Saunders 4710

NANCY DOLMAN (Vories, 1924),
D. Pale rose pink. L. T.

NANCY NICHOLLS (Nicholls,
1941), D. White flushed rosy
pink. No. 116 from YESO.

NANCY NORA (Bernstein, 1942),
D. Pink. M. AV. Walter
Faxon x Lady Alexandra Duff

NANTICOOK (Guppy, 1935), J.
Bright red. X.

NAOMI (E. Auten, Jr., 1933), D.
Creamy flesh pink. M. AV.

NATANIS (Guppy, 1929), D.
Crimson. Fragrant. T. Albiflora single x officinalis rubra
plena. X.

NAUVOO (Auten, 1937), D.
White. Fragrant. L. T.

NEHUMKEAG (Guppy, 1935), S.
Bright red. X.

NELLIE (Kelway, 1915), S. Rose
pink. M. DW.

NEON (Nicholls, 1941), J. Rose-
pink. No. 208 from Ama-no-
sode. M. AV.

NEW ERA (A. Franklin, 1939), D. White. M. T.

NICK SHAYLOR (Allison, 1931), Rose type. Pink. L. AV.

NINA SECOR (Secor, 1922), D. Pure white. M. AV.

NIPPON BEAUTY (Auten, 1927), J. Dark red, staminodes flushed yellow. M. AV.

NIPPON BRILLIANT (E. Auten, Jr., 1933), J. Red. T.

NIPPON CHIEF (E. Auten, Jr., 1931), J. Dark red. L. T.

NIPPON GOLD (Auten, Jr., 1929), J. Pink. L. T.

NIPPON MAID (E. Auten, Jr., 1931), J. Dark red. AV. to DW. L.

NIPPON PARADE (Auten, 1935), J. Red. AV. M.

NIPPON PRINCESS (E. Auten, Jr., 1931), J. Cerise pink. X.

NIPPON RED (E. Auten, Jr., 1931), J. Red. AV. X.

NIPPON SPLENDOR (E. Auten, Jr., 1931), J. Deep red. T. M.

NIPPON TRIUMPH (E. Auten, Jr., 1937), J. Red. Renamed War Hawk. M.

NIPPON WARRIOR (E. Auten, Jr., 1933), J. Red. Center tipped yellow. M.

NOKOMIS (Franklin, 1920), D. Light pink. Fragrant. X.

NORSEMAN (Pillow, 1923), S. Light red. X.

NYMPHAEA (Thurlow, 1919), D. Cream white, flushed pale rose pink. Fragrant. M. AV.

O

OCTAVIE DEMAY (Calot, 1867), D. Light old rose pink guards. Darker crown. E. DW.

ODALISQUE (Lemoine, 1923), D. Outer petals tinted pink, center cream white. Rose scent. LM. AV. X.

OHIRAMA (Origin unknown), J. Guards, bright rose pink. Fragrant. DW.

OLD HUNDREDTH (E. Auten, Jr., 1933), D. Creamy white. L. T. X.

OLD IVORY (Glasscock, 1950), S. White. E. Sunbeam x albiflora

OLD MAIN (E. Auten, 1939), Bomb type. Red. T. (off. hyb.) E.

OLD SIWASH (E. Auten, 1939), D. Flesh fading to white. M. Fragrant. T. Albiflora var.

OLIVER P. BAYNE (Smith-Krekler, 1954), D. Dark pink. E. DW.

OPAL (Pleas, 1908), D. Pale rose pink, becoming white. M. AV. X.

OPAL HAMILTON (Nicholls-Wild & Son, 1957) (seedling no. 1355), J. Pink. M.

OPAL IRIS (Pleas), SD. Light pink, salmon shading. M. T. X.

OPHA (Wild & Son, 1950), S. White. E. AV.

ORIENTAL GOLD (Japan, 1954), D. Yellow. M. AV. Also listed as Golden Dream and Yokihi.

OWEN F. HUGHES (Phillips, 1953), S. Light pink. LM. DW. Mischief x Clio

OZARK BEAUTY (Wild Bros., 1950) (seedling no. 4), D. Dark pink. L. AV.

P

PALLAS (Terry), SD. Flesh pink. EM. DW.

PANDORA (Guille, 1952), D. Rose pink. E. T.

PARADISE (Hollis, 1907), D. Flesh pink, paling to white center. Fragrant. EM. AV.

PARTY GIRL (Jones, 1957), J.
Pink. M.
PARTY GOWN (Kelsey, 1940), D.
White. LM. T.
PASSADUMKEAG (Guppy, 1935),
S. Dark red. X.
PASTEL (Nicholls, 1941), Rose
type. Light salmon pink. AV.
M. No. 217 from WALTER
FAXON
PASTEUR (Crousse, 1896), D.
Pale pink outer petals, center
almost white with green cen-
ter. Faint fragrance. LM. T.
X.
PATHFINDER (E. Auten, Jr.,
1939), D. Pink. Fragrant. M.
Albiflora var.
PATIENCE (E. Auten, Jr., 1933),
D. Cream-white. E. T. X.
PATRICIA (E Auten, Jr., 1931),
SD. Blush. E. T.
PATRICIA HANRATTY (Gardner,
before 1951), J. Rose red. M.
PATTY (E. Auten, Jr., 1939), A.
Near salmon pink. DW. LM.
Albiflora var.
PAUL BUNYAN (Lins, 1955), D.
Rose. LM. T.
PAULINE HENRY (Nicholls-Wild
& Son, 1957) (seedling no.
436), D. White. LM.
PAUL REVERE (E. Auten, Jr.,
1939), D. Dark red. LM. T.
Albiflora var.
PEACE (Murawska, 1955), D.
White. Not yet introduced.
PEACHBLOW (Shaylor, 1938),
SD. & D. Peach pink. E. AV.
PEDRO (G. Richmond, 1951), S.
Bright red. M. T.
PEGGY (E. Auten, Jr., 1931), D.
Deep pink. AV. LM.
PEG OF MY HEART (G. Rich-
mond, 1949), D. Cerise pink.
E. AV.
PELHAM (Auten, 1935), D.
White. Fragrant. LM. T.
PENNACOOK (Guppy, 1935), J.

Dark red. X.
PEORIA (E. Auten, Jr., 1931), S.
Red. DW. E. X.
PERRETTE (Dessert, 1921), D.
Faint pink, paling to white.
Fragrant. LM. AV.
PETITE D'OR (Murawska, 1944),
S. Blush fading to ivory
white. E. T.
PERE MARQUETTE (E. Auten,
Jr., 1933), S. Dark red. E. AV.
X.
PERFECT JOY (Kelway, 1929),
D. Coral pink turning nearly
white. Not listed in this
country.
PERFECT PICTURE (Kelway,
1928), SD. Pink. L.
Not listed in this country.
PERLE BLANCHE (Dessert,
1913), S. White. Golden
yellow stamens. EM. T.
PETAGRA (Franklin, 1920), D.
Light red. Fragrant. X.
PETER OLESON (Oleson, 1924),
S. Red. M. AV. X.
PETER PAN (Hollis, 1907), D.
Old rose. Rose fragrance. L.
AV.
PETITE (Falk-Glasscock, 1956),
SD. Red. E. DW. Officinalis
x albiflora
PHILIP G. CORLISS (Claar,
1955), S. Red. E. AV. Albi-
flora x lobata
PHILIPPE RIVOIRE (Riviere,
1911), D. Very dark crimson.
Rose scent. E. AV.
PHILOMELE (Calot, 1861), A.
Guards, dark old rose; collar
buff. Fragrant. E. AV.
PHOEBE CARY (Brand, 1907),
D. Old rose pink. Rose scent.
VL. T.
PHYLLIS KELWAY (Kelway,
1908), SD. Rose pink, paling
to white. M. AV.
PICO (Freeborn, 1934), S. White.
M. AV. T.

PIE PLATE (Wright, 1935), S.
White. EM. to LM. T. X.

PIERRE DUCHARTRE (Crousse,
1895), D. Rose pink. Rose
scent. L. AV.

PINK ANGEL (Christenson,
1948), S. Pink. VE. T.
Tomentosa x F2 hybrid

PINK BEAUTY (Risk, 1929), D.
Bright pink. Fragrant. M. T.
X.

PINK CAMEO (Bigger, 1954)
(seedling no. 6-45), D. White,
shaded pink. LM. AV.

PINK FORMAL (Nicholls-Wild
and Son, 1953) (Nicholls
seedling no. 877), D. Light
pink. LM. AV.

PINK GEM (Mann-Van Steen,
1936), S. Pink. EM. to LM.
AV. X.

PINK GLORY (Jones, 1938), S.
Dark pink with yellow center.
EM. T. Name changed to
Captain Jones.

PINK JEWEL (Winslow, 1951)
(seedling no. 1), S. Bright
pink. E. AV.

PINK LEMONADE (Klehm,
1951), D. Pink and yellow.
M. T.

PINK MONARCH (E. Auten, Jr.,
1933), D. Bright pink.

PINK MOUND (Klehm, 1952),
(seedling no. 780A), D. Pink.
M. DW.

PINK O'DAWN (Cooper, 1953),
D. Dark pink. L. Not in
commerce yet.

PINK OPAL (Sass, 1934), Full
rose type. Light pink. M. T.
X.

PINK PEARL (Submitted by
Interstate Nurseries.) No
description. Never listed.

PINK PERFECTION (Risk, 1929),
D. Pink. Fragrant. L. T. X.

PINK POMPOM (Freeborn, 1943),
D. Clear pink. E. Officinalis

rubra x Madame Jules Dessert

PINK RADIANCE (Allen Wild,
1959), D. Pink. M.

PINK SOLANGE (E. Auten Jr.,
1933). Fine pink. L. AV.

PIRATE FLAG (E. Auten, Jr.,
1933), S. Dark red. VL.

PITTI SINN (Vories, 1924), D.
Pink guard petals, yellow
petaloids, pink center tuft. L.
AV.

PIXIE (E. Auten, Jr., 1931), J.
Red. T. X.

PLYMOUTH (E. Auten, Jr., 1931),
D. White. Fragrant. AV. L.

POLAR STAR (Sass, 1932), J.
White. T. M.

POMPILIA (Earnshaw, 1920), D.
Ivory-white. M. AV.

PORPENTINE (Guppy), D. Red.
X.

POTTSI ALBA (Buyck, 1840).
Much overrated. Suppressed
by vote of the Directors. X.

PRAIRIE BELLE (Bigger, 1945),
D. Cream fading to white.
EM. AV.

PRESIDENT FRANKLIN D.
ROOSEVELT (Franklin, '33)
(seedling no. X-24, selected
1923), Rose type. Dark pink.
L. T.

PRESIDENT POINCARE
(Kelway, 1929), D. Ruby
crimson, spice scented.
Not available here.

PRESIDENT TAFT (Blaauw,
1909). Considered same as
REINE HORTENSE, which
see.

PRESIDENT WILSON (Thurlow,
1918), D. Rose pink. Spicy
fragrance. L. AV.

PRESTO (Auten, Jr., 1925), S.
Red. E. AV. X.

PRIAM (Sass, 1930), D. Dark
maroon red. M. T.

PRIDE OF ESSEX (Thurlow,
1916), D. Rose pink guards,

blush-white center. Fresh
fragrance. M. T.
PRIDE OF HUISH (Kelway,
1928), S. Peach pink. E.
Not avvailable here.
PRIDE OF LANGPORT (Kelway,
1909), S. Pale rose pink.
M. T.
PRIDE OF PAULDING (Neeley,
1920), D. Flesh pink. Rose
fragrance. L. X. Not good.
PRIDE OF SOMERSET (Kelway,
1928), S. Deep crimson. E.
Not available in U.S.A.
PRIMA DONNA (Franklin, 1939),
D. Light pink. E. M.
PRIMEVERE (Lemoine, 1907), A.
Creamy white. Moderately
fragrant. M. T.
PRINCE CHARMING (Glasscock-
Falk, 1955) (seedling no.
A1A46), J. Red. E. T.
PRINCE OF JAPS (Lewis, 1927),
J. Oxblood red. M. AV.
PRINCESS DULEEP SINGH
(Kelway), J. Dark old rose
pink, center buff. Fragrant.
EM. AV.
PRINCESS IMPERIAL (Kelway,
1929), S. Rosy pink, edged
lighter. E. Not available in
U.S.A.
PRISCILLA ALDEN (Originator:
Roberts, 1926), Reg. by: A. H.
Fewkes. Rose type. White. E.
AV.
PRUDENCE (E. Auten, Jr., 1933),
D. Lavender. Fragrant.
PURITAN MAID (E. Auten, Jr.,
1933), S. White. AV.
PURPLE CUP (Secor, 1924), S.
Red. E. X.

Q

QUEEN OF HAMBURG (H. P.
Sass, 1937). Bright pink. LM.
T.
QUEEN OF SHEBA (H. P. Sass,

1937), Bomb type. Bright rose.
LM. AV.
QUEEN OF THE BELGIANS
(Kelway, 1929), S. Creamy
white. AV.
QUEEN OF THE WEST
(Kelway, 1929), D. Rosy
peach. E. Not listed in this
country.
QUEEN VICTORIA (Kelway,
1929), D. Cream flesh. X.

R

RACHEL (Lemoine, 1904), D.
Light rose pink. LM. AV.
RADIANCE (Brant, 1931), S.
Dark red. T. E. X.
RAGGEDY ANN (Krekler, 1958),
D. Light pink. LM. AV.
RALPH (Pleas, 1913). Much over-
rated. Suppressed by vote of
the Directors.
RAMONA LINS (Lins, 1942)
(seedling no. S-1-4), D. Pink.
ML. T.
RAOUL DESSERT (Dessert,
1910), D. Shell pink. Rose
scent. L. AV.
RARE CHINA (Kelsey, 1940), SD.
White. M. AV.
RASHOOMON (Japanese origin),
J. Rose-red. Good fragrance.
M. AV.
RED BALL (Murawska, 1950),
D. Red. L. T.
RED BIRD (Franklin, 1921), A.
Rose-red. M. AV.
RED CHARM (Glasscock, 1944),
D. Red. E. T. Officinalis x
albiflora
RED CLOUD (Jones, 1941), D.
Red. LM. AV.
RED CROWN (E. Auten, Jr.,
1931), J. Red. T. X.
RED DAWN (Kelway, 1929), SD.
Dark maroon red. Not avail-
able in U.S.A.

RED ELIE (Winchell, 1948), D.
Red. M.

RED EMPEROR (E. Auten, Jr.,
1931), J. Light red. AV. M.

RED ENSIGN (E. Auten, Jr.,
1940), SD. Black-red. L. DW.
Off. hyb.

RED FEATHERS (Jones, 1941),
Bright red. LM. T.

RED GIANT (Glasscock, 1939),
Semi-rose type. Chinensis.
Dark red. M. T.

RED GLORY (Auten, 1937), S.
Dark red. Officinalis x
chinensis. VE. T.

RED HARMONY (Freeborn,
1941), S. Deep crimson. M.
AV.

RED JACKET (Krekler, 1955)
(seedling no. J19), D. Red.
E. DW.

REDKEY (Smith-Krekler, 1953),
S. Deep black-red. E. AV.

RED MONARCH (Auten-Glass-
cock, 1937), Bomb type. Red.
T. Officinalis x chinensis

RED SATIN (Sass, 1937), Rose
type. Cerise. LM.

RED SIGNAL (Freeborn, 1941),
S. Scarlet. Officinalis hybrid.
E. AV. X.

RED SPLENDOR (Mann-Van
Steen, 1936), J. Deep pink.
M. T.

RED STAR (Nicholls, 1941), J.
Vermilion. T. M. No. 80
from KARL ROSENFIELD

REGAL (Lyman, 1933), S. Black-
red. Never in commerce.

REINE BARONET (Millet, 1924),
D. Pink. M. AV.

REINE HORTENSE (Calot,
1857), D. Rose pink. M. T.

RELIANCE (Glasscock, 1950), D.
Bomb type. Pink. E. AV.
Otto Froebel x albiflora

REMEMBRANCE (Lyman, 1939),
A. Rose pink. Never in
commerce.

RENEE MARIE (Dessert, 1920),
D. Flesh white, shading to
pale pink. M. AV.

RESPLENDENT (Franklin, 1931),
Rose type. White. M. to L.

REVERIE (Jones, 1938), D. Rose
type. Pink with flush of
lavender. LM. T. X.

RICHARD CARVEL (Brand,
1913), D. Bright crimson.
Slight fragrance. E. T.

RICHFIELD WHITE (Franklin,
1939), Rose type. Midseason
Festiva Maxima. T. Seedling
G279

RIO GRANDE (Nieuwenhuizen,
1935). Dark red. M. AV.

RITA (Dessert, 1922), D. Rose
pink outside, flesh pink
within. Fragrant. L.

ROBERT (Gardner, before 1951),
D. Deep pink. LM. T.

ROBERTA (E. Auten, Jr., 1936),
J. White. LM. T.

ROBERT LEE DAVIS (Vories,
1924), D. Soft light pink. M.
X.

ROBIN HOOD (E. Auten, Jr.,
1939), SD. Red. M. AV.
Albiflora var.

ROMEO (Rosenfield, 1934), S.
Bright red. E. T.

ROSABEL (Sass, 1937). Rose red.
M. AV.

ROSA BONHEUR (Dessert, 1905),
D. Old rose pink. Rose scent.
L. AV.

ROSADA (Nicholls, 1942), D.
Rose type. Rose pink. T. LM.

ROSALIE (Auten, 1927), D.
Similar to American Beauty
Rose. DW. M.

ROSALIE (Glasscock, 1927), Rose
type. Medium red. DW. X.

ROSAMOND (Lewis, 1922), D.
Rose pink. Fragrant. AV. X.

ROSANNA SHRADER (Shrader,
1940), D. Rose type. Rose
pink. M. T.

ROSE BEAUTY (Richmond, 1949), D. Old rose pink. L. T.

ROSE BOWL (Keagey, 1946), S. Pale pink, fading to white. M. T.

ROSEDALE (E. Auten, Jr., 1936), SD. Dark red. E. DW. Officinalis x chinensis

ROSELLA MAY (Glasscock, 1927), Rose type. Deep pink. M. to L. T. Chinensis var. X.

ROSE MARIE (Auten-Glasscock, 1936), D. Dark red. Officinalis x chinensis. E AV..

ROSE MARIE LINS (Lins, 1958), D. Light pink. LM. T.

ROSE OF HEAVEN (Mann-Van Steen, 1936), D. Pink. AV. M.

ROSE OF MIAMIS (Jones, 1957), D. Blush white, some petals crimson edged. M.

ROSE SHAYLOR (Shaylor, 1920), D. Flesh pink, fragrant. M. T.

ROSE TRIUMPH. Submitted by Interstate Nurseries, 1937. No description. Never introduced.

ROSETTE (Dessert, 1918), D. Light shell pink. EM. AV.

ROSE VALLEY (Scott, 1925), J. Pink with yellow center. M. AV.

ROSINE (Lemoine, 1913), D. Bright rose pink. Rose fragrance. LM. AV. Not listed here.

ROSY DAWN (Barr), S. White, tinged pale pink. E. AV. Not listed here.

ROXANA (Auten-Lake, 1946), S. Pink red. E. DW. Richard Carvel x tenuifolia simplex

ROY ROBINSON (Winchell, 1941), no. 7A. Red-pink. M.

R. P. WHITFIELD (Richardson), D. Pale rose pink. Rose fragrance. L. T. X.

RUBIE BATTEY (E. Auten, Jr., 1933), J. Rich red. Yellow lines and dots on center petaloids very scanty. L. T.

RUBIO (Nicholls, 1941), D. Red. T. No. 135 from Torpilleur. M.

RUBY (Glasscock, 1927), D. Dark red. EM. Former No. 173. X.

RUBY KING. Submitted by Interstate Nurseries, 1937. No description. Never introduced.

RUSSELL EMRICK (Krekler, 1957) (seedling no. AT19), D. Blush. M. T.

RUTH FORCE (Shaylor, 1921), J. Cerise-pink. M. to L. AV.

RUTH GALLAGHER (Cooper, 1946) (seedling no. 10), Bomb type. Cream-colored. T. M.

S

SABLE (Glasscock, 1943), S. Red. Almost black. E. 2d generation OTTO FROEBEL hybrid.

SALEM (E. Auten, Jr., 1931), D. Red. Fragrant. X.

SALMON BEAUTY (Glasscock-Auten, 1939), D. Pink with   .. salmon cast. E. T.

SALMON GLORY (Glasscock, 1947), D. Salmon pink. VE. T. Officinalis rosea plena x albiflora

SALMON GLOW (Glasscock, 1947), S. Salmon pink. VE. AV. Albiflora x officinalis Sunbeam

SAMUEL HILL (Berneche, 1932), S. Pink. E. AV.

SANCTUARY (E. Auten, Jr., 1933), D. Cream white. T. M.

SAN DIEGO (E. Auten, Jr., 1931), J. Light red. M.

SANS SOUCI (E. Auten, Jr., 1930), A. Light violaceous pink. X.

SANTA FE (Auten, 1937), SD. Red. E.

SARAH (Pleas, 1913), D. Light pink. M. X.

SARAH BERNHARDT (Lemoine, 1906), D. Dark rose pink. L. AV.

SARAH CARSTENSEN (Terry, 1901), D. Light rose pink. M. DW. X.

SARAH K. THURLOW (Thurlow, 1921), D. Pure white. Rose fragrance. VL. AV.

SCARF DANCE (Auten, 1927), SD. Light pink and white. M. AV.

SCARLET O'HARA (Falk-Glasscock, 1956), S. Red. E. Officinalis x albiflora

SEASHELL (Sass, 1937), S. Pink. EM. AV.

SEBASTICOOK (Guppy, 1935), J. Dark red. X.

SECRETARY FEWKES (Shaylor, 1916), D. Pale rose pink, paling to white. M. T.

SEIHIN IKEDA (Harding, 1935), J. Reddish purple. M. T. Never in commerce.

SEIRIU SOMAE (Origin unknown), J. Creamy white. M. AV.

SENORITA (E. Auten, Jr., 1931), J. Deep cerise red. L. X.

SENSATION (Sass, 1937). Light pink. L. AV.

SENTINEL (E. Auten, Jr., 1931), J. Red. T. X.

SERENE (Franklin, 1921), D. Rose-pink. L. DW. X.

SHAWNEE CHIEF (Bigger, 1938), D. Dark red. L. AV.

SHAYLOR'S DREAM (Shaylor, 1918), D. Pale flesh pink, paling to white. Fragrant. M. AV.

SHAYLOR'S SUNBURST (Allison, 1931), J. Pure white. Pond lily fragrance. LM. T.

SHIRLEY ANN (Winchell, 1941), No. 12A. Red. LM.

SHO-YO (Harding, 1935), Semi-rose. Flesh-blush. Fragrant. LM. AV. Never in commerce.

SHIRINE (Brethour, 1936). Pink. T. LM.

SHY MAID (E. Auten, Jr., 1930), A. Pale lavender pink. E.

SIBELIUS (Rosefield, 1939), Rose type. Light pink.

SIGNAL STATION (Auten, 1938), J. Red. AV. VL.

SILOAM (E. Auten, Jr., 1933), D. White. L. DW.

SILVER CERISE (Porter, 1927), S. Cerise with silver-tipped edges. M. T. X.

SILVER KING (E. Auten, Jr., 1933), D. White. L.

SILVER WEDDING (Lyman, 1939), S. White. Never in commerce.

SILVER SWAN (Rosenfield, 1934), D. Rose type. White. L. T. Never in commerce.

SILVIA SAUNDERS (Saunders, 1921), SD. Rose pink. Extra E. DW.

SIR JOHN FRANKLIN (Franklin, 1939), Rose type. Red. Fragrant. L. T.

SISTER MARGARET (Cooper-Wild and Son, 1953), D. White. EM. AV.

SISTIE (E. Auten, Jr., 1933), D. Pink, fades white. Rose fragrance. L. AV.

SKY PILOT (E. Auten, 1939), J. Deep pink. T. LM.

SLEEPY HOLLOW (Auten, 1935), S. Blush white. E. T.

SMILES (Nieuwenhuizen, 1935), D. Light mauve, yellow petaloids. M. T.

SMOKE SIGNAL (Jones, 1957), J. Deep rose. M.

SNOWBALL (Franklin, 1933), Rose type. White. Seedling No. X-5, selected 1925. M. AV.

SNOW BOUND (E. Auten, Jr.,
1931), S. White. X.
SNOW CLOUD (Hoogendoorn,
1949), D. White. E. AV.
SNOW MOUNTAIN (Bigger,
1946) (seedling 22-37), D.
White. M. T.
SNOW SPRITE (E. Auten, Jr.,
1930), S. White. DW. E.
SNOW WHEEL (Origin
unknown), J. White. M. DW.
SOLANGE (Lemoine, 1907), D.
Cream white, suffusion of
buff and pale salmon pink.
L. AV.
SOME GANOKO (Origin
unknown), J. Dark crimson,
fragrant. DW. M.
SOPS OF WINE (Secor, 1922),
D. Dark red with purple.
L. DW. X.
SOUVENIR DE A. MILLET
(Millet, 1924), D. Amaranth.
LM. T.
SOUVENIR DE LOUIS BIGOT
(Dessert, 1913), D. Rose pink.
M. AV.
SOWADABSCOOK (Guppy,
1935), J. Dark red. X.
SPARKLES (Glasscock, 1946), SD.
Scarlet red. AV. E. Hybrid.
SPARKLING STAR (Bigger,
1953), S. Dark pink. E. AV.
Mary Brand x unknown
SPLENDIDA (Guerin, 1850), D.
Light old rose pink. L. T.
SPLENDOR (Sass, 1929), Rose
type. Dark red. L.
SPOON RIVER (E. Auten, Jr.,
1931), D. Creamy magenta.
Rose fragrant. AV. X.
SPRING BEAUTY (Nicholls,
1933), D. to SD. Rose pink.
E. AV.
STANDARD BEARER (Hollis,
1906), D. Dark old rose. E.
DW. X.
STANLEY (Crousse, 1879), D.
Light old rose pink. M. T.
Not listed here.

STEPHANIE (Terry, 1891), D.
Pale pink. M. T. X.
STONEY EDWARDS (Kelway,
1929), D. Rose and pale
cream center.
Not listed here.
STRASSBURG (Goos &
Koenemann, 1911), D. Pale
old rose. M. T. X.
SULLY PRUDHOMME (Crousse,
1898), D. Light flesh pink.
M. AV. X.
SUNBEAM (Hollis, 1906), J. Pale
old rose, fading bluish white.
M. AV. X.
SUNBRIGHT (Glasscock, 1939).
Red. E. AV. Chinensis x
officinalis Sunbeam
SUNCOOK (Guppy, 1935), J.
Dark red. X.
SUN FAST (Freeborn, 1945), D.
Bright red. E. Officinalis
ruba plena x chinensis
SUNMIST (Nicholls, 1942), Blush.
M. AV.
SUNRISE (Franklin, 1931), SD.
Rose pink. L. AV. X.
SUNSET (Risk, 1929). Light pink,
gold center. M. T. X.
SUNSET GLORY (Lyman, 1939).
J. Deep rose pink or red. M.
X.
SUN-UP (Auten, 1937), S. Dark
red. L.
SUZETTE (Dessert, 1911). D.
Rose pink. Fragrant. M. AV.
SWEET GENEVIEVE (Rich-
mond, 1949) (seedling no.
201-327), D. Deep lilac pink.
M. AV.
SWORD DANCE (E. Auten, Jr.,
1933), J. Rich red. M. T.
SYLVIANE (Lemoine, 1924), A.
White guard petals, pale
canary yellow petals in
center. M. Not sold in
U.S.A.
SYMPHONY (Brethour, 1929).
Light salmon pink. Fragrant.
EM.

T

TAMATE-BOKU (Origin unknown), J. Old rose pink. M. AV.

TANAGER (Sass, 1934). Red. L. D. T. Note: formerly registered as VESUVE, 1934.

TANYA (Jones, 1957), D. Dark red. L.

TARANTELLE (E. Auten, Jr.. 1929), J. Brilliant light red or deep cerise pink. AV. X.

TAR BABY (E. Auten, Jr., 1931), SD. Dark red. L. DW.

T. B. TERRY (Pleas. 1911). Suppressed by vote of Directors. X.

TECUMSEH (White, 1954), S. Red. F. AV. Marie Crousse x lobata

TEMPEST (E. Auten, Jr., 1931), SD. Dark red. T. M.

THE BARON (Auten, 1934), J. Red and yellow. M.

THE BRIDE (Dessert, 1902), S. Pure white. E. AV. Also listed as Albiflora, The Bride.

THE FLEECE (Kelsey, 1940), D. White. M. AV.

THE GEM (Pleas, 1909), D. Dark crimson. M. T. X.

THE JEWEL (Pleas). Considered the same as OPAL, which see. X.

THELMA BARNES (Franklin, 1933), Rose type. White. Seedling No. D-66, selected 1923. X.

THE MIGHTY MO (Wild, 1950), D. Red. M. T.

THE QUEEN (Kelway, 1902), S. White petals, flushed pink. M. AV. Not listed here.

THERESA GARDNER (Gardner, before 1951), D. White. L.

THERESE (Dessert, 1904), D. Old rose pink. M. AV.

THOMAS C. THURLOW Thurlow, 1919), D. Flesh pink, paling to cream white. Fragrant. M. AV.

THOR (Sass, 1937), D. Deep maroon. M. AV.

THURA HIRES (Nicholls, 1938) (seedling no. 8), D. White. Fragrant. LM. AV.

TILLIENOONE (Guppy, reg., 1932), S. Deep bright red. X.

TINKA PHILLIPS (Phillips, 1953), D. Rose salmon. EM. T.

TIRA (Franklin, 1939), Rose form. Pink. LM. T. X.

TO KALON (Kelsey, 1936), D. White. LM. AV.

TOKIO (Origin unknown), J. Rose pink. M. T.

TOM BERKLEY (Sass, 1941), D. Light pink. M. to L. AV.

TOM TINKER (E. Auten, Jr., 1930), S. Dark red. E. AV. X.

TONDELEYO (Lins, 1942) (seedling no R-2-101), D. Dark pink. ML. T.

TONTI (E. Auten, Jr., 1933), S. Light red. T. E.

TOP FLIGHT (Nicholls-Wild and Son, 1959), D. Blush. LM. T.

TOPEKA (Auten, 1938), Bomb type. Bright red. Officinalis x chinensis. E. AV.

TORCHLIGHT (Lyman, 1939), A. Deep rose pink or red. Never in commerce.

TOREADOR (Wettengel, 1923), S. Light red. Very L. T.

TORO-NO-MAKI (Origin uncertain), J. Blush white. Fragrant. M. AV.

TORPILLEUR (Dessert, 1913), J. Deep rose red. Fragrant. M. AV.

TOURANGELLE (Dessert, 1910), D. Light pink. Fragrant. L. AV.

TOWN CRIER (E. Auten, Jr., 1939), S. Light red. Albiflora var. E.

TRAGEDY (Hollis, 1909), D. Dark crimson. M. T. X.

TRANQUILITY (Nicholls-Wild & Son, 1957) (seedling no. 960), D. White. M.

TRINKET (Nicholls, 1941), D. White with yellow underglow. AV. LM. No. 72 from Laura Dessert

TRUMPETER (Sass, 1949), D. Dark red. M. AV. Fuyago x red seedling no. 10-31

TWO-IN-ONE (Bockstoce, 1955), D. Red. E. T.

U

UNA HOWARD (Kelway, 1929), SD. Carmine. Not listed here.

UNCLE BILL (Klehm, 1954) (seedling No. 77B), D. Dark rose pink. M. T.

UNCLE REMUS (E. Auten, Jr., 1931), SD. Black red. T.

V

VANDALIA (E. Auten, Jr., 1939), D. White. Rose fragrance. LM. Albiflora var.

VAUGHN DELEATH (Lanigan, 1945), D. Dark rose pink. M. T. X.

VENUS (Kelway, 1888), D. Old rose pink. Fragrant. M. T.

VERA (Gumm, 1923), S. Dark maroon-crimson. Fragrant. EM. AV.

VERITAS (E. Auten, Jr., 1939), D. Dark red. E. AV. Officinalis hybrid.

VESTA CLAUSSEN (Claussen, 1936), D. Pink. T. X.

VESUVE (Sass, 1934). Red. L. Changed to Tanager.

VESUVE (Dessert, 1905). Red. (Sym. 1921) E. AV.

VICTOIRE DE LA MARNE (Dessert, 1915), D. Dark pink. M. AV.

VICTORY (Thompson, 1944), D.

White with a dash of pink. L. T.

VICTORY CHATEAU THIERRY (Brand, 1925), D. Clear pink. Fragrant. M. DW.

VIKING (E. Auten, Jr., 1936), D. Dark red. L. X.

VIMY RIDGE (Brethour, 1937), D. Bright pink. X.

VINCENNES (E. Auten, Jr., 1939), D. White, flushed pink and yellow. E. T. Albiflora var.

VIRGINIA LEE (E. Auten, Jr., 1939), D. Pink. L. AV. Albiflora var.

VIRGINIA LOUISE (Walter J. Guille, 1948), D. Blush. M. to L. AV.

VIVID ROSE (Klehm, 1952) (seedling no. 76A), D. Bright rose pink. LM. AV.

VOGUE (Hoogendoorn, 1949), D. Rose. M. AV.

W

WABASH (Smith-Krekler, 1955), D. Pink. M. DW.

WALLY Z (Nicholls-Wild and Son, 1959), D. Light pink. EM.

WALTER (Krekler, 1958), D. Light pink. LM. T.

WALTER CAMPBELL LYMAN (Lyman, 1933), D. Shell pink. Fragrant. L. Never in commerce.

WALTER E. WIPSON (Murawska, 1956), D. White. L. AV. Le Cygne x Frances Willard

WALTER FAXON (Richardson, 1904), D. Shell pink, mild fragrance. M. AV.

WALTER MAINS (Mains, 1957), J. Dark red. E. T Albiflora x officinalis, anemoneflora aurea ligulata rosea

WAR HAWK
see NIPPON TRIUMPH
WATCHMAN (E. Auten, Jr.,
1933), S. White. L. T.
WATER LILLY. Same as MARIE
JACQUIN, which see.
WATERLILY (Brant, 1931), SD.
Pure white. Fragrant. M.
WAUKEAG (Guppy, 1935), S.
Dark red. X.
WEDDING DAY (E. Auten, Jr.,
1933), S. Flesh white. T.
WEE PHILIPPE (Smith-
Krekler, 1954), D. Dark red.
M. DW.
WENONAH (Franklin, 1920), D.
Dark pink, tipped with white.
X.
WEST ELKTON (Krekler, 1958),
J. Dark red. LM. AV.
WESTERNER (Bigger, 1942), J.
Pink. M. AV.
W. F. CHRISTMAN (Franklin,
1921), D. Blush white, shaded
with pink. Rose fragrance. M.
AV.
WHISKERS (Jones, 1957), J. Red
with bicolor plume center. M.
WHITE BEAUTY (E. Auten, Jr.,
1931), D. White. Fragrant.
M. T.
WHITE CAP (Winchell, 1956)
(seedling no. J-3-CJ), J. Dark
pink. M. T.
WHITE CLOUD (Auten, Jr.,
1931), J. White. E. T.
WHITE COCKADE (Keagey,
1946), S. White. M. AV.
WHITE CRANE (E. Auten, Jr.,
1939), J. White and yellow.
T. Albiflora var.
WHITE DELIGHT (Auten, 1935),
D. White. Fragrant. T. E.
WHITE EAGLE (Sass, 1937),
Rose type. White. EM. AV.
WHITE EMPEROR. Entered by
Interstate Nurseries, 1937.
Never introduced.
No description.

WHITE GOLD (Mann-Van Steen,
1936), J. White. T.
WHITE JADE (Harding, 1935),
Rose type. Rose fragrance.
White. M.
Never in commerce.
WHITE LADY (Kelway, 1900), J.
White. LM. DW.
WHITE MOTH (E. Auten, Jr.,
1933), S. Flesh white. T. X.
WHITE PEARL (E. Auten, Jr.,
1931), D. Shell pink with
lavender cast. E.
WHITE PERFECTION (E.
Auten, Jr., 1931), S. White.
AV. M.
WHITE PRINCE (Risk, 1929).
White with cream center.
Fragrant. L. AV. X.
WHITE ROSE (Shrader, 1942),
SD. White. LM. AV.
WHITE SWAN (Pleas, 1913), S.
White. E. AV.
WHITE WATER (Kelsey, 1940),
D. White. M.
WHITE WINGS (Hoogendoorn,
1949), S. White. M. AV.
WHITLEYI MAJOR (Origin
unknown.) S. Blush. E. AV.
WIESBADEN (Goos and
Koenemann, 1911), D. Flesh
pink paling to white. LM.
AV.
WILBUR WRIGHT (Kelway,
1909), S. Dark crimson-
maroon. M. AV.
WILD ROSE (Kelway), S. White.
Speckled pink. M. AV.
WILLA GIRL (Nicholls-Wild and
Son, 1959), D. Creamy white.
M. to ML.
WILLIAM F. TURNER (Shaylor,
1916), D. Very dark crimson
petals. Blackish sheen. EM.
T.
WILLIAM H. PARK (Freeborn,
1945) (seedling Chugai no.
29), J. White. M. AV.
WILLIAM SHERADEN

(Bockstoce, 1955), D. Light pink. E. T. Officinalis x lactiflora

WILL ROGERS (Franklin, 1935), D. White. AV. DW.

WILTON LOCKWOOD (Shaylor, 1915), D. Light rose-pink. Fragrant. M. T.

WINNEFRED DOMME (Brand, 1913), D. Dark maroon-red. M. DW.

WINNIE WINKLE (Franklin, 1931), Rose type. Pink. L. T.

WINNIKENNI (Thurlow, 1915), D. Rose-pink. VL. X.

WITCHES' DANCE (E. Auten, Jr., 1931), S. Dark red. T. L.

W. W. BLACK (Nicholls-Wild and Son, 1957) (seedling no. 1033), D. Pink. LM.

Y

YOKIHI
    see ORIENTAL GOLD
YONDER LEA (Fletcher, 1942),

S. American Beauty. M. AV. Unknown red double x Festiva Maxima. X.

YONG-LO (Harding, 1935), Rose type. Lilac rose. Fragrant. M. T. Never in commerce.

YORK AND LANCASTER (Kelway, 1928), S. Red and white. E. X.

YUKON (Auten, 1937), D. White. Fragrant. L. T.

Z

ZIP COON (E. Auten, Jr., 1931), SD. Dark red. DW. M.

ZULIEMA (Brant, 1941), D. Red. Fragrant.

ZULU BRIDE (E. Auten, Jr., 1933), SD. Dark black-red. M.

ZULU WARRIOR (Glasscock, 1939), S. Dark red. E. T. Chinensis x Otto Froebel

ZUZU (Krekler, 1955). Bluish pink. SD. M. AV.

INDEX

4'6"

3 FERNS

1 HEMEROCALLIS
Facinating
Soft Chinese Yellow
late June

6 DELPH
PACIFI
mixed co

6 LILIUM CAN
White - Ju

LILAC

3 HOSTA
p.s grandiflora
White
July - Aug

2 LUPINUS
polyphyllus
blue - June

3 CAMPANULA
persifolia
Blue
June - July

1 GYPSOPHILA
Bristol Fairy
White - all summer

3 AC

6 CHRYSANTHEMUM
Misty Maid
shell pink - Sept.

1 PAEONIA
LeCygne
White - midseason

3 ALYSSUM

Fence

1 DICENTRA
spectabilis
pink - May-June

3 HEUCHERA
Rosamondi
pink - May, June

3 IBERIS
Purity
White - May, June

1 PHLOX
Miss Lingard
White - June, July

5 IRIS SABLE
blue black violet
June

3 VERONICA
Blue Champion
June

3 IBERIS
Purity
White - May, June

Harold D. Stevens